NOTES FOR THE CHILDREN

NOTES FOR THE CHILDREN

A Journey on Life's Broken Road

PATRICK PRIESTNER

ROAD AHEAD

PUBLISHING

Published by Road Ahead Publishing, Edmonton, Alberta
www.wellbeing-canada.ca

Edited and designed by Girl Friday Productions
www.girlfridayproductions.com

Cover design: Natalie Alexander
Project management: Reshma Kooner
Project editorial: Bethany Fred
Image credits: All photos courtesy of the author

ISBN (paperback): 978-1-77835-292-8
ISBN (ebook): 978-1-77835-312-3

First edition

Dedicated, with love, to Daniel, Laura, Jenna, Lauren, Kaedra, and all my grandchildren. I wrote this for you.

For Diana, who walks with me together through life. I thank God every day for our love.

CONTENTS

FOREWORD

"If we could change ourselves, the tendencies
in the world would also change. As a man
changes his own nature, so does the attitude
of the world change towards him. This is the
divine mystery supreme. A wonderful thing it
is and the source of our happiness. We need
not wait to see what others do."

                    Mahatma Gandhi

My father had a great respect for Mahatma Gandhi. He considered Gandhi's belief in nonviolent change a critical aspect
of his vision for The Beloved Community—that place where
everyone is cared for, absent of poverty, hunger, and hate.

Like Gandhi, my father knew that the peace and enlightenment we strive for as a society begins not by confronting
those with whom we take issue but instead with an internal
journey. It begins with thoughts untouched by hate and anger,
thoughts left free to imagine what could be if our minds were
stripped of the barriers and restrictions we place on ourselves.

Real change begins with reflection. It begins with an honest, bedrock belief that we can aspire to something bigger than all of us, if we can only open ourselves up to the possibilities.

After all, how can you hope to understand and empathize with someone else's condition until you take the time to truly understand your own condition? How can you hope to inspire change for the better until you yourself have changed for the better?

Or, as the great author Leo Tolstoy once so wisely challenged us: "Everyone thinks of changing the world, but no one thinks of changing himself."

All great change begins by changing yourself.

But that's not to say it isn't difficult—and many don't feel up to the task. Too many of us struggle with mental health challenges. We struggle to find the help we need—to find the compassion we crave. We struggle because we were not taught the skills we need to thrive, and because we can't find the words to put to the emotions that we've bottled up. We struggle to find the resilience needed to continue our journey up the mountain.

Which brings me to this book. Socrates warned us that the unexamined life is not worth living—that it is our purpose as humans to find the meaning in what we do, to understand why we feel what we feel, and to find the reason for what we think. In *Notes for the Children*, Pat Priestner outlines his struggle to do just that—to understand the "why" of his life.

His story begins with abuse and addiction, but that's not how it ends. Pat asked the questions and, more often than not, found the answers. It helped him develop the resiliency he was looking for.

For Priestner, the tools he found most helpful were the words of the great musicians and thinkers who came before him. They inspired him. They helped give him clarity. They gave him reason and understanding and helped him rise above his circumstance.

Pat passes along all those lessons in this book—lessons about leadership; about how to be a better person, a better parent, a better husband; and about how to take responsibility for your happiness and change when a change is required. We all come into the world imperfect. It is our lot to try to find a better way. That's the story Pat tells in *Notes for the Children*.

I have to confess that I couldn't help but smile as I followed Pat on his journey through this book. As he heaps praise on the great minds that inspired him, he ignores the value of the inspiration he offers the next generation—the gift of his experience.

They say a society grows great when the old plant trees in whose shade they shall never sit, and if that's true, then we're lucky to share our journey with someone like Pat.

He is an example of how meaningful change begins—and where our path can lead if we are brave enough to keep asking why.

Martin Luther King III

RUNNING AGAINST
THE WIND

Tonight I watched a YouTube video of a seventy-two-year-old Bob Seger playing the last show ever at the Palace in his hometown of Auburn Hills, Michigan. His brilliant acoustic version of "Against the Wind" seemed a fitting "rumination on the march of time." Just watching the power of the moment in that arena had me take a truthful look at how I was living and enjoying life. Forty years have passed since that song was first released, and I remember well listening to it over and over again.

Of course, on the video, Bob Seger looked so much older and more vulnerable with those forty years of experience, as we all do. Believe me, kids and grandkids, you will all come to know this fact. Knowing how fast time passes should teach us to learn the habits that help make each and every day a great day.

A year after the song was released, I was a young man of twenty-six, starting a family and the first business I was a part owner of. It was 1981, and as the year rolled on, our big financial opportunity had turned into financial hell. I had always had it in my soul that we were running against the wind; sometimes that was actually true. This time was one of them, as bankruptcy and total failure seemed to be biting at our heels.

These days, the words "running against the wind" mean something a little different to me. I've come to hear the aging we all experience and how we try to keep moving forward navigating our challenges in a tough world. How we all want to be loving spouses and parents, good children to our own parents, and to have successful careers, even as we face hardships. How we want our partners, our children, and our parents to respect and love us. How difficult it is for us to be successful at all of this while keeping our sanity, our character, and our integrity. And finally, these words now make me think about how sometimes we have to face and run against the wind of our own destructive impulses in order to find the peace and happiness we want for our lives.

I have also tried to run against the wind of the many standard cutthroat, extremely competitive practices in business. Through it all, I can honestly say running against the wind has made my life better as a result.

I reside in a state of happiness almost all the time, though still with a slight bit of an edge running through me that I sure wish I could fully get rid of. Before I started practicing much of what I am going to speak to you about in these notes, that edge was more like a heavy thunder roaring in my head. This hurt not only me but also my family as well. Because of this edge, I still need to give myself frequent attitude checkups. If I forget, even for a day or two, this attitude veers a little over to the wrong side, and it takes some self-awareness to check in and improve my thoughts, feelings, and actions. It is important to remember that while each of us is a beautiful, unique individual, we are also works in progress. All of this is to say, I have come to realize a simple truth that I hope you take to heart: if we do not continue to work on ourselves as we travel through life, we should not expect things to go so well.

From the age of nineteen years old, I have provided sales and leadership training in the dealerships I worked at or later owned. That's approximately forty-eight years of contemplating and sharing my thoughts on attitude, resilience, anger, forgiveness, fear, gratitude, anxiety, and every other emotion that comes our way in the sales world, and I suspect in everyone's world. As well, throughout these years, I have been blessed to learn so much from the teams I have worked side by side with. In a competitive world, learning from others is a strength, not a weakness. Something else important that I learned early on, and which I continue to train on today, is that it's really easy to sell the truth in whatever it is we are selling. That includes our self-evaluations.

For some unknown reason, I kept many of these meeting notes in boxes for years on end, just regularly adding to the deck. Over the last twenty or so years, I've also kept personal notes on these subjects and many more, such as finding happiness and some peace in my life. Then about two years ago, when I was sixty-five years old, I started relooking at the notes I took from my staff trainings and the countless personal notes I've written over the years and decided to address them personally to you and gather them into a book, with the hopes they feel as helpful to you as these teachings and insights have been to me.

Among the many thoughts and feelings I had while re-reading these notes were vivid memories of the times when they were written and the emotional states I was in during those periods. If I am to help you on each of your journeys, being completely honest and forthright was a given here, even though I know some of my actions and mistakes were (and still are) pretty embarrassing.

It took a while, but I've come to understand that too much of my time was spent dealing with significant anxiety, situational depression, heightened anger, too much craving, incessant guilt, too much drinking, and constantly beating myself up. Like so many of us, I was trying to deal with all these emotional issues but not looking in the right places for the solutions that would have provided long-term relief.

I assume I was a fairly decent salesperson, trainer, and motivator at a young age, or I simply could not have been in my own auto dealership business at twenty-six years old. However, it took me another twenty-plus years until I was able to learn how to live with myself. I now fully realize that the pain I was causing myself was also causing pain to my family, and I am truly sorry for that. I did the best that I was capable of doing during those periods, but what I was doing to fix the pain and behaviors was not working. I am hoping to share with you some of the things I ultimately learned that did work. It is perfectly clear to me that you will benefit as much as I have if you do even a small amount of the work on yourself that we all need to do.

To that point, when I began to think about compiling and organizing the thousands of pages of notes that I had written, obviously, many thoughts came to the forefront. The first recurring thought was that you sure need a lot of luck and good fortune along the journey because the odds are so stacked against most people in the world in every conceivable way. That was certainly true for me, as I went from an unstable background with no money whatsoever to founding and running a significant company, finding true love, and being fortunate enough to have five marvelous children and four precious grandchildren.

The second thought was that I sure made an alarming number of mistakes along the way that should have doomed me. All I can say is "Thank you, Lord" for all the help.

The third and most recurring thought was that, boy, I sure needed to put in a lot of incredibly hard work. These notes have shown me just how much personal reflection and work on my own thoughts, feelings, emotions, and actions was done over the years. I could finally see what I needed to improve in myself and continue to improve over the years to get to the other side of happiness and success. I can assure you, children, without the inner work I did, my life would have turned out more like my father's, whom you will learn about soon, than the lives we live today.

My goals in taking on this project were profoundly clear:

- Can I help any of my three children, two stepchildren, four grandkids, or the future ones become happier and have better relationships with their partners, kids, family, and friends?
- Can I help any of you with some advice that could be of assistance to you on your career path, whatever that might be?
- Can I help any of you in any way to quiet your negative seeds and water your positive seeds?

I thought hard about how, today, Diana and I have the best marriage anyone could have, wonderful children and grandchildren, and a multibillion-dollar business with tremendous partners and friends alongside. The road to success has been long and sometimes dark and broken, with numerous land mines to navigate, and I am hoping some of the following notes will help you navigate your journey.

Children, the lessons learned and the serious mistakes I made are all going to be on the following pages for you. The truth is that at my age I have likely had my back against the wall a little more than you have. Please learn from my mistakes.

The best way to offer these notes, I thought, was to share

them in different chapters according to themes. I organized this book so it can be read from start to finish, or it can be picked up on any given day and randomly opened to find a note that may speak to you. However you read this, and hopefully continue to read over the years, I pray these notes help you along your journey and offer you companionship and comfort whenever you find yourself running against the wind.

GROWING UP

When I was speaking with my daughter Jenna about writing these notes for you, she asked me if I would include more about my life growing up, as she said I did not talk about it much over the years, and she would be interested in hearing more about my early life. Diana told me months ago that if I did not put some color behind why and how I arrived at these views on personal behavior and ways of living, it would not be very effective.

When I finally sent some of these notes to an experienced and self-aware editor, she told me the same thing Diana had. I have now decided to try to help you by telling you what really happened to me over the last fifty-five years or so, to help you understand why I think and feel the way I do.

This is not a tell-all, where I will dive into all the details of these stories. Rather this is an attempt to help you children know more about where I came from and what shaped me as a father and business owner. More importantly, to let you know the family legacies I want to carry forward and the ones I've tried hard not to pass on, in the hope that you never have to experience some of the hardships I am going to recount.

Organizing and shaping the notes to you has brought up
a lot of things that I haven't thought much about for many
years. Often, remembering these events, situations, and circumstances is very painful. Sometimes you just wanna stop
thinking about painful memories and pretend it all didn't happen, but of course, pretending it didn't happen doesn't make it
go away. If something this painful causes any of us this much
suffering, we must compassionately deal with this suffering,
like we would deal with the suffering of our children. For a
long time I did not do that for myself. Fortunately, I have since
worked on compassionately facing and overcoming much of
what I'm going to share here, and that work, over the course
of many years, has taught me so much and also helped me to
suffer much less in recent years.

So before I share the individual notes with you, I will give
you an overview of my backstory in this more traditional
chapter form. I suppose the best place to begin telling of my
upbringing and some of the stories I haven't shared much is
with my parents' history.

First, I want to say that some of the details I'm going to
share about my parents may reflect poorly on them. But I believe we should always consider someone's upbringing before
we judge them too harshly. For instance, my mother suffered
very much as a child. She was kidnapped with her older sister by her estranged father at five years old. He took the two
girls from Champion, Alberta, where they lived with their
mother (my grandmother), across the country to Toronto.
The girls were fortunate that their mother had the guts to literally chase them east and track them down. Try arriving as
a single mom in a city the size of Toronto in 1937 and looking for two kidnapped children. Thank goodness she knew
where the Hungarian immigrants and poor people lived at
that time, and mutual friends helped her locate my mother
and her sister.

Patrick's grandmother Teresa in Edmonton later in her life.

My grandmother told us she had watched her daughters and their dad and tracked their daily patterns. After watching for a few days, she pounced when she knew he would be at work, took them from their caretakers, and immediately got on a train to Hamilton to get away from him. Imagine not seeing your children for so long and then having to wait for the perfect opportunity to rescue them. My grandmother was a smart and determined woman who taught me so much.

Two years after they were taken from Alberta, they were living in a boardinghouse in Hamilton, but they were all together. Soon after, my grandmother met John Beres, a wonderful man whom she married, and he helped support the family and raise the girls. Years later, he also helped our family when we needed it. He was the best grandfather I could have ever had. Having said this, the newly formed family of four had a real tough go of it in Hamilton, and being reunited with her mother did not make my mother's life easy, as she was an eleven-year-old child who was expected to contribute to the meager family income by picking tobacco.

My father had just as tough an upbringing, with different circumstances but much of the same kind of pain. His parents were from England. His father, who made a living as a carpenter, was an alcoholic and tuned out the six children most of the time. His mother was living a very frugal life trying to make ends meet in Hamilton, and due to this financial hardship, she harbored ambitions of wealth and glory for her children. She was competitive and completely focused on attaining money and status for them.

Two things I remember my father's mother saying were, "It's just as easy to love a rich one as a poor one" when giving us marriage advice. The other was, as my sister Cathy was winning her first world championship speed-skating meet at around seventeen, our grandmother said to her, "Cathy, you should take up tennis, it pays way more money." Wow! She pressed her kids to be ultracompetitive, and I believe my dad had trouble meeting her expectations, but he learned the competitive nature of the world early. Unfortunately, he also grew up watching a father who was both mean and drunk a lot. As

I see it now, my parents were just two kids from difficult back-grounds trying to make a go of it against the odds.

I suspect life was difficult for them when they were first married, too, with my father working in the hotel business and my mom working as a seamstress and later a teacher. Having a set of twins and then another baby in thirteen months would have been incredibly difficult for any couple, let alone one with a husband who didn't arrive home until eight or nine at night, usually half in the bag.

Joe and Irene Priestner on their wedding day, November 7, 1953.

At the end of the day, my parents' journey through life was almost too difficult for them to handle, as more mistakes, more regrets, and much more humiliation came their way. I imagine a new life together for a young married couple was tough enough without so many self-inflicted wounds haunting them.

They were living in Hamilton with my grandparents when Dad had an offer to go work at a hotel in Windsor, Ontario. They left with the hopes of a better life and a perfect job for Dad, as he was a good talker whom people liked and a natural fit for the hospitality industry. Over the first couple of years, he did very well and was promoted to a management position at an early age. I am certain their return trips to Hamilton to visit their respective parents and siblings were good times filled with a sense of pride.

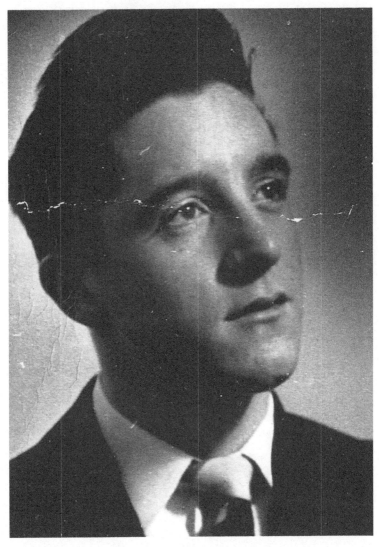

Portrait of Patrick's father, Joe Priestner, at around age twenty.

Well, alcohol and the pursuit of nicer things had Dad make the first serious mistake of his young life, a mistake that would repeat itself in years to come. He decided to skim some of the cash the hotel was taking in, and while this might have seemed to him to be easy money, the real world was busy making other plans for him. His bosses obviously began paying attention when money started going missing, and he was caught red-handed. Facing potential theft charges, Dad was fortunate when his boss said he was going to give him a break by firing him but not filing criminal charges.

My parents suddenly had to leave Windsor with three toddlers in tow. The drive back from Windsor had to have been embarrassing, shameful, angering, worrisome, humiliating, and anything else you might want to add. Pulling into Hamilton to move back in with Mom's parents into a small home with the three of us in this manner seems like one of the worst things that could happen in a new marriage. Can you imagine how humiliating it would have been for my father to have his in-laws help take care of his family because of what he had done? How about my mom, who must have been ashamed of what her parents thought of her marriage partner? A most arduous return. As fate would have it, his new job was selling cars at a GM store in Hamilton.

The way I sense it, Mom and Dad likely started drinking to relax, have fun, and try to forget about their troubles, believing it was all good. Next, they started using it to cope with their troubles "better," and finally, it was a daily problem of huge proportion. If Dad was like most alcoholics, he argued with himself about why he should or shouldn't drink each night, and the alcohol usually won. So the alcohol slowly took hold of their lives, and from there things started spinning out of control. They likely thought if they could catch a few breaks, they could turn things around and stop the destructive cycle they were spiraling in. But it was just a matter of time before it got really bad. I learned up close and personal very early in life that if you keep doing the same things and making the same mistakes, life is pretty darn tough for you and those around you.

During their early married years, Dad made decent money,

but they both wanted more from life and regularly spent well beyond their means. Combine this with my father's chronic drinking, and it was easy to figure out why things would unravel quickly. Then add in Dad being fired from two jobs for stealing (I'll tell more about the second time later), plus an incredible number of home and city moves over a short period (Mom says we moved twelve times before I was fourteen), and the result was a life of chaos and financial instability for the family.

I can still remember being twelve years old in the kitchen of our old house on Niagara Street in River Heights and being told I had to answer the phone in case it was one of the many collection agencies that were often on our case. Fifty years ago, our phones were the only way any of us could get in touch with anyone, including our friends, coaches, and teachers, or them with us. Unfortunately for our family, call display was twenty-five years away, so I was coached on how to answer the phone and tell anyone we did not know that my parents were not home. I was not sure they always believed me, but I was pretty certain this was not the way most of the families in the neighborhood answered the phone.

COMFORT FOOD

Another sound example of our day-to-day chaos follows. Many families throughout the world use food and dinnertime to share each other's experiences and bond together. We were fortunate to have a mother who was a terrific cook, and we looked forward to her cooking most nights. It was the conversation and bonding that missed the mark a lot of the time. She tried to make up for the constant chaos in our lives by often putting a large amount of time into preparing special meals, likely in hopes of us forgetting our problems for an hour.

However, when my dad was around, a drunken episode was likely, and some nights the fights between them would get out of hand. One night, like so many, stands out to this day. Mom was phenomenal at making comfort foods, like stews and things, and one night she decided to make a French version of one of her specialty stews, adding grapes and other unusual ingredients. I can't remember if the kids thought it was better than the regular beef goulash she had mastered, but I am certain we liked it. Either way, we all would have been happy, but Dad stormed in a bit late at a quarter to seven or so, completely loaded, and proceeded to try the night's version of Mom's phenomenal cooking. A couple of bites later, he told her it was utter crap, and he would not eat it. He then took his full plate, threw it into the kitchen sink, and demanded a proper meal.

We kids were just hoping he would move to the living room and fall asleep in his chair well before the screaming got worse. Mom, however, was no shrinking violet, and she was going to get even that night. He had just bought a brand-new set of cowboy boots that he was most proud of, and they were placed close to the stairs by the living room. She went to the kitchen and carried the remaining pot of stew to the living room stairs area and poured the remainder of the pot directly into his prized new boots.

Needless to say, the fight progressed until he finally passed out. For the rest of us, it was time to get our studying done. Another night in paradise. I sure learned a lot about the serious perils of alcohol for an individual, as well as a family, at a young age, but unfortunately, I did not see this clearly as an adult for too many years. Of course, I feel terrible about the times I embarrassed my kids while drinking.

KEEPING THE FAMILY TOGETHER

As barely a teenager fifty-plus years ago, I regularly called Sunday family meetings in our house to try to get the drinking and bizarre behavior to stop for a while so we could get through the coming week with as little chaos as possible. I would get my sisters to agree that we needed to discuss these matters and bring my twin brother, Mike, along before convincing our parents to talk with us. The success of these family discussions generally lasted a day or so at best. Despite the short-lived successes, I learned much about hope, leadership, and accountability at an early age. Through the years, those lessons on leadership and accountability served me very well, hope and false hope, not so well.

At the time, I had always hoped that our family problems could be worked out, and I had faith my parents would see what was really going on and make the changes necessary for all of us to be happy. Of course, back then I had no idea how difficult severe alcoholism is to deal with or about all the other problems that come with it. I just assumed if they wanted to, they could quit drinking, but as any adult knows, it's never that easy. Even though it never really worked, I was persistent in my family-meeting efforts to try to bring some order and sanity to the insanity.

Children, we had many family meetings that I called over the smallest things or events we were going to. Being who I was, I just assumed things could break into mayhem at any time if we did not talk about it beforehand. Susan was good-natured about it and was almost always rolling her eyes a bit with you all, as you should have. It's pretty funny that I still have a bit of a team meeting with the grandkids before we go out for ice cream or to the toy store. However hard the habit is to break, nowadays it's done for a bit of fun, as young kids seem to like team meetings. Life is probably better for us if it's the parents or grandparents calling the meeting, not the teenagers.

My sisters, Irene, Mary, and Cathy, recently told me that in those years, growing up, they felt I always tried to support them in any way possible. Most often when my three younger sisters had some problem to deal with, they asked me to help, as our parents were either not around or preoccupied with something else. I enjoyed helping in any way I could because they were all incredible sisters whom I loved, and like Mike and me, they were just trying to make it in a very difficult situation. As kids and teenagers, Mike and I also helped each other with everything possible; we were as close as any two brothers could be. The easy part for me in all this was that the girls and Mike were kind, smart, and very resilient.

Even so, Mary and Irene needed the most help, as they were treated poorly by my parents because they were not considered "championship" material in sports. Being treated this way by your own parents is a hellacious way to grow up, and I could certainly feel their pain at such a young age. The three of us were also expected to work after school and on weekends from the time we were twelve years old, to help with the family income.

When I was just turning sixteen years old, things went from bad to worse for our family. One morning Mom woke up to find Dad missing, with a note saying he was gone for good and was not coming back. Mom called us all together to say Dad had left Winnipeg, she had no idea where he had moved to, and he wasn't coming back. How could I ever forget her words "He left us with twenty dollars to our name"?

More problems were coming quickly, and we all knew it; we just had no idea what to do. The good news was that Cathy and Mike did not have to pay for their sports, as he was playing junior hockey, and she was on Canada's National Women's Team. A few days later God blessed us again when the family received a major break with Rene's school check bouncing. A nun from the all-girls Christian school called and told Mom her check did not clear, and we had to pay like everyone else. Mom finally broke down and said we had nothing, and her husband had taken off and left us broke; what could she do?

The nun was kind and asked her what she did for a living, and she said she was a stay-at-home mom with five kids. She also said she had her teacher's certificate in Ontario. With a wonderful display of decency and graciousness, she asked her to please come down to the school as they were one teacher short. That night we celebrated that Mom had a new job. Mary and I would continue to contribute everything we made to the family budget, and we would further cut all spending to the bone and make the best of it. For us it was just another day to put our heads down, work as a team, and be as optimistic as possible.

I believe this was really the beginning of me looking at things as half-full rather than half-empty, a lucky life lesson to learn so young. During this period Mary became understandably difficult to deal with, and Mom was running out of ideas. Our mom and dad started talking again about a year after he left, and for some unhinged reason, they decided to let Mary move to Calgary. Perhaps if she were to live with him it might have made some sense, but that was not possible, as he was living in a motel in Calgary for the year. So they let her move in with an American family Dad was working with and hardly knew. Even at my young age, I found it hard to believe they would let a thirteen-year-old do that, but I suppose they sold us on the fact we would all likely be moving there in six months anyway. I'm not sure it was a wise decision, and today I feel so sorry my parents were in such a difficult predicament they felt they needed to do it.

MOM'S PILLS

What a devastating impact a few pill bottles had on us as teenagers and young adults. Kindly, Mary recently shared with me some of the circumstances surrounding her teenage suicide attempt. I will not get into too much detail here, but she had been out a little late one night, as her ride home was delayed picking Mary and her friend up. When she arrived home, Dad did his usual screaming and trying to humiliate Mary; she was grounded for a month, etc. All she ever did was go to school and work every night to contribute, so I'm not sure why they grounded her. Mom and Mary had a pact that when my drunken dad did these cruel things to her, they would wait for him to fall asleep and usually he would have forgotten by morning. However, this night, Mom did not want another fight with Dad, so she sided with him and told Mary she was in serious trouble.

Back then Mary was given the monthly chore of picking up Mom's sleeping pills and had done it a couple of days earlier, so she knew the bottle was full. At about two in the morning, feeling in a desperate state from years from being in an erratic and seriously competitive home, she walked into the bathroom and swallowed the whole bottle. As usual our family dog slept with his favorite, and Mary said to him as he lay next to her, "I am so sorry, but I will not be here for you in the morning."

Early the next day, a nine-year-old Irene was told by Mom to go wake Mary up, as she must have overslept. Rene found her motionless, lying next to our dog, with an empty pill bottle from the bathroom. When Mary would not wake up, Rene started yelling to Mom, "Help, help," and soon an ambulance had arrived, and she was rushed to the hospital. Thank God she survived and was home a day or so later; the world is a better place because of Mary. Like most things in our home, this was never to be talked about again.

Nine years later, Mom's pills would contribute to another sad and painful event. Rene had been living with Mom since Dad's death a few years earlier. In fact, Rene was trying harder than most anyone could to get somewhere in this world by working at a motor-home dealership as an accounting clerk right after high school (she skipped a grade, so she was very young). She was also studying accounting at night on her own to convince the owner to make her the controller as her boss was soon to retire. At nineteen she had made it to the controller position, which is unheard of. She also paid the majority of the bills at home, as Mom was selling real estate only part time and needed her money to survive.

None of this seemed to be enough for Mom, as she continually tried to control most of Rene's life and lay guilt on her daily. Certainly, I can understand Mom's frustration and pain from the way life had treated her, but taking it out on Rene was unfair. It was only a few years until Mike and I were in a position to look after all of Mom's needs, but this time period was exceptionally hard for Rene, though I did not know at the time how bad it was for her, as we were living in Ontario.

One thing after another drove Rene to the brink, and one night she went for drinks with work friends until about eight thirty, arriving home to screaming from Mom as she exploded at her for going out. This was her breaking point, and she recently confided in me she had seen no way out of this life she was living. As with Mary years earlier, it was now her job to pick up Mom's pills and alcohol, and she had done so a few nights before. In a supreme state of grief and hopelessness, she went to the cabinet and then swallowed the full bottle of sleeping pills before going to her room. However, she quickly realized she did not want to die and ran out of the house down to Mary's home a few blocks away. She was met by a number of people over at Mary's and told Mary she was in serious peril because she had swallowed a bottle of Mom's pills. Mary immediately handled the desperate situation like the champ she is, knowing the quickest way to the hospital was to drive her full speed for about ten minutes. Because of her quick thinking and reaction, Rene was taken care of and sent home the next day. When she arrived home, she was hoping Mom would talk to her about the reasons and feelings that precipitated the attempt, but it never was discussed then or for the next forty years. For Rene it was back to work and looking after Mom. I am so very sorry for what Mary and Rene had to endure through their childhood and teenage years.

LET'S NOT TALK ABOUT ANYTHING HAPPENING HERE

When I reflect back many years and put my parents' hats on, it is clear they did not feel they had much to be proud of, having moved so many times and years later being in Calgary still completely broke and drinking more than ever. Cathy's speed skating and Mike's hockey were about the only things that gave them something to be gratified about. That changed a bit when I was the top Chrysler salesman in Canada at eighteen, but Mike's hockey career was coming to an end, so that probably evened things out for them. Obviously, this seems a sick way to parent, and it had a material effect on Rene and Mary more than the other three of us at the time. It likely had a profound effect on all of us as the years went slowly by.

I only recently heard of other things that happened after I left the family home. My sisters Irene and Cathy have spoken to me about the abuse they suffered growing up. This was particularly directed at Irene, but Cathy survived many other forms of deranged parenting. It's a testament to their strength of character that all three sisters have turned out to be kind, caring parents and had very successful careers of their own.

My sisters have reminded me of what I always knew, which is that no matter what happened behind closed doors, we were always pretending we were the perfect family in front of the world. No one ever spoke of the endless troubling behavior of two alcoholic parents screaming at each other or the constant guilt thrown the children's way. No one ever spoke about making us answer the phone and to coach us on how to lie to agencies coming after them. No one ever spoke about Mary being sent from Winnipeg to live with a family in Calgary we hardly knew and attempting suicide not long after. No one ever spoke a word about another suicide attempt by our other sister, Irene, when she was nineteen years old.

No one ever talked about the time in London, Ontario, when our mother got caught shoplifting, making a then-twenty-year-old Irene face questioning from store security and a police officer when she thought she was simply in the store shopping for groceries with Mom. She had no idea Mom had stolen food and left Irene to pay for some other goods while Mom snuck out of the store. After receiving a call from a panicked Irene, I immediately drove over from work, paid the bill, and helped make sure there were no police charges. Mom was banned from shopping for groceries there for good. This and a thousand other things were simply never to be talked about, lest someone from outside the family heard of any of this.

THE COMPETITION TORE US APART

Amid all this family chaos, pain, and public pretending, trying to be a decent big brother to my siblings was very important to me. I think most anyone would've done what I did in the situation we were in. I deeply cared about my siblings, and even as a young teenager, I also felt it was my role to try to keep the family together. It wasn't until years later that I learned there is a negative side to trying to keep an impossible situation together and to continue to try to keep twin brothers together through life regardless of the circumstances.

Cathy needed the least help, as she was Dad's favorite for being a world champion skater at sixteen and was also in Europe every winter from fourteen on as part of the Canadian speed-skating team. My parents saw stars and money when she made the Olympic team at only fifteen years old and won a silver medal at nineteen. She also won numerous World Cup meets during those years. Her reward was years of my dad's attention and heavy-handed guilt. Can you imagine your father saying before the 1976 Olympics in Austria that the only way he could quit drinking was if she won gold medals in the 500- and 1,000-metre events? Talk about pressure! Seriously!

Mike was also a star athlete, as one of the best goaltenders in Canada for his age, starting at about thirteen. He was playing major junior hockey as a fifteen-year-old in a league full of eighteen- to twenty-year-olds. Of course, my parents saw an NHL future with lots of fame and money.

I can tell you with every ounce of truth that I supported Cathy and Mike in every way I could when their stars were shining. When Mike was in goal, I was more nervous than him. I said a prayer each game while I watched in the stands. When he was playing junior hockey, all the games reporting would be in the *Winnipeg Free Press* newspaper the next day. How well I remember from fifty years ago the name of the sports reporter Keith Sharpe, who covered those games in 1971. The reason is that I would try to cozy up to him during intermissions by walking over and chatting him up. As Mike's twin brother, I figured he would lean a bit more to covering Mike well. I'm not sure that it worked, but if it didn't, it was not from a lack of trying. Not even my father was prouder of Mike

than I was, I held my head up high at the arenas, cheered him
on in every game, and was so proud that he was my brother.
At the same time, I was a decent player myself but was told I
had to work each weeknight and Saturdays as well to support
the budget. Having said that, my dad was one hundred percent
correct when he said I did not have near the talent and was
certainly never going to make it in hockey.

Our parents only attended children's sports if we were the
best player on any team that we were on, so Mike and Cathy
had 100 percent parental attendance, while the other three of
us would never see them at our games, unless I was playing on
the same team as Mike. I can honestly say it didn't bother me
at all, as I was also cheering Cathy and Mike along.

All I wanted was for the five of us siblings to succeed in
life and break the legacy of destructive family chaos, as Dad's
father was a severe alcoholic as well. Watching my siblings
do well was awesome for our family, and I never had a jealous bone in my body. Yes, I had some jealousy of other people
during the years I cheered Mike and Cathy on. We rented a
house by the bus stop in a nice neighborhood, and the folks
living there were in a far different financial situation than we
were. Yes, that jealousy forged some drive and inspiration in
me, but I loved cheering for my siblings and have never understood family jealousy.

The early morning before Cathy's Olympic 500-metre race
in early 1976 is still very fresh in my memory. Even though the
1,000 metre was her specialty, I thought she would medal in
this race and win gold in the 1,000 metre a day later. As her
race started early in the morning, I remember staying up until
about two a.m., and when no results were coming, I set my
alarm for four a.m. I immediately jumped out of bed and put
the TV on to find CBC TV was running an Olympic banner
on the bottom of the screen with results coming in on the various events. Twenty minutes later I saw her on TV as a silver

medalist, which was a big deal for Canada. It was the proudest I had ever felt being her brother, and I went into work that morning tired but elated.

Unfortunately, a minor injury occurred while cooling down from the 500-metre race, and she placed sixth in the 1,000-metre race the next day. While this was disappointing to everyone, we were still so happy that she won a silver medal at a young age and would likely dominate the events in four years.

When Mike's performance dropped off a bit as he hit his NHL draft year in 1974, he was close to spent, done, and not putting the required effort in. My father had treated him like gold during these years, but, like Cathy, the pressure on Mike was immense. I think he had a lot of emotional issues dealing with the guilt and extremely high expectations put on his shoulders as a teenager. No one in the world could blame him for that! The minute Mike quit playing junior hockey at around eighteen, my father's opinion of him changed considerably, certainly not for the better. That had to be difficult for Mike, who did not deserve to be treated like this.

Soon after Mike quit junior hockey, Cathy retired from skating at nineteen years old, well before her prime. Had she stayed skating, it was highly likely at twenty-three years old she would have been the favorite for gold medals in the 500- and 1,000-metre events. Why would you retire as a teenager in a sport where teenagers don't usually win? Here's a better question, with an obvious answer: Did she think she was better off not living her dream or living her dream while being forced to deal with our parents?

Well, once the two of them chose to leave competitive sports, I think the tide turned quickly. I was setting records at the car dealership that my dad and I worked at, and I certainly felt my dad's attention on me, as if I was becoming the new family star. At eighteen, I was the number-one Chrysler salesman in Canada, so Dad had another son to be proud of. To be clear, Dad loved us all, he just really loved watching the stars in action. At the time, I was not quite aware of how sick this all was, as I was busy learning how to sell people cars and then build a team and help them sell.

Years later I came to believe Mike had trouble accepting the fact that the star roles were now reversed a bit, and he might have resented it a little. I may well be wrong on this, but that is my feeling. Cathy, Mary, and Irene were very happy for me and unbelievably supportive. I can say with certainty and a loving feeling that my three kind sisters have supported me all my life with the couple of exceptions when conflicts with Mike were involved. Most brothers are not fortunate enough to be able to say this.

A few years after Mike quit hockey, he came to work at the same dealership I was working at. For a while things were going really well for us, and we eventually decided to go into a partnership along with one other fella who was a lot older. Together we invested $16,633 in buying our share of the company, and we worked together running that. Before long, we started to have many disagreements on how to run the business, but we always did well financially, and outside of work, we were still really great friends, just not so much at work.

As time went on, we continued to grow our business and take on more and more expansion. All the while, though, our differences and struggles to have a healthy, functional relationship at work or even outside of work grew worse and worse. It began to affect my life in a terrible way, and he likely felt the same. Eventually, there came a time when I had to look closely at the way I was handling my relationship with my brother and make some dramatic changes.

I remember vividly an incident that was the catalyst to some of the most profound changes I've made in my life. It was about eight at night in the early spring of 2007, and I'd just finished eating dinner, having arrived home from work around seven. I was trying to relax after another interesting day running a public company in the auto retail business. Just then, the phone rang. I walked over to my home phone, and the call display showed Mike calling. My heart sank a bit, and I did not have the willpower to pick it up, as I was pretty sure it would be another angry rant from Mike. By now these kinds of calls were coming weekly. Five minutes later it rang again, and I just could not answer it, as I knew I or my company must have done something to piss off Mike again. Perhaps a potential acquisition we were working on had leaked. Perhaps we were having a really good month on the manufacturer's midmonth sales results. Perhaps an employee from one of his dealerships had applied to work at one of ours. Obviously, I had no idea what tonight's potential tirade would be about and really did not have the energy to deal with it.

Thirty minutes later the phone rang yet again. After so many years of angry screaming between us, I just could not bear any more fights. So again, I resisted picking up the phone. I simply could not take any more emotional pain. Why did I put up with this kind of pain? I suppose I'll never know, but I do know I was weary from all the battles. There were many times I looked into his eyes, and it was like seeing someone I had never known before. Maybe he thought the same of me.

Anyway, I went to the fridge and drank a beer in record time, then repeated the formula until six beers and about thirty-five minutes later, when I thought I could relax. It was about this moment that my life changed in a near miraculous way.

It was as if I had the ability to step outside myself and really look at what was going on. I literally thought, *What on earth could make someone with everything I have so unhappy and so filled with anxiety?* Someone who had three wonderful and supportive kids in their early twenties, someone who had managed a couple of years earlier to get through a divorce with the very kind mother of our kids in a peaceful and polite manner, and someone who had survived a chaotic upbringing to have what I did.

As I sat in my family room with too many beers in me that night, something magical happened. I express it that way because I had been in the same situation hundreds of times before this and had never done anything meaningful to help myself. Saying that I was depressed and emotionally spent to the point of exhaustion from all this was an understatement. The truth was many, many nights my anxiety level was so through the roof that sleep was not possible without sleeping pills or alcohol to numb the pain. The resilience learned from my days as a child and teenager enabled me to get up early in the morning, forget about last night, and head into work to try to motivate the team to keep focusing on what we could control. This cycle lasted for years on end, and I am so sorry that some of my behavior hurt our family.

That night I proclaimed to myself that enough is enough. Had I not done that, the results of my life would not have been pretty. That night was the last time I ever had a drink of alcohol, which I am so thankful for. Otherwise, as I said, I could have continued managing my unhappiness and stress with alcohol, and ultimately wound up having the same destiny as my father.

Unfortunately, even doing the work, including quitting drinking alcohol, did not solve the problems with Mike fully until Diana entered my life. But for now, I will say the troubled upbringing we experienced along with the troubled years later with Mike proved to be very formative and ultimately beneficial to me. Without these struggles, I may not have been desperate enough to find and study Buddhism or been motivated to practice (and continue to practice) bringing mindfulness, gratitude, and self-compassion to every aspect of my life. As you will see in the coming notes, my personal life and even my business strategies have been deeply influenced by Buddhism.

Children, I hope these background stories I've shared will give you some context for my "notes" in the following pages as well as the life philosophies I came to cultivate and try to practice each and every day.

The famous Vietnamese Buddhist monk and spiritual leader Thich Nhat Hanh would say with remarkable consistency that in order to find true happiness we must also suffer in our lives. Without suffering, true happiness is pretty much a rare thing, otherwise we may not understand what happiness really is.

With this in mind, I can honestly say I am truly grateful for all the bad things that have happened in my life as well as all the wonderful things that have come my way. I count each of you and Diana as the most precious blessings that have come into my life. And the good has certainly outweighed the bad by a huge margin. I am indeed a lucky man.

DRIVE AND INSPIRATION

"Inspiration is hard to come by. You have to take it where you found it."

Bob Dylan

WHEN MUSIC WAS KING

Children, "Drive and Inspiration" seems to be the perfect chapter to begin these notes with, as it is simply impossible to reach our goals and dreams without both. It's sad to say, but without them, it is not worth pursuing anything that is very challenging, as we will inevitably give up early on our journey and end up even more discouraged than before we started. Inspiration is often easy to find at the beginning of our journeys; the trick is to keep going through all the ups and downs we will face along the way to fruition.

Inspiration for me began seriously in my midteens as I was realizing that if I did not work on my skills and improve my effort, I would likely end up living my life in a similar manner to my parents. Watching them struggle to stay sober, struggle to pay bills, and struggle to find self-respect made me very resolute in finding my way to the light. It was actually a lot of fear that had me moving, and I used the serious music playing in my head to channel this fear into inspiration.

One example of that was John Lennon's acid view of the wealthy and powerful in "Working Class Hero." It hit me pretty hard at sixteen years old. I was seeking a way out of the house and was trying to figure out who I'd be when I grew up. In a way, that song was such a scary cautionary tale of what could happen to you as an adult, it inspired me to be more brave and live life more on my terms.

> They hurt you at home and they hit you at
>   school
> They hate you if you're clever and they
>   despise a fool
> Till you're so [effing] crazy you can't fol-
>   low their rules
>
> When they've tortured and scared you for
>   twenty-odd years
> Then they expect you to pick a career
> When you really can't function, you're so
>   full of fear

Another example of finding my inspiration through music was this alluring line from "False Faces," a haunting 1977 Dan Fogelberg song:

> Oh false faces and meaningless chases
> I travel alone.

For many years I pondered so many things derived from the song. So many times running for first place, so many times chasing meaningless stuff, so many times wondering whose truth was a lie and wondering why I was so fortunate to be handed the escapes I was given to help me when perhaps I could not save myself.

We all need a spark to light the flame on moving forward toward our goals. For some, it's a terrible childhood; for some, the fear of loneliness; for some, the fear of ending up with a life like their parents; for some, to escape poverty; for some, to prove other people wrong; for some, the need to do some good in this world; for some, to make their parents or children proud; and there are so many more reasons.

Many years later I realized fear was my inspiration, and music was the spark I needed and used.

COULD YOU PLEASE MOVE THAT BUTT?

While growing up, I learned a fair bit about emotions from so many different situations that occurred around our house. I kept asking myself, "How normal is this?" I vividly remember working on a Saturday night as a sixteen-year-old lot kid (car washer and errand runner) and rushing home around ten that evening to get a quick shower and go meet up with my girlfriend. When I arrived home, I didn't see my parents and just assumed they were out partying somewhere. I cleaned up, walked down the street to the home of my girlfriend, and after spending a few minutes over there, we decided to go back to my house at about eleven.

This is where the adventure started. I can laugh about it today, children, but put yourself in my shoes and think how you might have felt that evening. I tried to open the front door, but it wouldn't open fully as it seemed to be bumping into something. I was a little perplexed, and after bumping it a few times, I quickly looked around the partially open door and, lo and behold, I had been opening it into the body of my

passed-out, five-foot-ten, two-hundred-and-eighty-pound father. It was his butt that kept the door from opening fully, but
incredibly he never woke up.

Heavy emotions run through your mind at times like
these, the first being embarrassment. What a glorious way to
impress a girl. All I could say was "This is my father," and of
course I had no idea what was running through her mind as
she watched this unfold. This was her first physical meeting
with either of my parents, and I can't imagine she was all that
impressed. Needless to say, the romantic moment and night
were lost. Soon after, her strict snob of a father said she could
not date me anymore, and that was all she wrote.

Like I said, many emotions and thoughts run through our
heads in times like these, but a few weeks later, it led to me realize it was time to start making my own way out of the house
and on with my life. It was not an easy way to find drive and
motivation, but it certainly was a memorable one.

NO EXCUSES, NO SURRENDER

In early May of 1978, I made the decision to quit my job
at the only dealership I had ever worked for and move to
Edmonton in order to further my hopes of owning my own
dealership someday. I was hired at Westown Ford to manage their new-vehicle department, and it was a significant
challenge at the time. I borrowed a van to move some things
from Calgary into the house I'd just bought in Edmonton.
It was a regular-size vehicle that had been customized for
camping and getaways, so space was at a premium. I had to
determine what was most essential for living, as I had room
for only a few things, so I included a mattress, a TV, a turn-
table, some audio receivers, and two huge speakers. It was
very clear to me what the priorities were, as there was no

way in the world that the van was going with a couch rather than my speakers.

The dealership was a huge store with the potential to grow even more, and it was well known, as the owner also owned the Edmonton Oilers, which had just signed a seventeen-year-old Wayne Gretzky. On a side note, Wayne came to the dealership to get a car, and he loved my baby-blue Thunderbird demo that I was driving and took it home for his first vehicle. I really wanted to keep driving this beautiful car, but it was the only one we had, and he wanted it, so I was happy for him. He was a very humble kid considering the fame he already had in Canada.

This was a very challenging job, and believe me, drive and motivation were really imperative to have in large supply. My second day on the job, Peter, who was not involved day-to-day happenings at the dealership, came into my office and welcomed me to the team. That was the nice part of the conversation before he told me that if I did not fix the mess the last new-vehicle manager left, I would be fired quickly. This was not exactly the same tone he'd used when hiring me a month before. I had sold my house in Calgary and purchased a new one in Edmonton to take this job, so the pressure was on.

About a week after my twenty-third birthday, on my way home from work I picked up the albums *Some Girls* by the Rolling Stones and *Darkness on the Edge of Town* by Bruce Springsteen, hoping to put the albums on real loud while sitting on the floor of my furnitureless living room. I was certainly expecting the Stones album to be a classic and hoping I might like Springsteen's. Boy, was I wrong. I was literally blown away by Springsteen's concepts of tough times, the rich and the poor, lost love, and trying to find hope and inspiration somewhere. As I was seeking to find mine, two songs played in my head on a daily basis and pushed me to not be left behind in this world. Here are some of the lyrics that inspired me from the songs:

"The Promised Land"
Working all day in my daddy's garage
Driving all night chasing some mirage
Pretty soon, little girl, I'm gonna take
    charge

The dogs on Main Street howl
'Cause they understand
If I could take one moment into my hands
Mister, I ain't a boy, no, I'm a man
And I believe in the promised land

I've done my best to live the right way
I get up in the morning and go to work
    each day
But your eyes go blind and your blood
    runs cold
Sometimes I feel so weak I just want to
    explode
Explode and tear this whole town apart
Take a knife and cut this pain from my
    heart
Find somebody itching for something to
    start

"Darkness on the Edge of Town"
You know some folks are born into a good
    life
And other folks get it anyway, anyhow
Well now, I lost my money and I lost my
    wife
Them things don't seem to matter much
    to me now

Tonight I'll be on that hill 'cause I can't stop
I'll be on that hill with everything I got
With our lives on the line where dreams
    are found and lost
I'll be there on time and I'll pay the cost
For wanting things that can only be found
In the darkness on the edge of town
In the darkness on the edge of town

Children, in 1978, when you started out with nothing, the only way you had a chance to be a car dealer was to have financial backing from a major manufacturer, such as Chrysler. The only way they would invest in you was if your track record running someone else's dealership was spectacular. So believe me, when I arrived at Westown Ford with my future on the line, there was simply nothing that would hold me back.

THE MUSIC THAT SHAPED ME

Between the ages of fifteen and twenty-five, many of us form our views and become real adults making life decisions. During those formative years, the following artists and songs moved me and helped me shape my life in the direction I wanted to go. So many of these songs were raging through my brain straight into my soul. I was fascinated by the lyrics and themes running through them. Through some of these songs, I came to realize that if I worked hard enough and believed in myself, I could really make things happen for my life. In a sense, these songs were the joyful inspiration that fueled so much of my drive and early success:

- The Beatles' "Help!," "A Day in the Life," "Helter Skelter," "Here Comes the Sun," and "Let It Be"

- George Harrison's "Isn't It a Pity," "All Things Must Pass," "Run of the Mill," and "Art of Dying"
- John Lennon's raging "Gimme Some Truth," "Working Class Hero," "Steel and Glass," "Watching the Wheels," and "I'm Losing You"
- Bob Dylan's brilliant songs "Like a Rolling Stone," "The Times They Are A-Changin'," "Positively 4th Street," "Dirge," "Sara," "Tangled Up in Blue," "Idiot Wind," "Hurricane," "Where Are You Tonight?," "Slow Train," and so many more
- The Rolling Stones' "Sympathy for the Devil," "Street Fighting Man," "Salt of the Earth," "Gimme Shelter," "Angie," and "Memory Motel"
- Neil Young's "The Last Trip to Tulsa," "After the Gold Rush," "Don't Let It Bring You Down," "Revolution Blues," "Don't Be Denied," and "Ambulance Blues"
- Bruce Springsteen's "Born to Run," "The Promised Land," "Darkness on the Edge of Town," "Independence Day," and "The River"
- Jackson Browne's "Late for the Sky," "The Late Show," "Sleep's Dark and Silent Gate," "The Pretender," and "Running on Empty"
- Pink Floyd's "Wish You Were Here," "Mother," "Hey You," "Comfortably Numb," and "Vera"
- Dan Fogelberg's "Aspen/These days," "The Last Nail," "Part of the Plan," "Times like These," "Loose Ends," "Same Old Lang Syne," "Nether Lands," and "False Faces"

At the back of the book I share with you some other songs that also shaped me through the last fifty years. Perhaps you'd enjoy listening to some of them, or maybe some will even inspire each of you to make a playlist of the songs that have most touched your soul and driven you to be the person you want to be. What an inspirational Apple playlist you could create.

Inspiration can be really tough to find, children. Please take a long look around to find yours, and when you find it, be sure to keep it.

STAYING HUNGRY

"The bird who has eaten cannot fly with the bird that is hungry." Children, this Native American proverb is an excellent way of recognizing we need to be hungry and stay motivated to hit our loftier goals and dreams. The lesson I learned early on about always running our business as if we are in a recession can't be learned enough times.

WATERING THE SEEDS

THE TWO WOLVES

Over the time I was assembling this book and going through the boxes of notes that I kept for decades, sometimes I found an insightful, thought-provoking one. One such night I came across the following Native American proverb that made me really ponder the choices we all make with our thoughts each and every minute of each and every day and the serious effects these choices mean for us. The exact origin of the story is uncertain, but it is often attributed to the Lenape or Cherokee people. This is the version I found:

> An old Cherokee was teaching his grandson
> about life. "A fight is going on inside me," he
> said to the boy. "It is a terrible fight and it is
> between two wolves. One is evil—he is anger,
> envy, sorrow, regret, greed, arrogance, self-pity,
> guilt, resentment, inferiority, lies, false pride,
> superiority, and ego. The other is good—he
> is joy, peace, love, hope, serenity, humility,
> kindness, benevolence, empathy, generosity,
> truth, compassion, and faith. This same fight
> is going on inside you—and inside every other

> person, too." The grandson thought about it
> for a minute and then asked his grandfather,
> "Which wolf will win?" The old Cherokee sim-
> ply replied, "The one you feed."

After I finished reading this, memories came flashing back, as too many times I've fed the wrong wolf inside me. The good news is if we are simply on a path of improving our self-feeding habits—not perfection here, just improving—we will feed the good wolf more, and our lives will be better to us.

GARDENING

Practicing mindfulness will help us recognize the wholesome seeds within ourselves, and we should try to water them every day. This is a very intelligent, enlightened, and kind life practice. We all possess the ability to obtain a fair bit more enlightenment; we simply need to nurture it. Obviously, our minds perceive many things both good and bad. Some of these thoughts bring us more happiness, some bring us more sorrow. Any of us who have lived on this earth for some time know this to be factual, and experience teaches us to spend a bit of time working on mindfulness.

I like to think of ourselves as gardeners of our own emotions; we decide which seeds to water and cultivate. Like a garden in our backyard, it is obvious the plants we water live and those we do not water wither away. The good news here is our mind and thoughts are exactly the same.

By practicing daily to focus on our positive emotions, we are not only helping ourselves, but we are helping our children and loved ones learn a wonderful way to live. Our example here will have a profound effect on our loved ones today and as they move through the many stages of their lives. This is a practice we are really doing for our children as well as our grandchildren, as it is possible to be learned in each generation. I think the most important gift a parent can give their children is their own happiness.

Unfortunately, the opposite is also true, as no child enjoys growing up in a home where negative emotions dominate the household. As I wrote about earlier in the book, it is very clear that my mother and father suffered very much in their early lives. I suspect growing up in the situations they did made it difficult for them to be good gardeners without tending to some important internal work.

It seems so obvious to me that our upbringing helps to form the many emotions, thoughts, and actions we unconsciously participate in, at least until we have done some work on ourselves so we can consciously see and manage our own thoughts and emotions. With a little consistent mindfulness and effort, our upbringing need not define us, and we can use it as a positive factor.

Please remember that it takes time and patience to get into the habit of watering our positive seeds and not watering our negative ones, especially if they were present in our homes growing up.

Children, someplace inside of us our healthy, positive seeds are born; we just need to water them and watch them grow. Please strive to be excellent gardeners.

WE KNOW

We know that we each have stored in our consciousness positive and negative seeds, as every human being does. We also know very much about watering our seeds.

> If we water them, they will grow
> We can choose which to water
> If we continue to water our positive seeds,
>   we will be happy
> If we continue to water our negative
>   seeds, we will suffer
> Our children know which seeds we water
> This is a significant life decision

I've learned from experience that it takes time and patience to get into the habit of watering our positive seeds and not watering our negative ones. The main reason it takes time and persistence is that very often the negative seeds are more powerful initially, and unfortunately, many times our upbringing was slanted to watering our negative seeds. Please think about this as you move through the different stages of your lives.

We really need to build a strong foundation, for the winds will surely change, and challenges will come. By always watering our positive seeds, we will have this rock-solid foundation in place to enjoy the life we are living.

ADVERSITY

WE HIT THE ROAD

Some things in life happen to us, and we never give it a second thought. On the other extreme there are those days that we can still somehow remember the feelings if not every detail of, years and years later. One of those days that I still vividly remember was the day we all left Hamilton, Ontario. It was sure a day as sad as they come, as we all packed into a large station wagon with my grandparents crying in front of their house on Fairleigh Avenue. Two parents, five kids, a dog, a lot of pain, and most everything we owned in one car. My grandparents had lived there my whole life, and we had lived with them off and on for a couple of those years, so they were surely going to miss us, and we were going to miss them.

Today I thought about this exact day in Hamilton fifty-five years ago as Diana and I said goodbye to Laura and her girls, Evie and Emily. Even knowing we would see them a month from now, it was still emotional for all of us, and there were a heck of a lot of hugs. Really can't imagine the feeling my grandparents felt so many years ago.

I can still somewhat remember the motel we stayed in halfway to Thunder Bay, four kids under twelve years old in one room, and my parents and a toddler in the other. Life was not making much sense to me. Why were we moving to the middle of nowhere in a northern Ontario city? We liked living close to our grandparents and had spent so much time with them growing up. All I saw as we were leaving was two extremely upset grandparents who were always kind to me and two parents ready to explode at each other. This was not a road trip anyone was too happy about. Years later I found out from my mother that the true reason we left Hamilton was my father's theft of money from the General Motors dealership he was working at as a sales manager there.

After much reflection years later, I can't imagine the pain, humiliation, and embarrassment my dad must have felt taking my grandparents' daughter and all their grandchildren away because he could not possibly get another good job in Hamilton after what he'd done.

As a twelve-year-old, leaving my grandparents and a home I loved was an early lesson in facing adversity that served me well years later when I would really need it. Often the challenges we face that certainly disappoint us are the ones that give us the wisdom we will need as we go through life. It was also the beginning of the teachings of empathy for me. Even though I didn't yet understand the circumstances, I could sense my father's humiliation as he sat behind the wheel of the station wagon, and I remember feeling sad for him.

A few decades on I would come to understand two important life lessons I was fortunate to learn from that terrible day and all that led up to it. When facing adversity, we need to take personal responsibility for our actions, and we better learn to become good leaders if we do not want to repeat this life when we have our own families. On that sad, sad day, I surely began to realize the cavalry wasn't coming anytime soon, and it was going to be up to me to eventually take my life in the right direction.

BOXING AND ADVERSITY

Boxing's biggest questions about the greatness of a top young fighter were the same one hundred years ago as it is today. How does a top young fighter handle adversity? How does he come back from the brink of no return when his mind and body cannot take any more? No matter the talent, no matter the speed, no matter the power, no matter the ability to not get hit much—at a certain point in one's career, each fighter will face their moment of truth.

Imagine you are still fighting in the tenth round and your opponent has taken everything you have and is still coming forward. Your energy is completely drained, and you are hit with a massive combination of punches. Your body and mind have never had to deal with this severe adversity, and you have two options: one is to go down and live to fight another day, and the other is to reach deep down in your soul and find a way to survive and fight back. What will you do?

The best fighters of all time have faced this adversity many times in their careers and conquered their fears and emotions to win most times. Are our lives not exactly the same? Do we not have major setbacks to come back from? Aren't there many times along the road when we want to give up on what we really want?

Of course there are—for all of us. As a young man I was fortunate to watch the prodigious Muhammad Ali conquer severe adversity and knock it on its butt. After watching and following Ali, how could I not do the same in my life, or at minimum try a lot harder to fight through the adversity? It was clear my adversity paled in comparison to Ali's.

I learned early on that it is not the adversity we face that defines us, it is how we handle it that defines us. This, of course, sounds like a cliché, but it is a significant truth of the lives we all live. Unfortunately, it is almost exclusively learned from life's many challenges we all face. A good example of this was in December 1982 as my family was going back to Edmonton for Christmas, and the dealership was almost bankrupt again. We knew we had to work even harder and smarter in 1983 to turn the dealership around once more, lest we fail in the first business we owned.

Facing and conquering adversity prepared me to handle it much better the next time it came around, which it did. It also gave me the strength I needed to take advantage of significant opportunities that came my way.

If we want to win the battle against adversity, it is not simply a cliché to declare that the way we respond to it will indeed define us and our lives. Remember, the things that disappoint us are often the events that teach us wisdom. Kids, please also remember adversity comes knocking on everyone's door, not just ours. Fighting back from adversity is a major life advantage for you.

THOUGHTS ON OVERCOMING ADVERSITY

I've been fortunate to have learned a fair bit about adversity and how to overcome it most of the time. Often that adversity was caused by myself, and that can be even trickier to deal with. I have watched so many people overcome severe adversity, much worse than anything I ever had to face. Seeing others have this kind of courage, dedication, and commitment often motivated me to overcome my problems, which were insignificant compared to others'.

I encourage you to learn from influential people, such as Helen Keller, who overcame oppressive adversity. One of my favorite quotes of hers is "When one door of happiness closes,

NOTES FOR THE CHILDREN 49

another opens, but often we look so long at the closed door that we do not see the one which has been opened for us."

In my life I have certainly experienced a door of happiness opening for me when another door has closed unexpectedly. Unfortunately, though, I've also experienced the tendency to look at that closed door and get so defeated and negative about it that I cannot see the open one in front of me. I have learned the hard way that focusing on the negative thoughts in our heads about our adversity will clearly not help us work through the problems and arrive at solutions that lead to opportunity.

It is so important to remember that being self-aware and in the right state of mind actually helps solve the adversity we are facing. I realize this is easier said than done, but believe me, I've done it both ways throughout my life, and watering the seeds of mindfulness, kindness, and wisdom has really helped me overcome adversity, while feeling sorry for myself and feeling that the world was against me actually made things much worse. The only thing that behavior accomplished was for me and anyone I loved around me to feel more miserable.

We need to think of these negative thoughts in our heads as uninvited guests in our homes. Gandhi said it so much better that I can: "I will not let anyone walk through my mind with their dirty feet." And this includes ourselves.

When we accept the fact that adversity is inevitable, we are in a much better position to move on from setbacks, big or small. Trying to resist adversity will not help us. Of course, well-thought-out plans can help us avoid some adversity in our lives, but it will come in some shape or form, regardless of our preparation.

An obvious plan to experience less adversity is to learn lessons from our previous adversity so that we don't repeat the same problems time and time again. Unfortunately, it took me far too many years to learn this. Living life will teach us that continually repeating mistakes is a choice, not another mistake. A perfect painful lesson I slowly learned was to stop repeating the negative story I would keep telling myself about how unfair life is and why I have this dreadful family situation that's ripping at me most days.

Too many good people I have known in my career think that adversity is a sign that the world is out to get them, and really that isn't the truth. We all have to watch the stories that we tell ourselves and be careful of how we view things. If we continually believe the world is out to get us, this will only make our adversity worse. Not thinking the world is out to get us will really help us move on from setbacks and serious problems and feel a lot better about ourselves.

Another plan for overcoming adversity is to recognize it as an opportunity to learn more about patience, humility, courage, resilience, self-discipline, and many other important character strengths. I have not met many truly successful people who have not faced and overcome serious adversity in some shape or form. A bit of failure is simply part of our successful journeys. These are wonderful tools to help us on our paths.

EDMONTON OILERS

It was one heck of a glorious run of hockey, beginning around 1983 in Edmonton, and the city was along for the ride. We were selling cars during the day and hoping we had the night off to watch the Oilers score a ton of goals led by a skinny kid under twenty years old named Wayne Gretzky.

Although we all knew he would become one of the greatest hockey players of all time, it was not accomplished by talent alone. Wayne led the team as the young Oilers took on the multitime Stanley Cup champion New York Islanders in the league finals. Though the Oilers suffered a devastating loss, the lessons learned from losing were well worth the cost. Rather than complain about it, they learned hard lessons from it and committed to making the necessary changes that led to numerous Stanley Cup wins starting only a year later.

Here are Wayne's words about losing the final to the New York Islanders in 1983:

> Only a few short years earlier we were watching Trottier, Bossy, Billy Smith, and Dennis Potvin and the other great players they had on TV. Then a few years later, we were playing against them in the finals. We were on a pretty good roll coming into the series and thinking we were invincible. We walked by their locker room in the corridor and saw after they won that they were too beat up to really enjoy it and savor the victory at that moment. We were able to walk out of there pretty much scot-free. We had so much respect for the Islander players and the Islander team that we learned immediately you have to take it to a different level in order to win a Stanley Cup. And that's what we did. We learned from it and often credit the Islander players and Islander team for teaching us exactly what it's all about and how hard it is to win.

Children, the Oilers won four of the next five Stanley Cup Finals, a feat likely never to be repeated by any team. Believe me, losing can be an awesome teacher and motivator for future goals. It's clear that it's our choice how we respond; we can either give up or learn from it. We can either be more committed to our goals as the Oilers were, or we can complain about it.

My childhood and the sibling challenges I met in

adulthood gave me many opportunities to face adversity and make a choice about how to deal with adversity. I certainly wasn't always a gracious loser or resilient enough when facing adversity, but over the years I have gotten better at letting myself learn from it and recommit to my personal and professional goals. I sure hope you just keep getting better; that's the ultimate goal we can ask of ourselves.

WHY ME?

Regrettably, for me and those closest to me, it took a number of real beatdowns to figure out how to understand and better deal with adversity. Many times in my life while going through some adversity, I heard, listened to, and believed the age-old "Why me?" running through my thoughts. I can tell you emphatically this never helped in any way to solve the issues I was dealing with. I am a bit embarrassed to admit this fact to you, as no one wants to be known as a "why me" complainer, but we all have this tendency in us sometimes.

The simple truth is I only helped the seeds of negative emotions like envy grow in me by watering them with an inner voice of "Why me?" or "Why is this stuff always happening to me?" My view here is that most humans experience reasonable adversity that can be overcome to a degree, at least with some work on ourselves. It is so critical to know we are not the only ones who have to overcome many roadblocks along the road.

Children, besides the strength and resiliency that it grows in you, one of the most beautiful things about letting go of the old "why me" narrative, and instead accepting and overcoming adversity, is the superb example it provides for your children to see and emulate. Watching a brave parent struggle and overcome adversity can be life-changing for children in the most positive way. What a blessing that is.

RESPECT AND DIGNITY

EVERY SINGLE PERSON DESERVES THIS

One thing I am very proud of is how we built our company on a platform of treating everyone with respect and dignity. We have focused on this for over forty-five years and fully believe it has been a significant part of our success. Of course, there are always some people at any large company that do not follow this practice, but we do try to change their thinking or weed them out. We must continually work on this, as it can slip if we are not focused on it.

My father was the one who first taught me that treating people with respect and dignity is the only way to move forward in life and business. His words about treating the lowest-paid person the same as the CEO in any company still ring in my ears. But it took me a number of years to fully comprehend what he meant by this.

His thinking was twofold: first and foremost, treating all people with respect and dignity is the proper way to live. He told me that if I ever date a girl who is rude and condescending to any server when we are out for dinner, you might want to get out of that relationship as quickly as possible. To this day, I try my best to treat each person in our company, or whoever we are dealing with, the same, which is with respect and dignity, regardless of their position or status in life.

The second part of his thinking was that treating all people the same is good for business. He would say that the local representative of Chrysler Canada you are dealing with today when you are twenty-six may well be a senior executive of the company when you are forty, and she will surely remember how you treated her when she was not in such an important position. That advice has proven true many times.

We have had a few executives over the years at our company who were the exact opposite of that. They would lavish praise and suck up to executives from the manufacturers we were dealing with, yet they'd treat people in entry-level positions at our or other companies like unimportant human beings.

It is not hard to see who lives by the values my father taught me and who does not. Always remember it is easy to be respectful to important people, as often, we are trying to make friends with them for our social circles or wanting something they can provide. The real test of character is how we treat those in serving positions and those well below our pay grade at work. Another character test is to see how you treat these people when no one is watching. Regardless of how well any of us have done in this life, the most important thing that speaks to who we are is how we treat other people.

CLOSE IT PROPERLY, YOU IDIOT

Although my dad's advice on how to treat others was very important to me, I also had to live and breathe some very uncomfortable situations to truly comprehend the power of giving others respect and dignity. As a nineteen-year-old kid, I had the misfortune to work for an owner who, after having a few drinks, would just tear into people, including my father, and leave them humiliated and often broken.

How can I remember a specific incident that occurred one evening around six in the summer of 1974? I can because it was so impactful to me and taught me to never in my lifetime treat another human being in such a way.

The dealership owner was driving from our lot to the main road out front, to head home, when his front hood popped open a bit. Generally, a person would think he would put his Imperial in park, get out, and close the hood like any decent person would. Instead, he saw about ten of us standing outside the showroom, put his passenger window down, and screamed at my father to come over and close his hood. Dutifully, my dad walked over and slammed the hood down; however, as soon as the vehicle was in drive, it opened again. This only made the situation that much more degrading, as the owner screamed at my father again and said, "Close it properly, you idiot." This happened again, so a few of us walked over to try to save him from any more embarrassment, but the owner told us my father would have to fix it and to "get back to what you were doing," which was standing outside waiting for customers. After a couple more attempts by Dad to close it, the owner got out and told my father to get him a new Imperial immediately, change the plates, and go put gas in it for him. When he returned with a fully fueled new car about twenty minutes later, the owner told my father that if his original Imperial was not fixed by 9 a.m. the next day, he was fired. He drove off as if this were normal behavior.

I walked over to my father, who was pretty embarrassed, and said something like, "Why do you have to accept being treated like a subhuman being by this creep?"

He replied, "I don't really have a choice, son, we need money for rent and food."

I certainly understood his predicament and felt beyond

sorry that this was his fate in life. Easy to see then why he drank so much and was depressed much of the time.

As this was happening, many thoughts were flooding my head, the important one being *Please God, make sure when I make it a bit in life, I don't ever treat people like this.* Situations like this were a very powerful situation for me to observe, and it ultimately motivated me to a higher place. Unfortunately, this time it was at my father's expense.

SEARCHING FOR DIGNITY

No complaints here, children, but it was tough at home with my father being drunk or often passed out anywhere in the house, including on many floors. Of course, it was worse when any of us had friends over, and we literally had to walk around or sometimes even over him. It was also difficult to watch my mom continue to belittle and scream at him, but she was in a tough position, and in those times it might have been impossible to imagine being a single mom of five kids. Think about that situation in 1968.

But where it started to take its toll on me was at work, where my father would be constantly drunk, glassy-eyed, and stumbling around. Often another staff member or I would have to wake him up as he was snoring in his office to appraise a trade-in vehicle, as that was one of his jobs. As a teenager trying to make something of myself in this world, the embarrassment of watching the sales crew actually laughing at his state of impairment many nights was tough to swallow. Years later I realized that he was fortunate that the owner was also an alcoholic, for a sober owner, even in the early seventies, would not have put up with that.

I, as well as my brother and sisters, did everything we

could to help him, but it would never last more than a couple of days. The embarrassment and guilt I felt over his drinking took until I was around forty years old to get over. Why did I feel so guilty because my father drank himself into oblivion most days? Many children of alcoholics have been wrestling with that question for years. I am pretty sure it affected my siblings in many distressing ways as well, and I am sorry for the pain they had to deal with.

I've learned a lot about respect and dignity from dealing with alcoholism including:

- Each and every human being deserves respect.
- Alcoholism is a disease, not a character flaw.
- Alcoholics need love and respect like everyone else.
- There is no dignity in treating people cruelly.
- There is no dignity in liking to watch other people suffer, especially when we do it to elevate our own self-worth.
- There is no dignity in beating someone down further when they are in the dumps already.

Alcoholism is like a lethal virus running through each family it invades. Having said this, it does not mean we should treat alcoholics poorly or without respect. It can also affect each of us who have lived it, for years after we leave the family home, and sadly, it seems to run through too many of the children's families as well. It is a compelling accomplishment when the second generation can eliminate this disease from wreaking havoc on their family.

EMOTIONS

NEGATIVE THOUGHTS LEAD TO NEGATIVE EMOTIONS

For too many years I looked at my emotions and the lack of control I had over them in an erroneous manner. Somehow it never seemed to help me when someone would say, "You need to learn to control your emotions better." I would say to myself, *Well, that's likely true, but how do I actually do it?* I also learned years later our toxic thoughts can actually harm us emotionally and physically, thus we need to pay close attention to them. This practice changes the quality of our lives.

It wasn't until I started looking deeply into what caused this or that emotion that I learned how to better control them. I began searching inside my anger, my regret, my frustrations, my jealousy, etc., to try to understand why I felt that way. Often during these times of heavy emotional stress, I would think, *The train of my life is coming off the tracks.* Over time I became more aware and mindful of how the negative thoughts were pouring into me and tried to address why they were coming in relentless waves, and more importantly, how to see and stop them so they didn't escalate into overwhelming negative emotions.

With much diligence and practice in noticing and

controlling my negative thoughts, most of the negative feelings the thoughts caused began to come and go more quickly. Thus my overall emotional state became more positive because each wave of emotion on its own was no longer overpowering and controlling me.

I've read that we have anywhere from 6,000 to 70,000 thoughts a day in our heads. The difference between these two numbers is not that significant because even 6,000 a day coming in with little self-awareness can cause us to have virtually no control over our emotions. This lack of awareness, of course, will not only lead to negative thinking, but it also results in negative actions and negative results. Children, it is imperative we find a way to notice and manage this nonstop noise in our heads. Mindfulness will show us the way.

TWISTS AND TURNS

How do we describe this journey of life we are all on from childhood to passing on? There are certainly numerous turns in the road and significant surprises we never anticipated, some good, some bad.

Many of these turns and surprises are actually opportunities that come our way. These opportunities have blessings in them, but we won't be able to recognize them or take advantage of them if we are in a negative emotional space and can't think clearly enough to see things as they are. I have had many excellent opportunities stare me in the face and missed taking advantage of them because of my negative emotional state.

For example, another embarrassing situation to relay to you children happened when I was really losing control of my emotions from so many family fights. This likely caused a very expensive miss for our company at the time. I will not mention the manufacturer by name, but they were going to have someone open a new dealership for them in Edmonton. These open points are worth millions of dollars and sometimes way more. Well, as they were fishing around Edmonton and other areas for a dealer to open the new dealership for them, all the smart people were looking for land and making pitches to the manufacturer for why they should get the dealership.

Sad as this is to say to you kids, I heard from someone months later that the point had been given to someone else. The truth was I didn't even know they were looking in my city. How bad is that? I was furious with myself and said a lot of hurtful things to myself. Within an hour it came to me that I missed the opportunity to participate in this fruitful opportunity because I was so preoccupied over the last year or so with family wars. I was not in control of my emotions; they were clearly controlling me. This was an insight I needed, and ultimately, it became another catalyst for the much-needed change I was about to make in my family relationships.

Life is often like the amazing emotional turns you see in a top streaming series. Many times what happens to us is so out there that people would say no one would believe the script if it was played out in a movie or TV series.

Children, I hope some of the notes I left here will help you clear your mind of negative thoughts and emotions so you have more room to see the blessings in all the unexpected plot twists that will surely come your way over the years and to take advantage of the opportunities, insights, and lessons these moments almost always offer.

THE UNRULY RIVER

In his outstanding book on happiness, Matthieu Ricard wrote, "If the passions are the minds of great dramas, the emotions are the actors. Throughout our lives they rush through our minds like an unruly river, determining countless states of happiness and unhappiness. Should we try to tame this river? Is it even possible, and if so, how? Some emotions make us flourish, others sap our wellbeing, others make us wither."

As Matthieu said, it is our responsibility to continue to work on developing our constructive emotions while trying to free ourselves of the destructive ones. Children, I have learned the hard way that taming our "unruly river" is an essential practice for long-term happiness. You would be wise to start practicing this sooner than I did as you go through life's journey.

OUR CHOICE TO MAKE

Believe me, I speak from painful experiences when I say my emotions were not under control for years of my life, and of course, this hurt the people closest to me as well. Another sad truth I discovered is that some people will learn how to provoke our weak spots to have us lose control of our emotions for their own benefit. It is even sadder that sometimes these people can be from your own family or group of friends.

Fortunately, we can practice ways to be more aware and mindful of our emotions and learn ways to de-escalate them, even when we are being provoked. If we don't work at practicing the mindfulness I am speaking about in these notes, runaway emotions, such as frustration, fear, anger, and jealousy not only hurt us, but they hurt those around us. Many relationships and careers have been lost to a lack of control of our emotions. Hopefully, some of the notes I am writing here will help you a little.

Over the last fifty years or so, I have learned four inescapable facts about emotions:

- If we cannot control our emotions, it is highly unlikely we can be in a healthy long-term relationship.
- If we cannot control our emotions, it is highly unlikely we can lead others on a long-term basis.
- If we cannot control our emotions, they will control us.
- The good news is the choice is always ours to make.

EMOTIONS, RELATIONSHIPS, AND RETAIL

Many of us have serious difficulties while working in any profession and trying to balance it with our home lives. But unlike other professions, when it comes to working in retail, this is a subject I can talk about with authority. The hour-to-hour and day-to-day stress of always having to sell something to earn any money can really take its toll on us and, of course, our loved ones. Unfortunately, I have witnessed the destruction of so many marriages in the industry where one or both parties could not deal with it properly. I suspect many other professions are similar.

I often offer these small bits of advice to our many associates while conducting training:

- Acknowledge that retail is often emotionally demanding, stressful, and chaotic.
- Acknowledge that retail and these pressures can and do affect us at home.
- Acknowledge that our spouses or partners and children also feel our emotional roller coaster ride each day, week, and year.

- Acknowledge that we all tend to take emotional stress out on those closest to us. (Please try not to do this.)
- Acknowledge that it is hard to leave work and then be completely present for our families. (Please try to let work go when you are away.)

You might be surprised by the number of really good people who have told me privately how they so much regret their poor behavior at home with loved ones after a really difficult day. Unfortunately, I have done the same too many times and regret my actions as well. Most of us have also done this in front of our children, as we seem to think it will benefit them in some way to see how tough life can be or how much we are facing when trying to make their lives better. I'm not certain that's a good idea, as children and teenagers usually have enough of their own issues to deal with.

Whatever career path you are traveling along, please remember to understand the challenges your partner faces each day. Kindness, self-compassion, and understanding can go a long way to keeping our marriages happy.

BUDDHIST THINKING

Watch out now, take care
Beware of the thoughts that linger
Winding up inside your head
The hopelessness around you
In the dead of night
Beware of sadness

George Harrison, "Beware of Darkness"

BEWARE OF DARKNESS

George Harrison's epic album *All Things Must Pass* was released in 1970, the same year the Beatles split up. For a fifteen-year-old kid wondering where my life was heading, this album had a pretty significant effect on my thinking. He had spent a lot of time in India looking at the spiritual side of Eastern culture, and this was heavily reflected in the album.

It certainly made me think twice about what we were being taught in our Catholic church and school and certainly had me entertaining new ways of thinking. The thing was I knew there was more to this world and that we could learn to think and act more positively, but I had no idea how to find it.

One of the first things I came to understand in my high school years was that beating yourself up like Dad did was not a way to be happy or successful. There was no honor in beating yourself up, nor being the tough guy insisting that you could take it. It is simply not a good way to live for ourselves or those we love. Unfortunately, it took me over twenty-five more years to fully understand how not to beat myself up.

Looking back, I suspect this was the start of my journey toward Buddhist thinking, and I remember well in university thinking about it a lot. Even so, for a number of years, I put this inquiry aside while chasing the dream of making real money and not having to be broke all the time like my parents. The ironic part of it was that as soon as I started being successful in the car business, I quickly found many new problems coming my way. It wasn't until several years later that I finally started doing some work on myself to try to ease the anxiety and stress of retail and a balanced home life. This is when I returned to thinking about Buddhist philosophies around suffering and happiness, and it kind of took me back to my university days. From then I read a fair bit and kind of understood what would be helpful to me, but I simply did not practice what I was learning—not even remotely enough. It was only years later, when I hit rock bottom, that I started reading and studying much harder, but more importantly, practicing Buddhist mindfulness and philosophies daily.

Imagine a way of thinking that could come to you as a Harrison song, to inspire you in your school years, and eventually return to you and guide you all the way through a midlife crisis and beyond. Not only has Buddhism been the backbone of my success in the highly competitive car dealer business, but it has also shown me the roots of my own suffering and liberated me in many profound ways so that I can love and deeply rejoice in my family and life in the most steady and appreciative ways possible.

SMARTEST AND KINDEST PERSON
I HAVE EVER READ

All the years I spent trying to understand why I was feeling anxious and so down on things was one heck of a long road. Believe me, many of the paths taken to try to improve myself never worked at all or faded fast. Some worked for a little longer, but I can honestly tell you that saying "I can do anything" or "I can conquer all" or any other simple, positive slogans never held. Growing up with the famous Catholic guilt certainly did not do me any good, and often when I was doing better, the guilt would kick in and I would actually feel as if I did not deserve the good things that came our way.

I have wondered many times if people who have a lot of guilt in their souls sabotage their own chances of success, thinking they are not worthy. I am no expert on this subject, but I do believe emphatically that guilt, anxiety, and many more of the afflictions we suffer need to be self-evaluated and worked on. With the experience of looking at many ways of making positive changes over the years, the only one that truly worked for me was the study of Buddhism. I understand that may appear to be in total conflict with selling cars for a living, but I do not think that is true at all.

My best suggestion for all you kids and grandchildren is to read a little of Thich Nhat Hanh's writing. I have met and read the words of hundreds of really smart people over the last fifty years, but nothing compares to the combined insight and wisdom of Thich. Please spend a little time doing this, as the benefits for your loved ones and yourself will be life-changing. I truly believe that learning even a little about how true Buddhists think and act would be helpful for your peace and prosperity.

For example, let's start with something the Buddha said

over and over, "I teach only suffering and the transformation of suffering."

A fact of life is that all humans suffer. The Buddha used suffering to liberate himself, and the Buddhist teachings make it clear we can do the same today with our lives. Of course, we may never reach the Buddha's level of enlightenment, but we can make good progress on our own personal journey. We have to always remember that even if we can transform 30 or 40 or 50 percent of our pain and suffering, this is a major life change for us. The Buddha's teachings can help us eliminate much of our anxiety, stress, envy, jealousy, regret, hate, worry, lack of energy, depression, etc.

For instance, my everyday anxiety over trying to be a proper husband while working to start our first business and raise three children was challenging, as my upbringing really hindered me in this arena of adulthood. Clearly, I should have looked in the mirror and started making positive changes sooner. When I finally found and used the Buddha's teachings, his wisdom helped me remove most of my crippling negative emotions that had plagued me for years. From then on, being a better husband came more naturally.

I've also wanted to be an excellent father to three children I love with everything I have and two stepdaughters who have blessed my life and whom I also love so very much. But I've made some awful mistakes along this path that I truly regret. Again, later in my life, the Buddha's insights made a very positive difference here.

It was important to me to have a successful career and eventually a thriving business so my family had everything we needed financially, and I could feel more like a winner. It was my ego that drove me to feel like a winner, and again the Buddha's advice worked well for my life to keep this ego in check.

Being a really good brother to my four siblings was clearly the most difficult role to succeed in throughout my life. One might think the first three I mentioned would be harder to achieve, but our upbringing and our own behaviors caused a catastrophic family dynamic that impacted far too many areas of my life and my siblings' lives. Children, I am sorry for my part in it, and I thank God for the Buddha's teaching that helped me see my part in the anguish this caused and free myself from it.

Having really strong relationships with all my friends and colleagues at work also set a high bar and was potentially stressful. With all my heart I can tell you, kids, the teams around me over the last forty-five years have been so kind, so skillful, such great teammates, and so much fun to be around and learn from. It is certain that the Buddha's words helped me a bit in my dealings with everyone, and I am certainly thankful for the help.

In fact, trying to be successful in all these things often had me following the wrong paths to get there, and it was only after studying and rethinking that my approach put me on the proper path, as imperfect as it still is.

The easiest way to understand Buddhist philosophy is to start with the Four Noble Truths.

First Noble Truth

Understanding we all suffer to some extent. We all need to recognize and acknowledge the presence of this suffering and touch it.

Second Noble Truth

The second truth asks us to examine the origins, roots, and

NOTES FOR THE CHILDREN

causes of our suffering. We need to recognize and identify how our suffering came to be.

Third Noble Truth

The third truth is we create our own suffering and need to find equanimity with our thoughts and emotions to help stop the suffering. With self-awareness much of our suffering will cease and be replaced with happiness. If that was not likely or possible, why put the effort in? To me, this third noble truth holds hope for a cure from our suffering.

Fourth Noble Truth

The fourth truth is that the path that leads to refraining from doing the things causes us to suffer. The Buddha called it the Noble Eightfold Path, or the Path of Eight Right Practices. They are:

- Right View
- Right Thinking
- Right Speech
- Right Action
- Right Livelihood
- Right Diligence
- Right Mindfulness
- Right Concentration

Let's always remember that most of us will never reach perfection, nor is that the goal here; daily improvement in our happiness, our relationships, and our careers is. I can personally attest to how much this has changed my life. Had I not looked at my own misery and begun studying the Buddha's writing, I would be in a completely different place today. Surely the business success I have enjoyed would not have happened, and it's simply a fact that the woman I love so much would not be here with me today. It's not likely that Diana would have married the old me.

I fully realize that Thich's teachings are hard work, especially at first. However, I ask you to please look into these words, as they will make such a difference. In the end, I believe the hard work we do is a lot easier than not doing it and continuing to suffer in different ways. Understand that children, work, and life in general make it hard to devote time to inner work, but you will be a much better partner, much better parent, and much better leader by doing it.

If we just pause for ten or fifteen minutes a day, and try to stop our incessant thinking, quiet our minds, and read a couple of pages of Thich's book *The Heart of the Buddha's Teaching*, I believe we will find much contentment in our day. Of course, in time, we might realize how much this practice is helping us and spend time in enhanced mindfulness study as well.

ARE YOU SURE THIS IS TRUE?

"The person who suffers most in this world is the person who has many wrong perceptions, and most of our perceptions are erroneous."

Buddha

I thank the Buddha for this insightful lesson. So often I held these wrong perceptions, and it punished not only me but those loved ones around me.

Fortunately, over time I came to understand that the key to a happy, peaceful, and prosperous life is to help ourselves overcome our poor thoughts and habits, which result from those incorrect, punishing thoughts running full speed ahead at us. Many years ago I found this perceptive question to ask myself when negative thoughts start invading my head.

"Are you sure this is true?"

"Are you sure this is true?"

This is such a powerful practice to avoid misperceptions of our thoughts and feelings. That is why we should quickly ask ourselves this twice. If we practice this on a daily basis, we will find that many, if not most, of the negative seeds coming at us incessantly are simply erroneous.

BUDDHIST WISDOM TO LIVE BY

Before you pray, believe
Before you speak, listen
Before you spend, earn
Before you write, think
Before you quit, try
Before you die, live

William Arthur Ward

CONSISTENCY

BUBBLES

It was May 2006, and the team of Bob Clark, Tom Orysiuk, and me were with our Bay Street bankers, trying to sell over $100 million of stock in an Edmonton-based automobile retailer, something that had never been done before in Canada. Bob was the president, Tom was the CFO, and I was founder and CEO. Each day started the same—a breakfast meeting with the bank team at seven, which I hated and will never do again, and meetings of precisely fifty minutes each between eight and six. The lunch meeting often had about thirty to forty people from the investment community to whom I would speak for about fifteen minutes, and then they would ask questions to get us off our game for about thirty minutes.

It was a pressure-packed two weeks, and the bankers tried to keep us on a chain but also wanted us all to have a few laughs along the way to ease that pressure. We certainly had some fun as our investment banker friends were good people who worked hard and wanted us to succeed at selling the stock. They had nicknames for all of us, and mine was Bubbles, which our bankers thought was appropriate because of the fact my first job in the business was washing cars and trucks. I certainly thought it sounded ridiculous, and I did not get into the whole Bubbles role but quickly realized investors really liked and admired people who started at the bottom. The bankers consistently played this up with investors, which was clever of them.

Anyway, after a very average first day, we hit the road Tuesday morning fully prepared for a day of meetings and full of enthusiasm. I don't recall if it was after we had not received an order for stock following five or six more meetings, but panic was quietly setting in. We were driving in a limo over to our final meeting of the day at five, and we did not want word to spread on Bay Street that the deal was not selling, since that can be a disease during a road show, which makes it that much harder to sell your stock at a good price during the rest of the sales trip.

Fifteen years later I can still remember being in the back of the vehicle somewhat in the dumps and taking a deep breath before saying something like, "Team, let's give this exactly the same effort and tone as we do in our most successful meetings. Let's stick to the plan and have a little fun doing it. This pension fund really wants to buy a part of a leading company before they go home tonight. Let's make it ours." Fortunately, we had a tremendous meeting, and on the drive back to the bank at quarter past six or so, our banker received a call, and we all could sense it was going well. A few minutes later we had a $20 million order, which was almost 20 percent of all the stock we were prepared to sell.

I truly thanked God that I had failed so many times earlier in my life when trying to sell a car that I was conditioned to keep going with the same successful plan that was proven to work even if we were rejected many times in a row.

Children, an important fact to understand about resilience and consistency is how these practices can help you out of the blue when you really need it the most. Of course, it sometimes takes months or even years before this practice really pays off in an immeasurable way, but is it ever worth it. We clearly weren't perfect, but no one can say Bubbles and the team weren't consistent and resilient.

NO WASTED SHIFTS

As a teenager I loved watching sports, and learning how successful teams win was always fascinating to me. Of course, many things factored into a team's success, but consistency on each down or shift was always a key factor. Although today's games are consumed by statistics, analytics, and percentages, consistency of play is still the most important factor for team achievements. In fact, the very successful coach Jon Cooper of the Stanley Cup champion Tampa Bay Lightning tells his team, "We can't cheat the game" if we want to win.

I believe he means the technical systems are in place with a winning strategy and the excellent players necessary to implement this. The only question is, Are we committed and resilient enough to keep our commitments through the whole game? If we do, we will likely win the game. I have preached the same to the teams I have led since I was nineteen years old till today; I just wasn't as detailed as Jon is. We focus on the following:

- No wasted shifts
- No wasted days
- No wasted weeks
- No wasted months
- No wasted years

This is consistency to our teams, and it works equally well in business and life.

How often does Connor McDavid or Tom Brady waste a

training session, a shift, a game, a season, an offseason, or anything else? Of course they don't always win, but it is not for a
lack of consistency or effort. The same goes for all of us if we
want our teams to win.

STAY CONSISTENT

Please, let's not let a lack of consistency creep into our lives.
In sales we must have a tremendous attitude on a consistent
basis, or we will never be truly successful. I suspect it's the
same in most professions.

Here are some tips on consistency we have regularly used
in training over the years that hopefully help you a bit:

- If we want consistent behavior, we need consistent thinking. Please remember our minds, with
  no self-awareness, will always veer over to what is
  easier to do. We need to be acutely aware of our
  thinking so that consistency can become a highly
  valuable habit.
- Let's not continue to doubt what we are doing, as
  that will hurt our consistency.
- To stay consistent, we have to show up every day,
  even if we are not having a great day, or even
  when something is actually bothering us. This is
  something I have been training on since I was a
  teenager and was not sure whether to mention
  it in the book because it can seem insincere, but
  it really isn't. There are days in sales that simply
  don't go well, making it hard to be fully engaged
  with the next set of customers, and we end up
  being off our game. I would ask our salespeople to
  always act like we are enjoying our time with the

customers when helping them select a car, regardless of our current mood. The funny thing is that if we do this, pretty quickly we will forget the negatives from earlier in the day and really help our customers out as our mood changes for the better. Certainly, the customers or clients in any business or service deserve this. While I believe sincerity is imperative, it's better to work hard and act a bit for a few minutes than to treat the client with a less-than-genuine effort.

- Using mindfulness to be actively present on the task we are doing assists us in staying consistent.
- We also have to realize that a new task or responsibility may be more exciting to perform at the beginning than it is two years later. However, the patient, client, or customer deserves our best enthusiasm and effort each and every time, despite the fact the task may not be that exciting anymore.
- Focusing on the process and not the outcome of our task most often translates into consistent, mindful work.
- Let's reward ourselves with a little something when we improve our consistent effort for a set period of time. Pretty soon this will be a positive new habit for us.

CRUCIAL FACTORS FOR EARLY SUCCESS

SLEEPING WITH MY BLACK BOOK

When I was starting to collect the many notes I had written over the years, one of the things that kept coming into my mind was *How the heck did I get so lucky so early in sales?* Please remember I was a scared, shy seventeen-year-old from a somewhat unorthodox upbringing. As I started thinking more about this, I realized luck and timing certainly played a significant part but so did a few other things. Trying to sort out which was the most important was not easy, but with hindsight a few stood out.

Patrick at around age twenty.

As nervous as I was, I was fortunate to be a self-aware and
motivated person at a young age, and that is really helpful in

sales. Until I started selling, I was not sure I was a self-aware person, but it became clear fairly quickly that I was. Almost immediately I could sense and understand that my customers were feeling nervous and somewhat overwhelmed with the process of buying a car, and I tried to make it easier for them. My thought process went something like *Let's be nervous together here; you need to purchase a car, and I need to sell one.* When people sense you are listening to them and understanding their emotions, they will open up to you. That is the point when you are on the path to a sale, and I did this each and every time. Being mindful of myself and of other people's issues played a big part in my early success. At the time I had no idea how significant a role mindfulness would play in my life so many years later. However, I had known for a few years how crucial motivation is to the success of anything.

A real problem occurred for all of us salespeople when about 20 percent of the people treated you like a pariah no matter what you did. This is something so many salespeople never get over, but I was lucky to understand that each customer is a new one, which allowed me to move on quickly from these daily setbacks, especially the emotional ones. This is where the resilience I attained as a teenager really benefited me, for when doubt would creep in, I could usually overcome it fairly quickly and get on with the next sale. Learning to be very resilient as a kid obviously turned out to be very beneficial to my early sales success.

I was also fortunate that our parents made it clear to us that you have to do your best; half an effort was not acceptable. I can't imagine any of the five of us wanting to go home and tell them we failed at whatever we were doing. Clearly, my parents helped me here, as this motivated me to keep going and try my hardest each day.

Having a really strong work ethic as early as thirteen, when I worked at the River Heights Deli after school each night, also

proved to be very helpful when I was beginning my sales career, as it was kind of normal for me to work harder than most
people did.

For these and other reasons, I was extremely demanding
of my own performance each day, and most of my competitors were not quite as driven. If most of the salespeople were
spending an hour a week studying inventory, used-car values,
and customer financing, I was spending five hours. I was asking questions daily of every smart person working at Chinook
Chrysler to expedite the learning curve. Many were frustrated
that I quizzed them so much but were kind enough to help 90
percent of the time. Wouldn't any of us improve more if we
spent five times as much time learning?

Knowing what a customer's trade was worth is somewhat
important in a sale, and with a thousand vehicles and option
packages available, it was impossible to know them all. For example, trade-ins could range from one to fifteen years old and
have between 10 and 100,000 miles on them, and back in 1973,
each week the dealership would get a new black book with all
the vehicles' approximate values, depending, of course, on options, model, mileage, and condition. The values changed a bit
each week, so the store would get five new books each week for
the managers, who held on to them like gold.

As soon as the new books came out, I would hassle one of
the managers to give me last week's book, as they were somewhat close to the new one in most cases. I feel pretty silly saying this, kids, but I remember living in my parents' house and
taking the black book to bed with me most nights, reciting out
loud and writing down the makes, years, and models of vehicles. I would then try to appraise these fake cars and write the
value I thought they were worth on my notebook while lying
in bed. Ten minutes later I would compare my estimate with
the official black book's number. Within a few months I knew
what most of the vehicles were worth. To this day, I do not

believe many people took their black book to bed with them. Like I said, working harder than your competitors usually pays off and so does not thinking we know everything after we have had some success.

THE BONUS THAT KEPT ON GIVING

Many times over the years, I have asked myself how I was motivated so quickly in sales when I never thought my future would be in selling cars of all things. I had finished a year of university, and my goal was to be a lawyer or a psychiatrist. I was terrified to start selling but thought I could do better than two dollars an hour as a lot man, and they gave me the chance. Even though I was seventeen and very afraid, I always went into things thinking, *I have to be the best in this job quickly, or I'm not gonna get anywhere and will end up as an embarrassed failure going back to being a lot man* (or "lot lizard," as they called us) *before I return to school.*

During the initial few weeks, I was so scared I just did everything I could to sell a car, but when I realized that I could actually sell a car, my attitude changed. I then said, "I am going to be the top salesman in this dealership within three months." When that happened, I said, "I want to be the best salesman in the province in another three months and the best in Canada within my first twelve months." I was pretty excited when that happened and realized that if I worked hard on myself, life was going to start getting better and university was in the rearview mirror. I was broke, so the short-term money I was making motivated me as well.

The first time I knew that I might be kind of a special salesperson was about six weeks into my career when the dealership management put a $750 extra bonus on for Friday and Saturday. This was huge money back in 1973, and they gave anyone who sold eight cars in two days this bonus on top of all the commissions you made selling the eight vehicles. Hardly anyone had ever made eight sales in two days, so most of the salespeople thought little of the bonus. I was extremely motivated to do it because I wanted to do something most had never done, and clearly the money was a big deal to me as well. I had sold thirty-one cars in my first month, so I did not think it was impossible but still highly unlikely. You also need a serious amount of luck to do this, but I got off to a hot start Friday by selling three and coming into work pumped up on Saturday morning.

My adrenaline was through the roof, and I would not have wanted to be a customer unless I really wanted a new car that day. Just joking, but if they were going to buy a vehicle somewhere in Calgary that day, it might as well be from me, as I was going all out to keep them happy. My shift was over at 6:00 p.m., and I had done four deals for the day. I quickly thought to myself maybe management would let me work with the Saturday-night team if I could get one of them to give me his shift. This was not hard since Saturday night after six was pretty dead, and the booze, girls, and bars were attractive and waiting for the salespeople, so one offered me his shift.

Management said I could replace him, but I was wondering at nine thirty why I worked so hard all weekend and missed by one. No one came in until about quarter to ten, and the other salesmen wanted to go home, so they said to take him. I said, "Thanks, guys," and went over to the car and introduced myself. By about ten thirty, I had a sale, bragging rights, and $750 in bonus money. To this day, I remember how proud I was to accomplish this, and when getting out of my vehicle at home that night, something popped into my head. I looked down the street to where my ex-girlfriend, who had seen my dad on the floor three or four months ago, lived. It was with pleasure that I held my bonus cash in my hand and said, "Eff you," to her dad. It was a happy night as I walked into the house on a cloud, and both parents were really proud of me.

This is when my confidence really grew, and I then became very aware of how much confidence helps us, especially with early success. Of course, working hard helps our confidence grow, as our effort usually drives our results.

ALWAYS LOOK AT THE BUSINESS WHEN THINGS ARE GOING WELL

I remember well when Mike and I opened our first business in January 1982 together with Chrysler Canada as the 75 percent senior partner. Of course, they had no problem letting us know who the majority partner was. Having them as a partner was difficult at times because a representative of theirs would come in every month for a few days to review the previous month's and year-to-date financial results. This was very stressful for a twenty-six-year-old kid, but learning to make the best of it really benefited the business in the long run.

The year before, in 1981, the dealership lost around $500,000 and was heading toward bankruptcy, so we had the opportunity to buy into it. The Chrysler manager would also hold us accountable to certain forecasts; they would also compare us with all the top-performing dealerships across the country, which they thought would either motivate or strike fear in us to keep up. I vividly remember about twenty-four months later that the dealership was performing well and now earning more than $600,000 in a year.

I also remember being a bit young and a little too full of myself and saying to George, the Chrysler manager, that we don't need to be spending this much time every month reviewing and comparing ourselves to everyone else. I can't forget the look on George's face as he got up and closed the door.

This was some difficult but brilliant advice that I have used for years. He said that you always review and renew your business when it is doing well. You do not wait until things start slipping before you make needed improvements.

I was fortunate to learn early on that momentum in retail, sports, and so much in life is hard to find, so when you get on a roll, work very hard to stay on it. It is always easier to stay on a roll than trying to recapture success when things are going downhill. Of course, if you think about it, this philosophy can apply to our personal lives and relationships as well. Around forty years later, I say, "Thank you, George, for setting me straight."

BEATING OURSELVES UP

ROOMMATES FROM HELL

Michael Singer, in his excellent book *The Untethered Soul*, described beating yourself up in an easy-to-understand manner. He refers to the voice in your head that never stops criticizing you as your "inner roommate." He recommends you look deep inside yourself and ask, *Would you let your actual roommates or friends talk to you like this every day?* If your friends continued to speak to you like this, surely you would remove them from your life and, hopefully, find new ones. We really need to treat our inner roommate the same.

For too many years I let this voice in my head beat the daylights out of me. Even when I was having considerable business success, this voice would always find something else to beat me up about. Experience tells me, unless tamed, this inner roommate will always have a problem with something we are thinking or doing. Before our current problems, there were always different problems, and going forward, there will be another set of new problems coming. We really need to practice a bit of mindfulness to eliminate most of the negative thoughts coming our way if we want a life of reasonable peace, prosperity, and happiness, which is precisely what I want for you all.

Most human beings will accept beating ourselves up, but

this acceptance changes considerably if someone is making life too difficult for our children. If a teacher, coach, or even a family member spoke to one of our children the way our inner voice or "roommate" speaks to us, we would take immediate action. Of course we would fight to the end to protect our child from this abuse and show sincere compassion for them. Do we not deserve the same compassion for ourselves as our beautiful child does?

Kids, please be kind to yourselves and treat yourselves as respectfully as you treat your loved ones as you walk through life.

A KIND AND HOPEFUL DAY

Most days over the last fifty years or so I have gotten out of bed with a fair bit of hope and positivity in my heart. But enough days have started with me getting out of bed with a bit of fear and a whole lot of anxiety running straight through me. These are the days when I become a master at beating myself up, making it hard to be around for my loved ones, and just feeling terrible about myself.

Children, enjoy the journey as you pursue your hopes and dreams while holding yourself accountable to results, but please learn life's heavy lesson that beating yourself up is a terrible practice that can become a devastating habit. As with many other negative emotions, beating yourself up also hurts the ones closest to you, as they hate to see you do this to yourself. Imagine what your child feels when they see you in this negative state, just as I used to feel with my parents or maybe you children have felt with me when I was beating myself up.

Below are ways I often try to respond to these feelings when they come on. I have also shared these words hundreds of times in team meetings at work:

- Let's remember to count our blessings today.
- Let's remember to be kind to ourselves today.
- Let's remember to be kind to everyone today.
- Let's remember to walk mindfully today.
- Let's do our best at work today and then let it go.
- Let's do our best at home today and then let it go.

THE GOOD, THE BAD, AND THE UGLY

"What a relief it is for the burdened man who has long walked through the world of suffering to lay down his heavy and useless load."

Longchen Rabjam

Man, oh man, children, this is something that has gotten the better of me for far too many years. Let us all lay down our own heavy and useless load. Certainly, continuing to beat ourselves up is actually like carrying this load on our backs forever. One of the most difficult and sometimes emotional situations that I have witnessed so many times in my career was watching people who were trying really hard and still beating the heck out of themselves.

We would be at work at 8:00 p.m., trying our hardest, and hoping a couple more customers would come to the dealership so we would not go home without a sale. On the other side of the coin, even if we had ten deals that day, we would do anything to make it twelve. Even though we were closed at ten, many of the team would stay open for as long as it took to make a deal. You could easily understand how someone who worked till eleven thirty and went home with nothing would feel. Tired, disappointed, and beating themselves up.

Time and again you would see this, yet the top-performing dealership I was working at never, ever mentioned this subject in sales training. We were judged and rewarded every single day of the week on what we individually sold, and if we did not sell anything for the week, things were bleak. To make things even worse, senior management would have a weekly meeting where they would have all fifty people working in the sales department in the room and hand out each weekly check, announcing the amount in front of the rest of the team so everyone could see your success or failure.

A year and a half later I was promoted to one of the four sales manager positions, and our treatment was similar. Following the embarrassment of many of the salespeople, senior management would then hand out the four sales managers' checks in a similar manner. The only difference was that the owner, who must have liked the movie *The Good, the Bad, and the Ugly*, would then name out loud each of the four of us in order of sales profit for the week as follows:

- First place was the good
- Second place the bad
- Third place the ugly
- Fourth place was the soon-to-be-fired

Even at such a young age, I could never decipher how this motivated any of us, and my approach to motivating others in a completely different manner started there and then.

I can still remember the owner of the business telling me my way of motivation would not work, and that fear and the threat of being fired were the only ways to keep your team in line and selling. To his credit, he said my sales results from the previous eighteen months entitled me to a promotion, and he told me he had never hired a manager under twenty-five years old in his business. I was certainly grateful for the opportunity.

Throughout the years I have had thousands of one-on-one

conversations with staff and had a similar number of meetings with our teams covering this issue. It is simply a fact of life that we humans tend to beat ourselves up. In nearly every one- or two-hour training session I have done over forty-plus years, I discuss beating ourselves up for at least a few minutes and sometimes much more. How can you move forward at full potential if you are beating yourself up constantly?

I always try to take a few minutes to go around the room and ask everyone to answer one question: "Who is the toughest critic on yourself day to day?" Except for the odd hilarious answer of "my spouse or partner," which gets the room laughing, virtually everyone in the room says "me." Even people who have been with us a long time will say, "I am working hard on this every day, but it's still me. The good news is it's very seldom as bad compared to when I started focusing on it."

Children, throughout this chapter I am trying my best to help you overcome beating yourself up. This issue has resonated with me since well before I was twenty years old. Sure wish that I had put more of this to use earlier in life and obviously hope you don't make the same mistake. I would not put these in my notes to you if they had not specifically worked in helping me stop beating myself up. Perhaps if you find yourself being too tough on yourself even years from now, you can take a quick look at this chapter and recommit to stopping this terrible habit. As I have said a thousand times to people looking for a bit of help to survive and prosper in our business, "I do not believe God put us on earth to beat ourselves up."

MEMORY MOTEL

The Memory Motel is not a place we want to check into on a regular basis. Children, please think very hard about this. I cannot tell you emphatically enough how many times earlier in my life that I would continue to relive terrible experiences that happened to me. Again and again, I would relive in my head things that occurred sometimes months and even years before. It's like for some reason I felt I deserved to be beaten up again by myself. In retrospect it was obvious to me that I did not know how much emotional damage I was doing to myself and those closest to me, or I would not have continued living like this.

Every time we reminisce about bad things that have happened to us, it is like stabbing a knife into ourselves and our emotional well-being. Like so many negative emotions this also affects those closest to us, as the pain we are causing ourselves spills out to them.

As with many emotions, practicing mindfulness will be a certain help to you here. Please consider trying these practices; they will work:

- Listen to and be a witness to our mean, self-attacking, negative thoughts.
- Don't judge them, don't condemn them, and please don't argue with them. The key here is to just let these negative thoughts enter and exit our head without attaching to them.
- We will soon accept that the majority of these negative thoughts in our head are not even true.
- When we can begin to smile and even laugh at some of these negative thoughts, we are well on our way.
- Remember, we all deserve love and that includes self-love, which is hard to accept for ourselves if we are beating ourselves up on a regular basis in the motel from hell.

WASTE OF PAINT

Gifted musicians and writers have a way of writing things many of us are thinking about but cannot express in words. Twenty years ago, Conor Oberst wrote a brilliant album called *Lifted* that had many excellent songs, but "Waste of Paint" resonated strongly with me. Here are some lines from the song:

> My head feels weak and suddenly
> It's clear to see, it's not them but me
> Who's lost my self-identity
> As I hide behind these books I read
> While scribbling my poetry
> Like art could save a wretch like me
> With some ideal ideology
> That no one could hope to achieve
> And I'm never real, it's just a sketch of me
> And everything I've made is trite and
>   cheap and a waste
> Of paint, of tape, of time

Seeing yourself as a waste of paint is a pretty negative feeling, to say the least. Unfortunately, many of us in this world have felt like a waste of paint at some point in our lives. I definitely felt this way about myself during the period in my life that followed the breakup of my partnership with my twin brother, along with hundreds of fights with all my siblings (mostly Mike) and mother over the breakup. I thank God I had done some spiritual and emotional work on myself prior to these times, or it would have been so much worse.

Many times I found myself alone, beating the heck out of myself. So many times I simply could not find the answers I was searching for and needing. Sometime later it became clear to me that many answers to our life challenges are easy to find if we know where to look.

Children, regardless of whatever happens to us, let's never beat ourselves up to this point. Please remember, the spiritual and emotional work we have done on ourselves will pay off when really difficult situations arise during our lives, which they surely will.

TAKING CARE OF YOURSELVES FOR YOUR KIDS

Looking back through so many years, so many murky situations, and so many roads to navigate is one heck of a challenging journey. Thankfully, the road through love and kindness helped me understand what is genuine and real. Most every time I have been kind to myself, I have been kind to my loved ones. But every time I beat myself up, I was not as kind and loving as I should have been to my loved ones. This is my life fact, and I suspect most people would agree this is the case in their lives.

I remember twenty-plus years ago working with a talented member of our team on this issue specifically, and I could not get through to him until I finally asked him what he thought his four children between ten and seventeen years old likely felt as they observed him continuing to beat the heck out of himself on a daily basis. He was clearly surprised that I would bring up his kids, but he finally accepted how damaging this was for himself and his family, let alone his career. That was the defining moment for him, and he got pretty emotional and made the changes necessary.

A simple fact of life is if we are not capable of taking care of ourselves, protecting ourselves from our inner negative voice, and nourishing ourselves with compassion, it is almost impossible to care for our loved ones as much as we would like to. Again, this is a lesson I wish I learned earlier. We all love our children, and if we can find a bit more forgiveness for ourselves, we are in a much better place to find even more love, kindness, and support for them. This is also an inspiring example and practice to pass on to your children.

BODY LANGUAGE

HOW WE SAY IT

Many experts believe that about 7 percent of effective communication is through spoken word, 38 percent through tone of voice, and 55 percent through body language. My father told me when I first started selling cars that it was not so much what you said to the customers but how you said it to them. I replied something to the effect of *What you say is obviously so important*, and he said, "Yes, *what* you say is important, but *how* you say it is much more important."

I quickly learned that saying the same exact words to a customer would have dramatically different results when delivered by two different people. Let's just say the customer's offer was $1,000 short of what we needed, and we had to bring someone in to explain the bad news to them. If the person going in to deliver the bad news to the customer was edgy, frustrated, lacking confidence, or had other negative-type emotions, the deal would likely not be made. The sale might well happen if another person went in with a genuine smile, a bit of empathy, some patience, and a kind heart. I discovered it was not always the money that made the difference to selling a car, it was more likely the person selling it.

In the company today, we are constantly communicating

things to the people we deal with, and some of what we say, they would prefer not to hear. You bet that we pick the right person to deliver these messages. Children, always be aware of your personal style of delivery and how it might be perceived by others.

SMILE A LITTLE

"Sometimes your joy is the source of your smile, but sometimes your smile can be the source of your joy."
Thich Nhat Hanh

Here are some simple but highly effective communication and body language tips I have shared in training sessions over the years:

- It's not only what we say but also how we deliver the words.
- Be very careful with our tone of voice.
- Too little eye contact shows indifference or lack of interest.
- Too much eye contact can be a bit creepy.
- Nodding quietly in agreement is very effective.
- Covering our mouths or eyes are signs of not telling the truth.
- Our facial expressions must show some enthusiasm.
- Crossing our arms makes us appear a bit defensive.
- Smile a little; it is a powerful weapon.

ANGER

FLUSHED FACES AND A SCARED DOG

Before we get into some of the problems that many of us deal with regarding anger, perhaps we should look at what a terribly hurtful emotion it can be. Anger is a natural response to a threat, even though the threat is often only perceived. It will cause our body to produce adrenaline, which will likely cause our face to flush, our muscles to tighten, and our blood pressure to increase. It will also make us much less attractive to others and will likely scare and emotionally hurt our children if expressed too strongly. Even our beloved dog cannot escape our anger, as she will cower and be upset to see us this mad. Scaring our own dog with outbursts must unequivocally tell us something about ourselves.

I really wish I'd had a better grasp of my anger when I was younger. When I was in a state of anger, my mouth was often moving quicker than my mind. Many things I did were not appropriate for my loved ones around me. I am sorry for those actions, and I did much of the work I talk about in these notes to help me overcome it. Kids, I truly hope the ensuing tips help you here.

ANGER AND GRATITUDE

Compassion and gratitude are really the opposite of anger, both are born from a deep understanding and from living our lives in a happy manner. Please think about the times you were truly angry. Do you remember being in a state of gratitude during that period?

It's highly unlikely we can be in a dual state of anger and gratitude at the same time. Not only does our anger hurt us and our loved ones, but it also deprives us of the opportunity of living in a pleasant state of gratitude, which is a very happy and fulfilling place to be. Clearly, gratitude and anger would not make for a happy couple.

Another important consideration about anger is that when we are angry, it is difficult for both our children and our parents to see us like this. These difficult emotions affect both a ten-year-old child and a sixty-year-old mother and grandmother. And it is likely that anger can run through generations. If my father was always angry, it's likely I will always be angry and pass this on to my son and daughter, and they'll pass it on to their children, and so on.

My goal, with all these notes to you, is not to be close to perfect in anything. I just want us to keep improving and moving in the proper direction. As usual, self-awareness will help us get there.

There are a lot of incentives for us to control our anger when we see things as they really are and look at the big picture, including being a leader in our family among the generations. If none of this works for us, perhaps looking in the mirror in the midst of an angry episode, as I suggest in the following note, might do it.

THE MIRROR

There's a clear difference between being angry and being an angry person. There are times in our lives when we all feel anger, and it's healthy to express a small bit of our anger, as long as we do it with some self-awareness.

My life experiences teach me that anger poisons our logic, our thinking, and our creativity. It also hurts our physical health and relationships. As we all have some anger in us, let's try to deal with it before we become an angry person. Angry people poison not only themselves but also the ones who love them.

We could learn something by looking in the mirror when we are in the middle of an angry moment. I think it is safe to say we would not look beautiful. I fortunately have done this numerous times and realized how terrible and even frightening I looked. As I was actually looking in the mirror, I was afraid *of* myself and *for* myself.

Mirrors do not tend to reflect anything but the truth. When we are angry, looking in the mirror can be personally very embarrassing for a few minutes and then very enlightening, if we are willing to learn from it.

A BETTER SOLUTION

Letting my anger get the best of me has happened so many times in my life I could not possibly remember them all. I only share this sad behavior with you because it affects our children as they watch us perform our angry act over small things. Many times I could not find the TV remote, car keys, dead phone, or whatever I was looking for. There was a decade or more when I would look for the lost item for a minute or so and then get angry when I could not find them pretty much immediately. After five minutes of yelling "Poor me," "Why does this always happen to me," etc., I usually never had much luck finding it quickly. I suspect my anger did not help my searches.

A better solution I prefer today is to quickly acknowledge I wish I had not lost this item but understand it's not my bad luck as most everyone loses stuff once in a while. I laugh, put my Columbo hat on, and retrace where it might be. Three things usually occur: one, I don't get mad; two, I usually find it much faster; and three, I am happy at the end.

Even if I found it the old way, after ten minutes of screaming, no one in the house is in a mood to watch TV or do anything positive with me. I realize this may seem a bit off, but getting angry over small issues usually equates to being an angry person on the bigger issues. I believe I live in the real world, and these types of situations happen or affect people everywhere. If someone you love has these kinds of anger issues and seems to have fallen into being an angry person, then mocking, making fun of, or yelling at them won't help either. Only kindness will.

Kids, if you have a bit of an anger issue, please forgive yourself and just try to improve. I am living proof it can be done.

FU*K IN YOUR BACKSWING

Writing this chapter on anger was very challenging and humiliating. A part of me prefers not to discuss or remember it too much, but I also believe that we all need to look at anger and how it can impact our lives if not dealt with in a healthy way.

While I was living in my competing worlds of elation and anger, I often golfed after work for a bit. After I relate this story to you, perhaps you will know why I started working even harder on my inner demons.

Whoever referred to golf as "a good walk spoiled" made a perceptible observation. I can remember standing at the first tee one night after a stressful day at work; there were four of us from the company playing. I was already worked up about something, probably having to do with business or family issues, when I put the ball in the water and of course ended up cursing. My good friend Joe, who is an excellent golfer, laughed a bit and said, "Do you know you swore in your backswing well before you even hit the ball?"

There really is something wrong when anyone starts cursing before they hit the ball. At the time I thought, *Seriously, this can't be right, who does this?* Well, apparently, I do. Another telltale sign I have work to do on myself, not my golf game. When anger like this arises in us, we need to think of the consequences of our reaction. We need to train ourselves ahead of time to be prepared for when it comes and just let it go through us without making an attachment to it.

Events like these sure made me look at my anger and why it was festering. It's obvious I had not done enough self-reflection or studied mindfulness in a meaningful way up to that point.

I believe most of us can move on from excessive anger or whatever is hurting us to being pretty darn happy if we just take some time and try to understand a little mindfulness and the gift of self-compassion. Please take these tips from a former expert at being angry.

DARKNESS DOWN THE HALL

Another example of my anger getting the best of me happened when we lived in Winnipeg. Although financial times were difficult, and banks were hard for us to deal with during this period, there was nothing to be gained from being extremely angry and much to lose, including my self-respect. I recall being incredibly angry one day in my den after getting home from work, yelling like a total idiot, when Susan came in and said the neighbor's window was open, and they could hear everything I was screaming.

Talk about embarrassment for Susan, the kids, and me. Also, pretty sure the kids and Susan must have cringed a few times watching me. Sorry again, as this was abhorrent behavior by me.

Sometimes the stress is overwhelming, and it is easy for us to explode, but it is never the answer. What the heck do children ages eight to eleven years old think about this embarrassing behavior from one of their parents? I very much regret these times and the effect these actions of mine had on our family. Today I seldom get angry about anything besides technology not working (ha ha). It's simply all the work done over the years that changed me so much that I could go from Winnipeg to today.

The Greek philosopher Epictetus said about anger: "Whenever you are angry, be assured that it is not only a present evil, but that you have increased a habit."

I am hoping the notes in this book will help you avoid my severe reactions to the stress I was dealing with when major stress comes to visit you.

WORKING AT BEING ANGRY VS. CARING FOR OUR ANGER

A very important fact to understand about being angry on a regular basis is that it actually takes work to be like that. Believe me, earlier in my life I often did the hard work to set the stage for my own anger to occur. Why would anyone want to work at being angry? We all may have our own theories on that, but I inevitably worked hard at it for too many years. I suspect feeling disrespected, feeling powerless, wondering "Why is this happening to me?" and so many more things cause us to feel as if we don't deserve to be happy, and we often punish ourselves for no sane reason. Too often I allowed my anger to arise and, in fact, have even encouraged it by watering the angry seeds inside myself.

I had tried so many things and read more books than I can remember to help me from getting mad, but most of it simply did not last. It was only after reading more Buddhist texts that I was able to shift my destructive relationship with anger.

The most profound thing I learned was that the Buddha never told us to suppress our anger, he told us to go back to our anger and ourselves and take good care of it. He told us we should care for our anger like a mother cares for her crying child. This is brilliant, life-changing advice if followed.

When I took care of my own anger, I had a nice win for myself and for the people who loved me. For me, this started to be effective only when I actually started caring for my anger the same way we would care about our children. As corny as this sounds, it is compassionate and really works, as the anger came from something in our past and needs care. I started to separate my anger from myself and would actually look at my anger as separate from me. By doing this, I became capable of observing my own anger, no different from watching an actor's anger during a movie.

When we are mindful enough to simply let our anger enter our thoughts and quickly let it dissipate, we are making progress. After a while it becomes very easy to do, and we do not become attached to the emotion like before.

I now know we are more than our anger. We all have the ability to use mindfulness to understand when anger is coming on and to deal with it in a calm, soothing manner, which everyone will appreciate.

ENLIGHTENING BUDDHIST SUGGESTION

From all my years of reading and learning, I believe Buddhists look at anger a little differently from most people. Not only would they suggest we look deeply with compassion at our own anger, but they would also suggest practices to help us do this. Through Buddhism, I have learned that conscious breathing calms our anger, and our mindfulness penetrates it. Please remember that anger is just an energy form, and energies can be transformed, especially when we practice self-compassion and mindfulness. Let's always try to understand this as we go through life and remind ourselves in times of stress that we have the power to transform our anger, we just need to use it.

MINDFULNESS

OUR PERFECT TIME IS NOW

We are always in the perfect time of our lives, moving to the next stage one step at a time. We must live mindfully each hour, each day, each week, each month, and each year.

This is also a much more pleasurable way to live. For example, we are on a plane ride home to Edmonton for a few hours. Isn't it much more fun to be enjoying the time flying home rather than sitting here wishing we were home already? Certainly wishing we were home already does not change the fact we are three hours away. Most of life is the same. It's much more fun to accept and enjoy the moment we are in rather than resisting it or waiting for it to be over before we can be happy.

As long as we recognize that everything is impermanent, we can enjoy each stage of our journey to the fullest.

JUST BE AWARE

Just being mindful and aware of our emotional issues, such as jealousy, anger, regret, or frustration, will help us work through these challenging feelings more easefully. We don't even have to think about or analyze them, just be aware of them. Watch how much calmer our minds will be when we practice this kind of mindfulness.

I believe our schools will be teaching mindfulness in the future, and I am pretty certain your children will be doing this by the time they are teenagers.

IT'S SO LOUD INSIDE MY HEAD

Children, one of the most important things we can learn studying even basic Buddhism is to observe the functioning of our own mind in a detached and calm manner. This practice will really help us calm our mind, and therefore, calm our emotions. Just as importantly, it will also help us gain insight into our own behavior, including our destructive behavior.

When we are actively aware of our thoughts, words, and actions, our mind naturally becomes more still, and we are better prepared for life's ups and downs. Often, we joke about the noise inside our heads, but it is a simple fact we are all much happier with a calm and quiet mind. I suspect the words "it's so loud inside my head" would fit very well in a terrific punk rock song but not so much in our own lives.

TURNING IN THE RIGHT DIRECTION

Buddhists believe if we listen to and understand our inner suffering, we can solve most of our problems. I couldn't agree more, as I have seen this so clearly in my own life. When I did not understand my own suffering and its causes, life never seemed to work very easily and would often slide in the wrong direction, helping make things miserable for myself and those around me. The truth is I didn't really have anything to be miserable about, and when I started to understand how much

I created my own pain, my life turned in a meaningful way in the right direction.

I know many of us can look at this approach as too philosophical, but my own life changed for the better in all areas, including personal relationships and business success, simply by practicing mindfulness.

DON'T GIVE UP TOO EARLY

WHO GIVES A FU*K, PAT?

I still remember many of our sales team from our first dealership in 1981, where I had an ownership position in London, Ontario. We had a team of misfits to start with, and within a week of being there, we had only three salespeople. About four months later we had a decent team of ten who were motivated to change the attitude and sales numbers at the store. Having said that, I remember there was still lots more work in that area, as each day I would continually listen to salespeople tell me why the customers were not going to buy a vehicle today. I would say, "Please take them for a demo ride in the vehicle, and I will help with the sale when they return in twenty minutes or so."

Patrick's first dealership, London, 1981.

If they would come up with another objection, which was often the case, I would say without maybe realizing what I was saying, "Who gives a fu*k, please let me talk to them."

After a few months I had a new nickname courtesy of our salespeople, which they joked about behind my back. Pretty soon they started joking with me about it. They would say to me, "Hey, who gives a fu*k; could you please talk to my customers?" I always shrugged and took it as a compliment, as the team was confident I would sell their customers the vehicle or at minimum give it my absolute best effort. This was a fun way to start working on the tough deals, and it showed I was not the type to give up too quickly or early in the process. Please remember Thomas Edison said, "Many of life's failures are people who did not realize how close they were to success when they gave up."

DRIVING BLIND, HEADING FOR THE WALL

It was the spring of 1985 when I was forced to grow up really quickly as a businessman. Obviously, I knew how to sell cars, manage a team, and make a losing business profitable. However, I had no experience or expertise in understanding how business partnerships worked or the myriad of legal issues surrounding shareholder and franchise agreements. My brother and I each held 33.3 percent shares in the car dealership, as did our partner.

Because we were a franchise of Chrysler Canada, they had a rule that only one person could be the dealer principal of the dealership, and that person would have a fair bit of additional power in the agreements. Because Mike and I were only twenty-six years old when we started at the dealership and our partner was a twenty-year veteran of Chrysler Canada who was about forty-five years old, he had the additional power and leverage. As two young, inexperienced shareholders, we found out quickly that he was more than happy to use it.

Four years into the partnership, my brother pulled off a questionable move by firing our partner's son while our partner was on vacation. I agreed with Mike that of course he should be let go as he had not shown up for work for three days, but we should wait until his dad got back from Mexico. Mike did not listen to my advice. Well, John returned from vacation a couple of weeks later, and I received a call from the dealership's receptionist at 8:00 on that Monday morning saying John had called an important management meeting that I needed to attend. My brother received a similar call. Arriving at work about forty minutes later, I had no idea what was going on, and John had his door closed. When he opened it at 8:55 a.m., all the managers walked into his office, and there was

John and his recently fired son. I sat down in his large office and knew this was not going to be pretty. Mike walked in and sat down a few minutes later.

John started off the meeting with the statement that a tragedy had occurred with the firing of his son and the way Mike handled it. I will never forget the words he used, he said the twins were about to find out the golden rule of business: "He who has the gold makes the rules."

Sitting there quietly, I was somewhat dumbfounded, as my thinking there was that thirty-three out of a hundred did not seem to be enough gold to pull this stunt off. He then went on to say he had special powers as dealer principal, and if the "boys" did not apologize and get in line, we were going to be fired. He then finished the meeting by reinstating his son as business manager and saying everyone would now fully understand who was in charge and let's get back to work.

After clearing my head, I spoke with Mike and said, "Well, we can either take this or stand up and fight for our rights." He agreed, and we went into John's office to discuss this humiliating episode. John pulled something out from a law firm he had spoken to the week before, as he had come back a bit early from vacation and plotted out his strategy. The letter to us clearly stated he had the power in our shareholders agreement to do this, and he also said he had spoken to his friends at Chrysler Canada, who were backing him with our franchise agreement. He then said, "Your power is very limited, so you better go along with this, and we will call the managers back in to listen to your apologies to my son and me."

I paused for a moment, then said that will not happen and I needed a few days to think this over. A lack of experience really hurts in situations like this, but it sure teaches you to grow up quickly.

Using simple logic, I first thought that I was working with the team selling most of the vehicles at the dealership and was the leading driver of the business, taking it from 350 new cars in 1981 to almost 800 in 1984. These additional sales also took the store from losing $500,000 in 1981 to making about $600,000 in 1984. My brother and I quickly figured out that people at Chrysler must know who was doing the work, as they spent a day once a month at the dealership and must have been aware John spent his entire days sitting in his big office not really doing much.

I found this calculation was spot on when I called an executive at Chrysler to explain what was happening at the store, and he was immediately concerned the store would be back to being a terrible performer if we were forced out. Six months later and after much fighting with lawyers, John was gone as a partner, and the business thrived for years. Lessons learned from this challenging situation were plenty, and here are a few of them:

- If we do the work to make us valuable, people eventually recognize this.
- Having good relationships and showing respect to people along the road will help us when we need it most. In this case, our staff and our franchisor, Chrysler Canada.
- We never want to exercise our power over others, but we need the guts to use it when we really need to.
- Don't ever give up too quickly.

COMPASSION

BE A GOOD FRIEND TO YOURSELF

Kids, unfortunately I have learned the following lesson the truly hard way and pray you can avoid much of this in your life. If we don't love ourselves, we cannot really love someone else. If we cannot treat ourselves kindly, it's difficult to treat other people kindly. How can we show compassion for our children and parents if we are unable to find compassion for ourselves? If we can't accept our own faults, how do we accept the faults of others? If our compassion does not include ourselves, then how can it be complete compassion?

By finding self-compassion, not only do we help ourselves, but we help those around us, and that is a beautiful thing. Let's remember that in moments of suffering, this pain is part of life, and please remember to be kind to yourself in this moment. Please give this suffering the compassion it deserves, the kind of compassion you would give to your own child.

You might well ask yourself, "Why does he write about self-compassion so much?" The clear answer is that it is often harder for all of us humans to find compassion for ourselves than to find compassion for others. Over time, it has become clear to me that we all need self-compassion to have the best lives possible.

Even so, this is an area of life I personally failed in for years on end. After a lot of years and a lot of pain, I still don't completely understand why self-compassion is so hard to find. I'm not sure we will ever know the exact reasons so many of us do not practice enough self-compassion, but I expect many of us have this one thing in common: for whatever reason, we simply do not think we deserve it. This is a crucial delusion that costs us and our loved ones dearly. Practicing mindfulness will help us here, as we all suffer from defeats, mistakes, and misfortune, and a little self-compassion goes a long way in helping us find more beauty, kindness, love, and happiness.

THE GIFTS OF SELF-COMPASSION

Self-compassion often sets the stage for us to be the following:

- Better partners
- Better parents
- Better friends

It also leads to the following:

- Better health
- Better careers
- Better lives

DOWN WHERE THE SPIRIT MEETS THE BONE

Lucinda Williams's song "Compassion" urges everyone to have compassion for our fellow humans, and these words ring very true in the world we live in.

Always a sign of things no ears have heard
Always a sign of things no eyes have seen
You do not know what wars are going on
    there
Down there where the spirit meets the
    bone
Down there where the spirit meets the
    bone
Down where the spirit meets the bone

We all know too well the pain we suffer from and most often rise above, but we can't know the same of most people we encounter. We simply have no idea of their pain, their issues, their hurt, their background, or so much more. Perhaps we know a little of their life story, but it's difficult to know it all.

I've tried to live with the practice of compassion for others as much as possible, though I have often failed here. I have always had an enormous amount of compassion for the downtrodden in the world, and it's likely having watched my parents up close and personal and the misfortune they faced that made me feel like that. Unfortunately, my compassion for the well-off was not as easy. For some unknown reason, probably jealousy and envy, I felt that if they had more money and power than most of us, they did not deserve much of my compassion. I was simply wrong. You know, it's a funny thing, but when we have more compassion for others, we are happier ourselves.

THE MICROPHONE

I recently looked up the definition of "compassion" in a dictionary: "a strong feeling of sympathy and sadness for the suffering or bad luck of others and a wish to help them."

Of course, this is an apt description of "compassion," but

what it fails to mention is that compassion is truly meant for both others and for ourselves. I have no idea why it took me so long to understand and accept this fact.

It's a bit embarrassing to admit to you that I gave the terrible thoughts in my head a loud microphone. Whether it was the unfairness of my upbringing, the unfairness of our wealthy competitors in business, or the unfairness of my family situation, they all took up a loud space in my head. How many times did I hand them the microphone and let them live rent-free, roaring in my head? How dumb was I to do this? And at the end of the day, none of these thoughts were true, for how many hundreds of millions of people had it one hundred times worse than I ever had? Kids, simply let these thoughts come in, have their brief moment, and let them pass on. It sure beats handing them a microphone.

SELF-COMPASSION IS NOT A SELFISH ACT

Children, I wasted many years of my life not having remotely enough self-compassion, and I paid a heavy emotional price for that. Unfortunately, so did many of the people closest to me, and for this I am very sorry. How can it help a twelve-year-old child to watch their father getting extremely angry? How does it help watching their father get drunk and act stupid and belligerent? How did it help Susan with me being so frustrated so often? Obviously, I let our family down by not controlling my emotions properly.

I am very sorry I hurt all you children with this poor behavior. After each of these situations occurred, not only had I hurt you, but I hated myself for acting so foolishly. Had I found self-compassion earlier in my life, I know these actions and behaviors would not have occurred nearly as often, if at all.

The more we reject ourselves, the more exhausting it is for

us and our loved ones. Please do not think practicing compassion for yourself is a selfish act; it is a necessary practice for all of us. As a result of doing this, we will develop even more kindness, love, and compassion for others.

With the world being as competitive as it is, we can always feel inferior to others and berate our own shortcomings. We will always have more peace and less anxiety and stress by being kind to ourselves.

Children, remember you are very much loved by all of us; remember you are very worthy of contentment and happiness in your life. Remember to learn from my mistakes as it took me into my early fifties before I could find this crucial self-compassion. Do not watch your children watch you being unkind to yourselves, along with the actions that often follow.

WHICH VOICE NEEDS MORE OF OUR ATTENTION?

One day I was talking with my daughter as we joyfully watched one of her daughters control the room around all of us. I said to her, "The only thing as loud as the voice of a four-year-old is the voice in our head." We laughed together, but later I wondered, which of these voices needs more of our attention? At first it felt like an easy question to answer because, of course, the grandchild is a beautiful young person whom we love being with and watching grow up. We can't say the same about the voices in our heads, which are often negative and self-critical. The more I pondered it, though, the more I realized they both need a lot of our kind and compassionate attention.

WALKING MEDITATION

THE PATH OF WALKING MEDITATION

Again, this is something that I wish I had learned years earlier in life—a small amount of walking meditation can improve our personal and career goals. Here are examples of walking meditation practices that are very easy to do and very helpful for all of us:

- As we are walking from one part of the office to another for a meeting, we can take that one or two minutes and intentionally feel our feet as they touch and lift from the ground beneath us. What a perfect space to be in as we go into the meeting. If we walk into most meetings in a peaceful state, whatever the situation, the stress level inevitably drops, and success is more likely.
- When walking outside, we can simply try to enjoy the feeling of the air moving against our skin. This is so easy, we can also enjoy it while walking the dog.
- Many times while walking outside with a quiet mind and full of mindfulness, a message quietly

comes through to us, often helping us find solutions to the issues we are trying to solve.

- When in our home, we can practice this mindfulness as we walk from room to room. When our feet are touching the floor, we can feel the sense of happiness and contentment as we make our way. This is a commendable habit to practice when we are walking across the room to help our child crying or walking down the hall to her room at three a.m. to comfort her. She will sense and feel your calmness as you are helping her. I sure wish I had learned this when my children were young and regret not being more aware.

Kids, remember the small changes you're making will make a huge difference, but they will not happen overnight. This is the same with any form of mindfulness or meditation. The first few times we use walking meditation is going to be difficult. We'll likely lose concentration, and our mind will slip back into being inundated with thoughts. You might say all this is silly, but with diligent practice, it becomes part of our healthy lives. Just keep doing it. Over time it will work extremely well, and you'll be much happier, much less stressed, more successful in both work and home, and a much kinder parent.

MOVING CASH AROUND QUICKLY

I have used walking mindfulness for many years, and I cannot tell you enough how much it has helped calm me and bring me back to a good place. Along with spending a few minutes each night contemplating gratitude, walking meditation is the easiest way to help us water the seeds of joy and happiness in our lives.

An excellent example of how walking mindfully was so helpful to me was during the 2008 credit crisis. Our entire team was in a constant state of stress because we were facing bankruptcy on a daily basis for approximately six months. Almost all these problems were out of our control, for our main manufacturer was in bankruptcy as was its credit division. I do not want to bore you with the details, but suffice it to say, the head office was in a constant state of emergency. And we moved money around from one store to another the minute the credit source would do an inventory and leave. We were fortunate that our stores on the east coast were four hours ahead of our west coast ones, and the team cleverly used this to our advantage. We would then take all the money from the recently audited dealership, send it to another store, and pay off some sold inventory from that store before the creditors showed up there.

The irony of it all was that our credit source was actually in bankruptcy, not us, but they were on our case every single day. No other bank would give us credit because our lead OEM (original equipment manufacturer) Chrysler was in bankruptcy and in the news every day. Even though our company earned about $20 million that year, we were planning for a potential bankruptcy of a public company—not a fun place to work.

When I woke up early in the morning to read whatever bomb had dropped afresh, I would at least walk with mindfulness to my computer and make a cup of tea. Arriving at work each day, I practiced walking mindfully from office to office and meeting to meeting in order to keep myself from being depressed and to hopefully rub some of my mindfulness off onto the team in a bit of a positive manner.

The attitude and skill of the entire head office team, led by an extremely smart CFO and chief legal counsel, were incredible. The results were a stock price, which were at the time under one dollar per share, growing to over fifty dollars per share a few years later. Investors are extremely happy with that kind of return.

I believe walking meditation dramatically helped my state of mind throughout this miserable time. It also helps the team stay calm under enormous pressure if the leader is somewhat calm.

WE WALK ANYWAYS

Down the hall at home
Down the basement to work out
To the pantry
Anywhere we walk at work
Walking into the grocery store
Walking the dog
Wherever we walk, anywhere we walk,
let's think about our good fortune. We are
walking anyway, what a precious combi-
nation to help us be happy. Walking and
meditation work so well together.

FIRST FIVE MINUTES

WIN THE FIRST FIVE MINUTES

I can remember hundreds of meetings with team members discussing the average amount of time we would likely spend with each of our customers looking to purchase a vehicle. Although today it is a bit less with the internet playing a larger role, certainly we have most on the team say anywhere from ninety minutes to perhaps two hours in total. After we agreed on that amount of time, I would always ask the same question. "If we are going to invest that much time and effort trying to help people, why would we blow the first five minutes and their initial powerful first impression of us?" I would then remind the team that the first few minutes are the most important part of the sale, that's when the customers decide they like us or they don't like us. This is a very significant time, and we do not get a replay.

Here are some sales tips we would discuss and frequently remind everyone of:

- Use walking meditation on the walk over to greet them. It sets up the proper attitude and mindset for us. This is a real advantage over competitors

who don't give themselves an attitude bounce
before meeting with customers.

- Please show customers we are actively listening to
  them.
- Reasonable eye contact builds trust with
  customers.
- Smile a bit during those first few minutes (this is
  underused by many of us).

If we are perceived by customers as either trustworthy or
a bit suspicious within the first few minutes of meeting us,
it makes perfect sense to work hard early to win their initial
trust. I suspect this works just as well when meeting people
doing just about anything in this world.

Our training over the years has focused our staff on how
important the first five minutes are, especially the first thirty
seconds. If we are looked at as trustworthy right from the start,
then all the work we do over the next hour or so will likely be
beneficial to both the customers and us.

Children, I know I am talking about this a fair bit, but only
because it really works. Let's always try to win the first few
minutes and make an excellent first impression.

I LIKE YOU

Boy, you grow up quick when your dad tells you as a seventeen-
year-old kid to go on the showroom floor and try to compete
with a seasoned, hyper-aggressive, money-motivated crew of
approximately forty people between the ages of twenty-four
and sixty. I had both the advantage and the disadvantage
of being a lot boy for this nasty crew, as I had cleaned cars,
changed license plates, and picked up hamburgers for them as
a sixteen-year-old.

Knowing what they were like was helpful, but knowing how they behaved was also intimidating. There were many things to ponder and worry about as I left the car wash bays behind to start trying to sell cars.

One consideration that seemed crucial to me was, How can I make some kind of connection with the customers and get them to like me a bit as we start the sales process? Believe me, even before they arrive at the dealership, customers have already determined that you are not really there to help them. In fact, most of these customers have a "meeting" in the car on the way over with their significant other to remind each other to not believe anything we say, to not to commit to buying anything today, or to remind themselves that the last time they purchased a vehicle they felt they were taken a bit.

I woke up quickly to the fact that customers can find a way to dislike and not trust you in only a few minutes. I remember being around twenty years old during a sales meeting trying to explain to our salespeople that the customers often had a strategy driving over to the dealership. We chatted back and forth, and I said to the team, "Just like we are having a meeting about how to sell them a vehicle today, they are having a meeting about not buying one today from us." My view was that we had a lot more practice than they had, as we did this every day. If we were positive and respectful, we should sell a lot of cars.

Back when I was a shy, eighteen-year-old kid, I really needed to find a way to make that all-important first five minutes not so uncomfortable when approaching and meeting customers. This is something that is difficult for seasoned salespeople as well, but even more so for a very young person the customer might perceive as too green and inexperienced for them. I cannot tell you how many customers questioned me when I approached them on the lot as a very young man with long hair or eighteen months later when I was introduced to them as the sales manager.

It is a hard way to start or finish the negotiations when the buyers are hesitant to deal with you in the first place. At its worst, some customers thought it was a joke that I was introduced as the manager, and a very small number of them even refused to deal with me. I was fortunate that 95 percent of them were good people and treated me well. Learning the "I Like You" way of approaching people was a lifesaver for me.

Kids, before you laugh a bit and say this sounds pretty corny, know that this was the first significant process that I ever used when selling cars. The "I Like You" process came from a rather average book I read as an eighteen-year-old, but this sales point was incredible to learn. In hindsight, the success of using this process made me start to focus on the psychological side of selling automobiles early on, and I bring it up in almost every sales training meeting I have done over these many years.

By now, most of our team knows the "I Like You" process very well, and I often ask people who are skeptical if they can think of a better way to approach someone who is very defensive coming into the store. I ask them, "What's your plan to get through those uncomfortable first few minutes with a customer?" No one has ever come up with a better way than simply using the liking-them idea in your head.

I have also found this equally effective with any person in any situation within the sales and service business or outside of the dealership business completely. I practice it with the utmost consistency today, whether in person, on the telephone, or in a Zoom meeting. Whatever your situation, when you add up the number of interactions we have each day, taking an extra thirty seconds to use the "I Like You" process is invaluable.

Here's how it works. When I am about to greet someone in any business situation, which could include dealership people, bankers, Toyota employees, government officials, accountants, lawyers, institutional investors, potential business owners we are trying to purchase, or anyone else, I diligently do the following:

- I try to look at them a second or so before they look at me, bow my head a little, and say to myself, "These are good people, I like them." It is simply amazing how much this lowers the tension when we meet seconds later.
- We have to truly believe we are the best person to help them with whatever we are working toward, so I humbly say to myself, "I am the best person for you or your team to work with." Then we put our best effort forward to complete our deal, which is beneficial for both parties.

If we really believe the two points above, our sincerity and honesty will shine through. I often tell our team members that if you can't believe these two statements, you should not be working with them because it is likely not beneficial to either of you.

Years and years of experience tell me the only reason people won't do this consistently enough is because it does not work 100 percent of the time, because, of course, nothing does. Again, we should not be looking for perfection in anything as it usually is unattainable.

If this process improves our closing ratio by 20 percent and each situation is less stressful for both parties, this is a good practice. Let's not let a small minority of people who are impossible to deal with stop us from using our best plans that work so much of the time. Please remember, children, how effective this can be for you and how respectful it is for the person or people you are about to deal with.

ACCOUNTABILITY

WE ARE THE NUMBER-ONE FACTOR

I can't remember who I learned this from as a teenager, but all I can say is "Thanks for the brilliant advice." I have practiced and taught it since I was nineteen years old. This topic has been covered in our company meetings for about forty-eight years, and we believe it is a powerful tool for success. We genuinely plead with whatever team it is to please accept two facts about sales and retail:

- The number-one reason customers purchase from us is you.
- The number-one reason customers do not purchase from us is also you.

Of course, there are some exceptions, including inventory availability. Today more of the process is online or sometimes on the phone with the customer, but your part in the success still determines the success of the result.

My years in retail, including running a publicly traded company, taught me that those who understand how important they are to the success of any endeavor undoubtedly do the best at rising to the top of their field. Without this acceptance

NOTES FOR THE CHILDREN127

of accountability, your chances of being at the top of whatever you choose to do are very slim indeed.

OWN YOUR NUMBER

Whatever field you choose for your career, please remember and acknowledge it is our responsibility to make a connection to the people we are dealing with. A saying learned as a rookie salesman has been very helpful to me:

"They drove here to buy a car; we work here."

This must always be top of mind for us if we want to be the best in our field. I was told it is my responsibility, not the customers', to make the relationship work. You would be surprised how many salespeople did not believe or follow this advice. It is also our responsibility to put our "blinders" on at work and leave any home stress and problems behind so we can be accountable to our customers and make the connections positive.

Another excellent example of being accountable is a training phrase I started using after I became a sales manager, which was simply "Own your number."

I am not sure where I learned this, but it was another game changer for me. For the first year or so working at the dealership, so many of the salespeople and managers would be standing around, talking about the economy, the unemployment rate, the wrong color of many of our new vehicles, and so much more. Of course, the first year, I was so excited about selling cars that I didn't spend a lot of time talking to everyone else, but shortly thereafter, I started to fall into this rabbit hole of a sales trap (salespeople know what I mean).

Always remember, kids, sometimes experience can work against you if you become a bit jaded and bitter about the work you are doing, and a young person with a better attitude ends up doing a much-improved job. It is always our responsibility to own our number rather than blame outside circumstances for our lack of success.

Anyway, before I could join the team as a complainer, I was so lucky to learn this phrase about you owning your number. I determined that if my bosses assigned an 80 unit target this month for our sales crew, we were going to do between 80 and 110 vehicles, come hell or high water, as we said back then. We would meet as a team to start the month and divide the sales target among the salespeople, some would have 9, some would have 14, and some might have 18, depending on their ability and track record. The point was that each team member "owned their number," and because I was the team leader, I "owned" the total number. We agreed to the number, we committed to the number, and by doing this, we certainly hit our targets better than any other crew.

I remember the words of a good friend, and one of the best salespeople I have ever met, during the massive recession of 2009. Trying to pump up the sales team was certainly a challenge those days, and during one meeting we were all talking, and Bob Janis said to the group, "The recession is on the south side of the city." The dealership we were in was on the north side of the city, and his words said everything you will ever need to know about "owning your number." You simply cannot be better than Bob when it comes to salesmanship, accountability, and resilience. I still smile today about his words and insights.

On the reverse side of owning our number, a few times in my career I definitely did not own my number and would blame outside issues and problems for not hitting these targets. Each time I did this my career and company would take a significant hit because of my poor attitude.

A recent example of owning our number happened in March 2020 when COVID-19 devastated the country. We knew things might become very bleak in retail very quickly. Of course, we cut costs as fast as we could, but it was the young leaders in our company who had all been taught for years to "own your number" that kept saying we would sell cars even if 70 percent of our employees had to stay home. I was pleasantly surprised how well they did those first few months, while many competitors, with good reason, kind of gave up a bit. What a team of leaders at each store. We have the best people in Canada working at our dealerships, and for this, we are truly blessed.

Children, please learn this incredibly valuable life lesson. Whatever your target and responsibility is and wherever you work, you take full accountability for your success. This means even if you have poor leadership and policies to navigate around, we take full responsibility to get the job done and "own our number."

I NEVER REFUSED TO SELL A CAR IN MY LIFE

I can still vividly remember a weeknight from about forty-nine years ago in Calgary. It was about seven p.m., and I was with a few salespeople standing outside by the front door of Chinook Chrysler when one of the team came back in after working with a family for an hour or so.

One of the sales managers said, "What happened? I thought we were close to a deal as they had been here awhile and loved the vehicle."

I cannot remember the name of the salesperson, but I somewhat remember his face as he quickly replied something I will never forget. "Don't blame me, I have never refused to sell a car in my life."

Something hit me on the spot those many years ago, and I remember thinking, *Wow, this is the best we can do? "I never refuse to sell a car." When it's our job, not the customer's, to sell the car.* This would be like a quarterback talking to his coach after an interception and saying, "Don't blame me, Coach, I've never refused to throw a touchdown pass in my life." An unbelievably poor attitude seen up close and personal.

What a terrific life lesson on being, or not being, accountable for our own results. Hope you understand why this hit me hard and has stuck with me for a half century.

DISCIPLINE

PRACTICING SELF-DISCIPLINE

While learning the practice of self-discipline, please consider a few suggestions here that I have used in sales training for years:

- Ups and downs in performance and consistency are usually the result of poor discipline.
- The secret of our success is really found in what we actually do each and every day. We must be mindful and honest with ourselves about what we are really doing every day.
- Self-discipline is a lot like momentum: it's much easier to stay on a roll than get back on one. Let's make sure we are diligent with our discipline.

From sad experiences, I tell you, children, that the times in my life when I was not practicing self-discipline or trying to fool myself into thinking I was, my results quickly headed south.

MINDFULNESS, GRATITUDE, AND RESILIENCE

I have found it very enlightening to learn that simply practicing the daily habits of mindfulness, resilience, and gratitude increases our ability to remain more self-disciplined. Practicing mindfulness keeps us aware of the tasks we need to be disciplined about, practicing gratitude keeps us in a better state of mind to accomplish them, and practicing resilience keeps us from giving up too early on our road to better self-discipline. When we are on the path of cultivating more self-discipline, it is amazing how many benefits we derive from these three core practices.

CLOSEST THING TO DYIN' THAT I KNOW OF

Even though I am pretty disciplined, how can I speak like an expert on the subject effectively compared to the true champions? My discipline pales in comparison to Muhammad Ali and Joe Frazier.

I recall being sixteen years old and listening to the "Fight of the Century" between Muhammad Ali and Joe Frazier on the radio. Of course, I had wished I was at Winnipeg Arena watching on closed-circuit TV, but the money for that ticket was not something I could afford.

Ali had been unfairly stripped of his championship title and been inactive for a few years because of his stance on the Vietnam War and had only two comeback fights before the Frazier bout. Though I liked and respected Frazier, I wanted Ali to win. With an estimated 300 million people worldwide watching, Joe ended up winning a fifteen-round decision in an incredibly tough fight for both. However, Muhammad won their second fight on January 28, 1974, in a twelve-round decision, and the trilogy fight was scheduled for October 1, 1975.

On the Fight City website, Michael Carbert wrote in 2021,

> More than four decades later, one still hears
> the echoes, the reverberations of that final,
> epic struggle between two boxing legends.
> After all, it was more than a heavyweight
> championship boxing match, much more.
> It was a monumental clash of wills, a last
> battle between bitter rivals, the final, in-
> disputable proof of a champion's greatness,
> and the night when, on the biggest possible
> stage, the whole world saw how boxing,
> when distilled to its very essence, is not a
> game or a sport at all, but something else
> entirely. Simply put, boxing is life and death,
> legalized gladiatorial combat, brutal and
> merciless, the roped square a domain where
> warriors have the unique chance to lay claim
> to true glory by overcoming the greatest of
> tests.

It was one of the most grueling fights in boxing history, and neither man was ever the same after it. Both men fought their hearts out, displaying courage most of us could only dream of. After the fourteenth round, Frazier's trainer, Eddie Futch, told Joe he had taken too much punishment and was asking the ref to stop the fight.

Joe said, "I want him, boss, don't stop it."

To which Eddie said, "Sit down, son, it's all over. No one will ever forget what you did here today."

The world can be cruel and unfair, as while Joe was asking his trainer not to stop the fight, over in Muhammad's corner, he was ready to end his evening as well. Had Joe's corner waited fifteen or so seconds longer before telling the ref it was over, Frazier would have won the fight, as Ali's corner would have been the first to stop it.

Regardless of who won, both men were beyond skilled, courageous, disciplined, and resilient, and both men will go down in history as two of the best of all time. Years later Ali would say, "It was like death. Closest thing to dyin' that I know of."

Boxers have taught me over and over again through the years how much self-discipline, sacrifice, and resilience mean to your success. Most come from abject poverty and ex-tremely difficult life circumstances to become world cham-pions. I have enormous respect for every one of these fighters and over the years have said to myself a thousand times, *If these men can endure and survive this kind of upbringing and rise above it, how can I not put forth my best effort and dis-cipline to find my success, which is clearly miles and miles easier?*

Without witnessing the drive I watched in these boxers, I do not think I would have had the drive, discipline, and cour-age to achieve what I have. They certainly showed me the way to reach a little deeper each and every day. We all need some sources of motivation and examples to follow, please look for your examples and inspirations.

HOW FAST CAN IT GO?

In Hamilton, Ontario, June 1949, a young Joe Priestner was one of eleven boys chosen from the high schools in Hamilton and the vicinity to be one of the new "execs" working at the premier retailer in Canada, Eaton's. Back in 1949, having your picture in the *Hamilton Spectator* was a very big deal, and I imagine everyone in his family was so proud as the oldest child received this recognition.

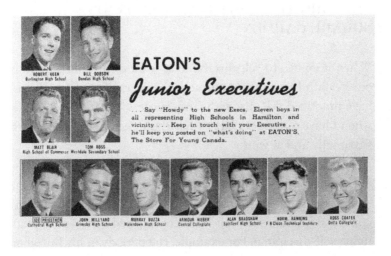

Article clip from "Eaton's Junior Executives" in the Hamilton Spectator, featuring Joe Priestner, 1949.

Less than ten years later, Joe and his family of five were driving from Windsor back home to live with his wife's parents after Joe was caught stealing money from the hotel where he was a manager. How can things go so wrong so quickly? His five siblings had all finished university and were on their way to successful careers, which was unusual coming from a lower-middle-class family. Though addictions and serious emotional issues surely played a part in my father's early troubles, discipline was also a big factor. It's my belief he had all the talent and then some to be very successful, but his constant lack of discipline throughout his years caused more and more problems.

We all need to learn from those who do things right and from those who do not. Can't say for sure in which area I have learned more from, but it's clearly both sides. Kids, let's try to learn from Dad's struggles with discipline and continually practice self-discipline in our daily lives. I know Dad would have wanted us to.

THE BRIGHT LIGHTS OF MADISON
SQUARE GARDEN

When it comes to self-discipline at work or at home, there is one certain fact running through the years of my life. When I have practiced self-discipline, my success has been immense; when I have not practiced it, I have suffered many losses, both personally and at work.

My view of self-discipline comes close to many dictionaries' definition of it, and my life experiences tell me the same story. Our ability to mostly control our emotions and overcome our weaknesses can be accomplished only while practicing self-discipline. For example, the periods in my life when I did not spend even fifteen minutes a day reading, learning, and indeed relearning how to water my positive seeds and ignore my negative ones were times I invariably suffered more. I have also learned to control my thoughts and behaviors better in the face of temptations that we all face.

Self-discipline is a habit we must learn, practice, and master if we want our life's goals to materialize. I have met far too many people who have had some pretty good ideas but next to nothing to show for them—innumerable times a lack of self-discipline was the main reason. Often, even having a consummate character and an excellent skill set cannot overcome a lack of discipline.

Former heavyweight boxing legend Joe Frazier said, "You can map out a fight plan or a life plan, but when the action starts, you're down to your reflexes. That's where the road work shows. If you cheated on that in the dark of the morning, you're getting found out now under the bright lights of the ring." Who could say it better regarding the importance of self-discipline in whatever field we are in?

We may never be under the bright lights of Madison

Square Garden, but in our world, the lights we are under are just as important to us. Practicing self-discipline will go a long way for all of us.

BITTERNESS

TOXIC BITTERNESS

The *Cambridge English Dictionary* describes "bitter" in a few ways:

- "Someone who is bitter is angry and unhappy because they cannot forget bad things that happened in the past"
- "A bitter experience causes deep pain or anger"
- "Expressing a lot of hate and anger"

Clearly, bitterness is not a state any of us want to reside in, and as with all negative emotions, this also affects those closest to us in a serious manner. Kids, I lived for many years with a touch of bitterness, mostly from growing up in a chaotic home, realizing that life was not always fair. The taste of bitterness really snuck up on me when we started our first business in December 1981. It became abundantly clear that most of our competitors in the auto retail business in London were wealthy second-generation families who certainly had a superior opinion of themselves. To them, we were simply peasants who came to London to make it, but like many before us who started with nothing, we would likely fail, and they would laugh about it. To your face, they were half-polite, but you would have to be completely stupid not to see their real feelings underneath.

While I played the underdog card well to further motivate myself, this also caused bitterness to creep back into my soul. My favorite words under my breath for all of them were "eff you," and I'm not especially proud of that today. Fortunately, bitterness started to hold less of a grip on me with each passing year, and this is a nice burden to not have to carry around.

Bitterness is so toxic for us, and had I not been so lucky in my business life, the odds are I would have ended up a bitter person, as I had once used it as motivation. I'm not sure that is a healthy thing to do. Can you imagine what we as parents do to our children by living with bitterness inside us and them having to see and feel it?

Had I held on to my bitterness, I know Diana would never have dated and married me. I am pretty sure she would not want to bring her daughters, Lauren and Kaedra, into a relationship with someone whose being was anchored in bitterness.

I am sure I did enough things that hurt people in some way, and I am sorry for that. Being bitter at the time did not help my actions then. We all have enough things we wish we had done differently in our lives, but we don't need to add bitterness to the pile. We have all known many people who are bitter, and we can see how this has affected them. Please take a quick look at some of the notes over the following pages to hopefully help you avoid this emotion as your journey through life progresses.

BITTERNESS PILLS

All bitterness ever did for me was to cause many problems, including a lack of sleep, fatigue, low self-esteem, a lack of confidence, personality shifts that were not positive, and relationship issues. I have worked with and known so many good people who ended up bitter about so much in their lives. I suspect they received many of the same dubious benefits I did.

The truly sad thing about bitterness is that not once did I ever see this emotion help anyone solve any unfortunate situations. Worse yet, bitterness can be awfully hard to shake. It is also extremely difficult to watch, or sometimes even be in the same room as, a loved one who exhibits so much bitterness. Unfortunately, if we are not careful, we can also be that one person people don't want to be around in that room.

It's normal to feel angry or bitter once in a while, but holding on to our anger leads to a degree of bitterness that is like poison. Please remember that for bitterness to grow it needs sympathy, and often that is found in the negative stories we tell ourselves. Though I do not see any signs of this in any of you, I ask you to please be aware of this throughout your lifetime. From my experience, bitterness has a way of creeping in if we are not mindful of it.

A RAW DEAL

I can't believe how often I got to the point of bitterness from believing I had been given a raw deal in life because of my family's problems and the home we had all grown up in being a painful place to live.

The belief that people have been given a raw deal may well be true, and it may well not be true. In my case, hindsight tells me it was not true; I was not given a raw deal. Even if it is correct, we cannot control what happened to us in the past; we can control only our actions and plans going forward from it. This is a life truth I sure wish I had learned earlier, kids, so take a tip from someone who has failed here for way too long.

Bitterness is never the favored path to move forward from unfortunate events that inevitably occur in our lives. Along the way, I discovered four firm decisions I could make to help me move further away from bitterness whenever it creeps into my life:

- Let go of grudges completely (a very achievable task).
- Forgive people for what they have done (also very achievable).
- Stop worrying about negative things in the past (a little tougher to do).
- Stop talking about negative things in the past (a little tougher to do).

HUMILITY

A CHRISTMAS LESSON NOT TO BE FORGOTTEN

Real leaders know that it is the little things you do better than your competition that help you win. The importance of all the small basics in your business being done very well cannot be overemphasized. Bragging about them to anybody who will listen to you is not the answer.

I still recall forty-three years ago being in one of the first meetings I'd ever been in with a bunch of competitive owners of dealerships in London, Ontario, for a special dealers Christmas event. As a young, somewhat-broke kid, I felt like I did not belong among the wealthy establishment family dealers in the city, let alone an event at the London Club.

I distinctly remember one dealer who was very successful at the time, and after a few too many glasses of wine, telling anyone who would listen that he actually "had the magic." I am thinking, *Wow, do some of these rich people really have the magic? What the heck do I need to do to find it? Please someone teach me how to find it.* As he rambled along about his brilliance, I can remember thinking, *I am not sure he has it, but I best keep that opinion to myself with this crowd.* Two thoughts entered my head as I drove home that night:

- *If I ever make it and have a lot of success, please don't become like him.*
- *If I become this full of myself, I will likely lose everything over time.*

Not that it brings me any joy whatsoever, but ten years later, he was out of business. Today it might take anyone with that attitude about a year or two to lose it all, not ten. Good lesson to be learned here.

SEARCHING FOR HUMILITY

Sometimes we learn so much from watching people up close and personal who are the exact opposite of what we are trying to be in life. I was fortunate to see many of these situations up close. A couple of instances that happened over twenty-five years ago still reside in my mind.

About a week or so after we moved to Edmonton, I watched in horror as a couple of the sales managers at the dealership we had purchased put on sales meetings. They obviously had an arrogance that had no limit and believed they were the best in the county. During the sales meetings I attended, you might think being a bit humble would occur to them, as I was the new owner, and it was my first taste of their leadership. With about thirty-five people in the room, one of the sales managers actually said during his incoherent rambling, "If any one of you can't sell three cars this weekend, why don't you just go into the corner and lick your nuts like a dog." He also claimed his training was so superior that anyone working for him could sell three cars in a weekend.

I was sitting there pondering how this could possibly motivate anyone and how this could qualify as effective training of people. Needless to say, that's the last training meeting he ever did at our store.

A few weeks later I listened to another tell the sales team in the used-car building, "If I can't close your customer today, God could not." As I was walking back over to the new-car showroom, I thought to myself, *How can someone say this to their team, let alone when their new boss is standing there?*

These two individuals were among the first to go from a dealership that had lost over $1 million the year before we bought it. The lesson here is that we learn from everyone, good and bad.

HUMILITY FIRST

Children, one of the things I so much admire in all of you is the personal humility you continue to show. This is such a splendid quality to have and, of course, sets such a good example for your children as well. We must always remember that true humility is the deep and very solid foundation of all virtues. Though some may disagree, I believe humility is clearly not a sign of weakness but one of underlying strength.

Most people prefer to follow a humble leader, not a bag of wind. As you move through the next stages in your life, please remember to stay as humble as you are today. Also, keep in mind the old proverb, "When someone sings his own praises, he always gets the tune too high."

EARLY BASICS

SEVEN FUNDAMENTALS THAT REALLY WORKED

As I read through so many of my old notes from years ago, several common themes resonate throughout them. I realized many of the themes were the basic covenants of what I was trying to accomplish in my training sessions then, and many continue to this day. In hindsight, I might not list these now in the same order as I did then but have decided to share them with you in exactly the same order as I have done for years.

There are seven fundamentals that I regarded as essential if someone wanted to flourish in any sales environment. I also believed at a very young age that training would be much more effective if looked at from a more conscious manner with an ample amount of inner reflection. Many of the salespeople working with us would at first say, *Please just train me to be a top salesperson by giving me "the best lines to use on customers."* But I persevered with what I thought was a better way, and most of the time, people would try some of these things and find rapid improvement.

I did not know at the time that these early fundamentals would transfer seamlessly to just about any career. I will list them here, and you will see that throughout these notes I've expanded a little on each:

- Don't give up too early.
- Expect more from yourself.
- Take one step at a time.
- Listen, listen, listen.
- Focus, focus, focus.
- Don't beat yourself up.
- Put the other person's hat on.

When we have done the first five things as best as possible, let's do the sixth one and not beat ourselves up. It took me a number of years to add the seventh rule, but it is one of the most valuable ones, and so very needed for us all.

THE SAME FUNDAMENTAL TRUTH

Another insight that came to me as I contemplated these notes was the incredible diversity of people from every stage of life I have worked with and learned from and how each of them shared the same fundamental truth about surviving in business. Before I speak to this truth, I want to give you an example of the variety of situations and people I've worked with:

- Working in a small family-owned delicatessen from twelve to fifteen years old
- Working as a lot porter (they called us lot lizards) washing cars, changing plates, and doing anything else they needed at sixteen years old while I was in first year university (Mike and I had skipped grade three, so I started university young.)

- Working with thirty other salespeople as a car salesman from seventeen until nineteen years old (The average age of the salespeople at that time was about forty years. This was a *zoo* for a shy kid studying philosophy at university.)
- Working as a new-vehicle sales manager, leading a team of about eight salespeople from nineteen until twenty-one years old
- Working as a general sales manager, running the entire sales operations (approximately fifty people) of a large auto dealership from twenty-one until twenty-four years old
- Working with my brother and another partner with Chrysler Canada to have my first actual ownership position in a dealership (The three of us had one-third of a $25,000 initial investment, which was $8,333 each. Today my brother has his own extremely successful business, and the other partner retired thirty-five years ago.)
- Working closely with executives at General Motors, Toyota, Ford, Honda, BMW, Audi, VW, Lexus, Acura, Lincoln, Fiat Chrysler, Nissan, Infiniti, Hyundai, Mazda, Mercedes-Benz, Kia, and others
- Working closely with executives of the financial companies of most of these manufacturers
- Working closely with senior executives at almost every Canadian bank
- Working closely with the Capital Markets division of almost every bank in Canada
- Working closely with most of the large securities firms in Canada
- Working with so many investment firms in

Canada and the United States while running a
public company
- Working closely with some of the largest accounting firms in Canada
- Working closely with some of the top legal firms
in Canada
- Working closely with a number of significant
advertising firms in Canada
- Working closely with a number of executives at
newspapers, radio stations, TV stations, and online agencies in Canada
- Working with a Canadian federal cabinet minis-
ter during the 2008 Chrysler and General Motors
bankruptcies
- Working very closely with approximately eighty
business owners on business purchases ranging
from $10 million to over $600 million each (The
sellers are often divesting their only significant
asset and have to navigate their own family estate
plans as well as negotiate the transaction with us.
You learn things about people and their family
history that are very enlightening; most people
are decent with difficult decisions to make.)

It has been truly fascinating to watch so many different
types of people and how they attempt to accomplish their
goals and priorities and to see the techniques they use to be
successful. I began to notice one common theme when it came
to having a successful career and business.

I can tell you with full confidence that a senior investment
banker sweats as much selling a $2 billion deal to investors as a
new entrepreneur sweats getting their first $10,000 loan. Early
on, I hoped this pressure might lift the more successful I became. But when I started finding financial success at a young

age, I quickly understood that this pressure was never going to go away if I chose to stay an entrepreneur. The same fundamental truth applies: you need to sell to survive. You must learn to live with that or get into another field of work.

Most successful entrepreneurs wake up after a successful sales day or month, and the first thing they think is *We have to do it again today, yesterday's gone.* This was another early basic tenet that I saw in the successful people I observed, so I tried to emulate it the best I could. Early on, I started introducing this fundamental truth about survival in business into my sales meetings, lest anyone think this would ease up with more money or experience.

My son-in-law Justin is a terrific husband and father and a heck of a leader. After a number of years in the military, he joined our business and did very well in each position he was put in, and everyone liked and respected him. One day about three years into his sales career, he said, "I am going back to the military." We joked that he sometimes found it easier to be in Afghanistan than deal with the constant pressure of the need to sell today to survive. The navy is lucky to have him.

ATTITUDE

WORKING AT THE SCHOOL BOARD

I don't quite remember how or why I developed a bit of an attitude during my high school years, but it was there. Perhaps I started to understand the world a bit, and I got a chip on my shoulder about how schools seemed to favor the wealthier kids whose parents knew how to play the game. Perhaps it was just my perception, but it sure seemed to me things were not exactly fair, and many times I let them know. I'm not sure that ever helped me, but I was young, angry, and pissed off. Years later I learned, indeed, that life is not fair, but it is still fascinating.

After I finished grade twelve in Winnipeg, we were going to move again, this time to meet up with our dad, who had moved to Calgary a year or so earlier to get another job. I did not attend my graduation, as I protested the music they were going to play, so it was a beautiful late June afternoon as I was about to take my last walk down the school hallway and out the door for good. I knew I was never coming back to visit.

As I was walking along the hallways, I decided to kick the living crap out of all the lockers before exiting the school. Little did I know someone was about to rat me out. My actions did not go over well with the school, and a day later

Mom received a call that said they were going to withhold my grades, which I needed to register for university. The school board determined I would have to work at their warehouse for the two weeks before we left for Calgary to pay for the damage I had done. Then they would release my grades. I was not a happy camper about this.

When my sentence was finished, the four kids and Mom left Winnipeg for good on the long drive to meet up with Dad and Mary, who were already living in Calgary. We moved into Dad's motel on Macleod Trail and wondered what might be next. A few salespeople were also living in the same motel, and it was clear on arrival that the city might have changed, but the drinking was the same. Fortunately, we soon moved into our home, which was nice.

It's pretty clear to me today that my attitude was horrible, but I believe it was because of all the changes that kept happening to us, and obviously, rebellion was on my mind. Even so, acting out my attitude destructively didn't make my life situation better or reap me any rewards whatsoever. Would not recommend any of you handle the situation as I did. Thankfully over the years my attitude has improved somewhat.

SHOWTIME

When I was first selling cars, I distinctly remember learning something very important about being prepared for each set of customers we would speak with. Meeting customers as they came into the dealership, I quickly realized how apprehensive they were. Of course, there was a small percentage who were rude and arrogant to us no matter how we approached them. However, the majority were good people and actually pretty nervous. I realized that it was my job to get them to like and trust me enough to be able to work through a stressful process for them. Most often, if I accomplished this, they were likely to purchase a vehicle from me. I also realized quickly that if they were neutral with me and had little trust, then the chances of a sale were slim.

There had to be a better way than what the managers were currently teaching us, which was basically threefold:

- Look the customers in the eye.
- Smile.
- Make sure you are in control and lead them around the lot while you are showing them vehicles; never follow them.

Our bosses really believed if the customers were not following us around the car lot, we were losing control of the sale. If one of the managers saw a customer walking in front of you, kind of going his or her own way, they would call you out at the next morning sales meeting and make fun of you in front of the whole group. Control of the customer was the essence of what we were taught.

Even as a teenager I could not understand this managerial strategy that we were being taught. From my perspective, if you treat people well and with respect and have a positive attitude yourself, people will follow you.

I mostly disregarded what we were being taught, knowing that my attitude toward the customer during the first few minutes set the stage for success and a likely sale. So this meant I had to figure out how to have the best attitude possible before meeting each and every customer.

Figuring out how to do this well was challenging. While it is a noble goal to be happy and treat every customer perfectly when they walk through the door, often our own attitude or lack of confidence would get in the way.

For instance, ten minutes before you met these new

customers, your finance manager might tell you that both cars you sold on the weekend were not going through because the financing fell apart, or perhaps ten minutes before you met these customers one of your old customers came in to complain about the problems with the new vehicle they just purchased three weeks ago. It's not that easy to have the best attitude and make the best first impression each and every time.

There were also many salespeople who would try to kind of sabotage your deal by walking by the customers and you and saying something rude to his friendly sales partner. They would have their big laugh and walk away, while the customers were in a bit of suspended disbelief. The managers of this business thought it was all friendly gags and pretty much let it go. Can you imagine that today?

The vital lesson I learned in my first year of retail has stayed with me for almost fifty years, and without it, I am one hundred percent convinced my career would have been much less fruitful. The lesson I am speaking of is twofold: you are not likely to have the right attitude with the customer if you do not have the right attitude and state of mind within yourself a minute or so before greeting them.

So as a young rookie, I would say to myself each time a customer was coming in, "It's showtime," and I would put the blinders on and think of nothing but this customer. Thirty years later I would use mindfulness before each encounter with a customer, employee, banker, or anyone else so that my attitude reflected calm, presence, compassion, and kindness. "Showtime" was a pretty basic way to acknowledge that this customer was what we needed to focus on, nothing else. Mindfulness is a much more intelligent and sophisticated way to practice. Furthermore, in our homes and personal lives, mindfulness helps us and those around us so much more than a silly slogan.

I know my own attitude was paramount to my success or failure then, as it is today. So is yours.

TWENTY-ONE-POINT LEAD

As we move through the different stages of our lives, we need to fully understand how our attitude and state of mind help us find our dreams or lose our way. Let's understand that our attitude determines our facial expressions, our tone of voice, and our gestures and actions. This is how people see us, and they make an important early first impression of us; in fact, they usually make their own minds up about us in mere minutes. This impression of us is not easy to change over the course of our negotiations or dealings.

This is like playing against a Joe Montana–led team and spotting them a twenty-one-point lead. Not a particularly intelligent strategy to use. I have discussed this in hundreds of meetings to help us get out of the gate with a quality first impression on our customers. Kids, another beauty of this is that we do not have to work one more hour to do this; we just have to be a bit smarter.

LET'S HAVE A LITTLE FUN

Speaking of attitude, do we really think if we're not having any fun that our spouse is having a lot of fun being around us?

Do we really think if we're not having any fun that our children are having a lot of fun being around us?

Do we think our children are learning this type of behavior from us when we're never having fun?

Do we think our coworkers are thrilled being around us when we're never having any fun?

Let's always try to have a bit of fun along the journey.

PEOPLE TALKIN'

A small tip on attitude that will really help us all regards gossip. Again, I can talk from the wrong side of experience here. One day when I was running the new-vehicle department at Westown Ford, a few of the team were standing with me by the east door, and we were acting as hockey armchair quarterbacks discussing the previous night's Oilers game. I was talking about a player they had just traded for with Boston and was telling the team I could not understand the trade and that he certainly did not play well at all last night. Little did I know he was waiting at reception to see me because the Oiler's management had him come down to pick up a new vehicle at our dealership, which I would help him with.

Talk about embarrassing, as our receptionist called me over and said, "Tom" was here to see me. As tough a player as he was, I thought he might say something to me about my comments that he had certainly heard. Thankfully, he was a real nice person, and we found a vehicle for him, and off he went with a new Bronco. He certainly showed more manners and class than I did. Real-time life lesson for me about talking out of turn about another human being.

If we want to carry a great attitude with us, partaking in gossip is a sure way to lose it. Forget for a minute the damage we can do to other people who we gossip about, and let's be honest with ourselves. How do we feel inside ourselves when we just finished a round of gossip? Likely not very good and a bit ashamed. Let's use our time saying positive things to ourselves and about others. I believe many of our mothers or grandmothers often said, "If you can't say anything nice, don't say anything at all." I can tell you from experience that our children do not like to hear us gossip, and when we do, it really gives the kids the direction to do the same.

THE GREAT DISCOVERY

Oprah Winfrey said, "The greatest discovery of all time is that a person can change his future by merely changing his attitude."

Even though I do not think I have ever watched a full episode of Oprah's, I couldn't agree more, and I plead with you children to take this to heart. Our attitude and willingness to learn determine our fate.

CLOUDS

Children, please remember when our attitude and mood start to go toward the negative side, just let it come and let it go without any self-judgment. The most effective way that has worked for me is when a negative thought comes into my head, I simply let it pass right on through without any comment whatsoever. Take a deep breath and let the thought or emotion just drift away.

As Thich Nhat Hahn would say, "Feelings come and go like clouds in a windy sky. Conscious breathing is my anchor."

PRECIOUSNESS OF LIFE

Man, oh man, I truly wasted thousands of days of my short life immersed in a bad attitude—being upset about something, feeling jealous of what others had or appeared to have, continuing a feud with someone or some organization, and however many other negative things you can think of. Some of us seem to think that if we do not have some kind of enemy, no matter how minor, we are not working hard enough. Sometimes the angry feelings or perceived feuds were the result of a terrible situation that needed to be remedied, but often it was something like dealing with the cable company that had us upset.

Life is precious each and every day, and if we are always waiting for tomorrow to be happy, let's remember tomorrow is not always like we hope it will be.

Children, here is a certain fact of life that is not depressing, negative, or morbid: each and every one of us is going to get sick, and each and every one of us is going to die; we just do not know when. All but one of your grandparents have died. Your parents are over sixty, and their time is limited. Your siblings and you will pass away at some point. Though it's hard to contemplate for any of us, your sons and daughters will pass on some years from now.

I remind you of all this so you can examine how precious life really is and to make sure we do not waste much of it captured in a state of anger, jealousy, regret, or other negative emotion. Let's try to live each day in a state of reasonable happiness, contentment, compassion, and other positive emotions. Many of the notes in this book will try to help you achieve this. Please also know the way we live our lives and carry ourselves will reflect heavily on how our children see their lives and carry themselves.

BROTHERS ONCE

A DEVASTATING JOURNEY

How do you possibly write a chapter called "Brothers Once"? I suppose I should start with explaining that when I first contemplated *Notes for the Children*, I realized I was going to have to include background about my relationship with my twin brother. I wanted you to understand the things that shaped my life and share how various experiences led me to do the work that I needed on myself to get to the happiness I now have.

My relationship with my twin brother, Mike, has certainly been one of the major influences for the changes I decided to make. However, for the sake of privacy and to not hurt anyone, I've decided not to go into a lot of detail in this book.

It is beyond belief to me that twin brothers who were extremely close to each other and best friends for almost thirty-five years could end up in such an estranged and contentious relationship. To describe how close we once were, perhaps Mike's wife, Patricia, summed it up best some forty-five years ago. Soon after she and Mike were married, Patricia told my mother that if Mike, Patricia, and I were on a boat and there were only two life jackets as the boat was sinking, Mike would have saved me, not her. That must have been a devastating feeling to have for someone who had just married Mike, and no one could ever blame Patricia for feeling the way she did. I suspect that type of deep feeling did not help our brother relationship going forward and was likely an undercurrent to the problems to come.

We both grew up in a very difficult situation, and each of us learned how to deal with our family's issues and problems in our own way, so I can tell you only the truth of things that happened to me, and he has the right to tell his story as well. I am sure Mike would have a different view from mine, and that's normal.

Without sharing specifics, I can say that, for decades, I was repeatedly following unhealthy patterns of communication and behavior with my brother. While we were in business together and even after we split up our partnership, the patterns of severe anger and verbal abuse between us just never seemed to end. We went from being the closest two brothers could be to brothers screaming from the rooftops at each other on a regular basis. Many years and lots of personal work later, I realized this was so similar to the abusive cycle we continually witnessed during childhood when our parents would have no money and be drunk and scream for hours at each other and later pretend it didn't happen.

For Mike and me the cycle would include some friendly chats about hockey, the kids, and family stuff, as if nothing happened two days before. Often, we would go up to his cottage to watch a game or listen to some music and enjoy the night. Two or three days or a week later he would hear about something my company was doing and tell me again how everyone hated everything about me and that I was "a pathetic piece of sh*t."

At the time I couldn't see that we were probably caught in an abusive pattern we witnessed throughout childhood; all I could see was how badly I wanted to make it work between us and stop the fighting. This likely came from the family peacekeeper role I assigned myself as a fifteen-year-old kid, calling Sunday family meetings to try to get our parents to stop drinking all day and screaming at each other.

Undoubtedly, I missed the mark with Mike many times, but I did everything possible within my heart and soul to try to stick together as brothers and as best friends. Years later, I realized that as a young kid, it should not have been my responsibility to try to fix our parents' problems and try to keep the home somewhat functional. Similarly, I started to see that it wasn't my sole responsibility to make things work with me and Mike, especially if "making it work" meant tolerating an ongoing abusive situation between us.

The positive news here is we generally do the work on ourselves to be happy only when we have hit very close to rock bottom. The partnership and family fights drove me there many times. However, I didn't finally finish the work I needed to do on myself until 2009 when Diana, Lauren, and Kaedra moved from Richmond, Virginia, to Edmonton. That was the beginning of the end of the madness for me.

From left to right: Lauren, Patrick, Kaedra, and Diana, 2008, shortly before moving to Canada.

I had warned Diana before we married that I had an extremely volatile relationship with my brother, and it was pretty stressful. I certainly owed her that, but I am not sure anyone could have known what it was like before they were in the actual situation with me. Sure as winter is going to come to Edmonton, it was not long before my company must have done something Mike did not like, though I was never sure what the actual issues were most of the time, and he was at it again in full force.

Thankfully for me, Diana would not put up with two minutes of this insanity. If Mike started screaming again or engaging my sisters to come after me, Diana would rationally encourage me to stop participating in all the dramatic feuding and try to resist succumbing to my emotional habit of always keeping the family peace at any cost. She was astounded by how the family would continue to go through hell and a few weeks later pretend nothing happened. This is an eminent lesson for you children to always see things as they really are in your life and to not pretend otherwise.

Shortly thereafter, Diana's wisdom and kindness saved us when she said, "This is madness, and it ends now." This is when I finally finished the work I had to do with my relationship with Mike, making the hard decision to cut off communication with him and no longer engage in family feuds. I finally saw that I could never take Diana back into the darkness with me, I could never let my kids see me suffer again from such toxic relationships. I especially could not let Lauren and Kaedra see this darkness. Could you imagine two brave young girls having to go to school in a new country as part of a new family and everything that goes with that and additionally having to deal with listening to Mike and I fight like dogs? They would have been crying in their rooms each night wondering how and why the heck they moved here. And I certainly did not want any grandchildren down the line to see me engaging in this behavior.

As hard as it was to cut off communication and change my part in the broken-down relationship with Mike, this enabled Diana and me to have an extraordinary marriage, a warm and loving relationship with five incredible children, and the same with our beautiful grandchildren.

The way I see it now, Mike and I grew up in an abnormal home and found business success at a young age. Beyond doubt the combination of the two was too much for us to overcome as twin brothers. I am so, so sorry for the pain this relationship has caused Mike, and I should have done things differently but did not know how to. I take my share of the responsibility for the things that went wrong and the stupid things I said, including too many curse words.

Earnestly, I hope Mike has come out on the other side of this in a happy and content place as well. From the outside, it certainly looks that way, and his children are prospering and doing very well. I am happy and thankful for that, as our behavior could have affected all our kids more. It was never fair to any of our children.

For many years you children witnessed only the fights and anger between Mike and me, but I wanted to share the stories that follow, which speak to how bonded we once were and the closeness that drove me to try so hard to attempt fixing the relationship over the years, albeit unsuccessfully. I hope the future will get better for us, but there's a lot of heavy baggage there. We could have gone through life as true brothers, not brothers once. The following three stories are only a few of the many wonderful times we had together.

POSITIVELY FOURTH STREET

I can remember so many fun times Mike and I had together as we were growing up, way too many to count. I always thought if we had each other and our sisters, we would be OK. To this day, I remember the moment the two of us heard Bob Dylan for the first time, and I can remember exactly where we were sitting. We were in the living room in our house on Palliser Drive in Calgary listening to the radio playing a song we had never heard before. After a minute or so of getting used to the odd voice, the lyrics kept going on and on until, "Yes, I wish for just one time you could stand inside my shoes you'd know what a drag it is to see you."

After the song finished, the DJ said, "'Positively 4th Street' by Bob Dylan." We looked at each other, and I don't think either of us ever thought of music the same again.

We had just turned sixteen and were short of money, so we asked Mom for a five-dollar loan and the keys to her car so we could go buy the album at the local drugstore, where they sold records as well. This was one of the hundreds of times we would pick up a new record and go listen to it together, and this pattern lasted until we were close to forty years old. Awesome memories to say the least.

FEELING SO PROUD

I can still vividly remember being at River Heights Arena in Winnipeg as a thirteen-year-old kid watching in the stands as the Winnipeg Ambassadors all-star team (Winnipeg's best thirteen-year-olds, selected from all the teams in the city) took on the River Heights team of fifteen-year-olds, who were expected to give the young Ambassadors a little more than they could handle. The arena was packed to the rafters as people came to see the young hotshots take on a pretty strong team in the River Heights bantam team.

Watching Mike stand on his head for save after save throughout the game was making me feel prouder and prouder. As I walked around the arena during the first and second intermissions and listened to all the talk, most of it was of the thirteen-year-old star in the Ambassadors' net. My pride grew and grew.

It's kind of funny and ironic, but I had tried out for the same Ambassadors' team and was rightfully cut, along with some other pretty decent players. I can say with unequivocal conviction that I did not have an ounce of jealousy in me. I am also proud that I felt nothing but happiness for him.

One twin the star, the other the cheerleader. I thought we were forever a team, but clearly I was wrong.

EMPTY BEER CASES

Looking back to the time we lived in a nice neighborhood of Winnipeg, in our rental house with the bus stop behind it, brings back a lot of memories. Mike and I shared a small bedroom in the basement that seemed to be all we ever needed. We had the rec room around the corner mostly to ourselves, and we would spend many hours each week talking about life as young teenagers and listening to as much music as we could. We would talk about the lyrics and meanings of the songs till we went to sleep.

On a bit of a comedic note, we also smuggled a fair amount of beer we had managed to acquire down there as well. We had this small garage at the back of the house that was not used for a car, and no one ever went into it, so it became where we would hide all the empty beer cases.

About a year after we started hiding them, Mom came downstairs one night and said, "Boys, I went out to the garage this afternoon, and there are all these empty beer cases there. What do you think happened?"

One of us said, "Well, it does not have a lock on it, and I suppose some of the neighborhood kids must be using it to get rid of their beer."

Mom said, "That must be the case, so I will try to get a lock for it."

Two thoughts come to mind here:

- Mom was a very intelligent woman who obviously had blinders on for her two boys to believe that story.
- For the life of me, I can't remember whether it was Mike or me who came up with this story, but it sure was a good one.

These were certainly fun times growing up as twins and always sticking together. I am very grateful Mike was the best brother anyone could have had for the first half of my life.

DISCOURAGEMENT

EARLY YEARS OF SALES TRAINING LESSONS

I remember early in my career attending so many different motivational and sales training sessions and feeling something was missing in them. The sales trainers were very good at what they presented, but they invariably talked about how to pump yourself up with a bunch of words and slogans like, *Do what I say here today, and you will be so successful.*

Even at that young age, I would ponder the reality of how easy this was for everyone to do on a consistent basis. Also, if that is all you have to do, well, everyone would spend fifteen minutes a day reciting slogans and laudatory phrases to make twice as much money. Who wouldn't? Why wouldn't everyone just do that to be successful?

It took me about five years to come up with a solution that worked on a more gratifying basis and lasted so much longer. The goal for the team and for me was to achieve a more favorable mindset each day in a retail business where we simply did not get paid if we did not sell. For this to happen, I realized it was imperative we find out how to stop being discouraged all the time, which was like a toxin in the business. It was either elation on a good day or total discouragement the rest of the time; it's no wonder an inordinate amount of alcoholism and family problems prevailed in the industry. In the coming pages, I will leave you some notes on how I believe our habits can lead to being discouraged and the things we can do to move forward from it.

LOSING HELPS US WIN

Children, one of the ways I have battled discouragement is to reframe losing and see the gifts it has given me. I am happy to have experienced losing and even repeating the same mistakes and poor habits I had during those times. The reason I am happy about these losses is that I have learned from them and, as a result, have become happier and humbler when winning. Believe me, the knowledge I gained from losing was sure worth the price of the pain.

Here are some other wins of losing:

- We really don't learn anything about ourselves when we have somewhat easy wins; we need to lose to truly learn things about ourselves.
- Having lost makes our wins much more gratifying.
- Winning becomes so much more humbling if we have learned to lose with a bit of grace.
- It's OK to lose; let's just learn from it, and let's not keep making the same mistakes.
- The lessons we learn about ourselves when we lose and come back from it are priceless, literally priceless, and give a beautiful example for our kids to follow.

FROM BAD TO WORSE

A few too many times in my life I did not act like someone with a good attitude, and it hurt me each and every time. I am embarrassed to admit this story to you, but it is true that this happened in a time of significant discouragement in my life. I pass on this humiliating display of "poor me" only in hopes you never act in any way like I did.

Things were going from bad to worse for us in Winnipeg, stemming from an acquisition and move we should not have made. I will not bore you with the details that led to this financial crisis for our company, with the exception of taking personal responsibility for it. The fact was only two people, my brother and me, had made this decision, and we were responsible for the current situation. A week or so earlier, our bank had called all our loans, even though we were current on all our payments. Things were rapidly sliding into a state of hell as we had six weeks to pay off the loans or face bankruptcy. Finding a new bank quickly was not an easy proposition, nor was finding the money to pay a crack legal team to negotiate with our bank.

Be that as it may, this is a perfect real-life event that shows us precisely how we have a choice on the way we handle the problems life throws our way. Of course, the way I handled the problems that day was exactly the opposite of what might have been successful.

I recall specifically coming into work one morning in Winnipeg and proceeding to sit at my desk in my office in the corner of the showroom. This is a place where optimism and enthusiasm must be front and center in retail, as all sales went through this office. Well, I was so convinced bad things and bad luck were coming our way that I took out my notepad and proceeded to write down every bad thing that was going to happen to us during the morning. One by one I added to my list, predicting more misery by the minute. An amazing strategy: let's get to work and get ready to log all the bombs about to drop so I can feel especially sorry for myself and feel even more discouraged. I suppose I wanted written proof to convince myself further that our luck was surely terrible. Two important things resulted from this self-inflicted stupidity of mine that day.

The first was, thank God, I learned that I had done enough work on my attitude for so many years before this trying situation that I recovered my attitude fairly quickly after that terrible day and made the moves necessary to recover and get moving in the right direction.

Second, it reconfirmed my view that if someone who'd been trying and working hard for years on having a positive attitude could sink so low, so fast, as I had, this must happen to pretty much everyone sometime in their lives.

As it is easy to sink so low into discouragement so fast, we must be vigilant to be aware of what is happening inside us so we can do the work of turning our discouragement around. It's crucial we focus all our attention on our plan to recover rather than sitting in a bit of self-pity, as I had done.

THE PAIN STOPS ONE STEP AT A TIME

As I started to compile and read so many notes across so many decades, I came to fully realize that practicing mindfulness and continuing to grow as a human being have really saved me—saved me from a life of family strife, career disappointment, financial struggles, and having a poorer relationship with those I love the most. Practicing also helped me find the love of this or any other life, Diana.

By the time of my university days, I was constantly reading and learning, first from philosophers like Bertrand Russell and then on to more study on human behavior, particularly in sales. Working in a very competitive, brutal retail world, I learned well the daily struggles of all of us at the dealership. It was becoming very clear that we were either really high emotionally or sinking low very quickly. Usually, we would move between the two emotions many times during a single day.

I could feel not only my pain but also the pain of others who were much older and more jaded than I was. I kept thinking to myself that I better figure out a way to deal with this, or how could I possibly stay somewhat positive and survive working and living like this until I was even forty? It never occurred to me what age sixty-six might mean, though I remember as a kid listening to the Beatles' "When I'm Sixty-Four," thinking that it must be about the end. Little did I know then that sixty-six would come, and I'd be writing these notes to you and fortunately feeling more alive than the man in the song.

So early on in my career, I really focused on understanding discouragement and motivation, despite the fact that every sales coach or trainer I heard talked only about motivation. None ever brought up discouragement, the single biggest killer in sales and, really, in life. Just imagine what our children and grandchildren think and feel when they see us in a state of discouragement.

The pressure of dealing with so many obstacles along the road plays heavy on all of us, and we must think for ourselves and look deeply for our answers. Reading and studying Buddhism and the way Buddhists think changed my life in an incredible way. So I wanted to share with you the practical wisdom I learned from Buddhism about how to beat discouragement when it comes knocking. I believe these suggestions can help all of us avoid being discouraged, children. I have used these in training sessions for too many years to count:

- We need to count our blessings each and every day and, in fact, a number of times a day.
- It's much harder to be discouraged when we are feeling gratitude.
- The easiest way most people find to practice gratitude is to acknowledge it as soon as we wake up, just before we go to sleep, and use walking meditation a bit during the day.
- Our morning and evening ritual should take between one and two minutes each, and walking meditation takes no extra time, as we are walking anyway, even if it is from one office to another at work or from one room to the other at home.
- We can choose to look at our social media accounts or practice a few minutes of mindfulness while walking; that's always our choice. These few minutes of counting our blessings each day will change our outlook on life considerably and lower our time spent in discouragement.
- If we are truly committed to staying positive and staying away from being discouraged, it's important to make sure the people we are hanging out with the most are doing a bit of the same. Realizing this is a potentially sensitive subject is obvious, as our loved ones may be part of the group that is very negative. Unfortunately, most of us when we are down and discouraged can't help but share our pain and problems with those around us. Believe me, I do not want any of us walking away from chronically discouraged friends and family, but we often just enable ourselves and them to be negative. When we talk about this in training, many will say to me later that they finally had a talk with some of these

people in their lives and said something like, *Hey, perhaps we have both been a bit too cynical and negative, and this is not helping either of us. Let's try to be more optimistic, and because I am in sales, I have no other choice.* This is an intelligent and fair way to make sure we are spending time with people who are somewhat positive and up-lifting, or at least trying to be.

- Staying away from being discouraged always requires us to say positive things to ourselves each day. We all know the majority of thoughts in our head are of the negative persuasion, and we need to practice mindfulness, let the poor thoughts just drift away from us, and continue to water the positive ones.

The only way to do these practices is one step at a time. Let's simply take the first step on our journey, then the next, and so on. Soon we will be on our way to enjoying each step and each day without feeling very much discouragement at all.

HABITS THAT FEED DISCOURAGEMENT

These are a few bad habits that, over the years, I have learned the hard way contribute to our being discouraged. Please stay away from these at all times:

- Comparing ourselves to others clearly leads us to being more discouraged. Our industry makes us do this virtually every single day of the year.
- Beating ourselves up, which I talk about considerably, assuredly causes us to feel discouraged.
- Let's keep an eye on our expectations and how

long our hopes and dreams take to actualize.
Many of us expect results too quickly and get discouraged far too soon along the road to success.

Many of us also see a significant setback as the start of
being very discouraged. We must look at setbacks as a learning
experience that will help us going forward and not let a few
of them hold us back. Always remember that every successful
person has had more setbacks than you can imagine.

CAREFUL WITH OUR DISCOURAGEMENT

Discouragement to me is best described as being demoralized
by how events and life in general treat us. It leaves us with a
loss of confidence and enthusiasm. Of course, that is the an-
tithesis of the optimistic way we would like to be living.

Often discouragement interchanges with our expectations
that may not be in proper alignment with the reality we are
facing today. I remember so many times as a teenager hoping
and believing on Sundays that things would change for the
better the coming week. History and past behavior gave me no
evidence that things would ever change. However, it was likely
the youthful exuberance of hope that made me believe in an
outcome that was seemingly impossible. Years of tough failures and dashed hopes eventually taught me to stop choosing
a plan that had next to no chance of success and then becoming discouraged when success did not happen.

We also need to be very honest with ourselves. Are we
putting enough well-thought-out plans and commitments in
place to get us to where our expectations are? Many times I
did not have either of the two in place, and yet I was discouraged when things didn't go well. Clearly, my discouragement

was misplaced. Please, children, always be self-aware about the roots of discouragement and the ways we can avoid it.

KNOCKED DOWN AND NEARLY OUT

Being in a state of discouragement is a large barrier in any career situation we face. As a young teenager, I watched my father face numerous career challenges, many of his own making. His response to this adversity was to feel a bit sorry for himself and drink himself half to death during the crisis. Alcoholism certainly played a significant part in his response. Obviously, this behavior only made things worse, and I learned much watching it. However, it took a lot of internal work on myself to not repeat the same mistakes in my life. It is very unfortunate that my father in 1970 did not have the same resources to obtain the help he needed as we do today.

Life often brings us all some compelling crises, and during the Global Financial Crisis of 2008, mine came calling like a lightning bolt. Our company faced the bankruptcy of our main OEM Chrysler Corporation and its finance arm Chrysler Financial, who was holding all our loans. Believe me, in a major crisis, being too focused on discouragement is a pernicious disease. Like most battle-scarred business leaders, I was fortunate to have experienced some of it before. Each of those situations educated me so much, and I am thankful I had the chance to experience them.

This was almost completely out of our control, which made it most difficult to manage and not be discouraged to the point of giving up. This type of crisis was truly a one-of-a-kind situation with Chrysler that was unlikely to happen again within fifty years.

The company was earning approximately $20 million in

2008, but that was not considered when the banks decided to run for the hills. Not one company I had ever owned in my entire career had ever missed a payment to anyone, but that meant flat-out nothing to any of them. To say it simply, no bank would go near us, and for a public company, that was the kiss of death.

Our stock plummeted below one dollar a share. It is very painful and somewhat surreal to actually be able to watch your life's work and financial net worth sink so fast, so deep, so publicly. Reasonable sleep was next to impossible, and hope was in short supply, but my years of training and studying helped me keep going and not give up. So did having a creative-thinking and talented team around me. I have often given thought to the millions of good, hardworking people worldwide who lose their dreams in a comparable situation because they did not have the luck we did.

Not that I needed any more motivation to help solve this crisis, but I was fortunate to have an added incentive, as Diana had just moved to Canada with Lauren and Kaedra a few months earlier. I can't imagine what my emotional state would have been had we indeed been forced into bankruptcy, and I thank God every day that Diana was firmly beside me through these sad and humbling days. It is another perfect example of how important it is to have the right partner in life. Mine certainly arrived at the exact right moment for so many reasons, and if we do the work and put some time into ourselves, we often get the help we need. Please remember, kids, we do often get the help we need when we need it most.

With incredible skill and commitment, the team did a remarkable job of saving us from a near-certain bankruptcy, and without so many of them, we would have failed. The simple truth is that this near-death situation for the company we were dealing with could be overcome only as a team who all kicked discouragement in the butt and kept going. I will be eternally grateful to each of you who helped steer the company through this sad mess of a time; you were the meaning of a brilliant team.

Children, I hope you never have to experience something like this in your life, but whatever you face, always know how important the team around you is, including at home. Please remember it is all the work you have done over numerous earlier years that will help you overcome discouragement in these exact moments.

CONTROL

WHISKY BOTTLES

As a younger man I had somewhat of a controlling personality, which I hated. Regrettably, it took me too long to understand why I was like this. Children, if we do not do a bit of self-study and honest emotional and spiritual work to help ourselves, it is difficult to even understand our behavior, let alone improve it. When I started to do the important work to understand my behaviors, it became very clear the past was still haunting me.

Of course, being controlling was natural for me because as a twelve-year-old all I ever witnessed was bombs dropping around our family pretty much every other day. In fact, that started well before I was twelve and lasted until I moved out of the house at eighteen, at which point I realized it was not normal. I simply knew that if I was not trying to control some of the chaos, it was not going away by itself. Not that it worked.

Each Monday, I suspect that all five of us were hoping for a more sober week. I saw the futility of my mother trying to control my father's drinking by controlling his liquor supply. Even as a kid I realized how silly it was for Mom to go around every nook and cranny in the house, including vents, to find and throw out all his booze.

This happened countless times, and all my young, logical mind would tell me was "There goes another fifty dollars we don't have." At the time I kept thinking, *Why were we wasting money throwing alcohol away when we were always close to being broke and surely Dad would just buy it again the same day he found it thrown out?* Dad would come home from work half in the bag, look for his whisky bottles, then scream and yell for fifteen minutes. All the family got out of this was a lot of commotion and anger before he would drive over to the liquor store and buy it again, and as a bonus, we were short fifty dollars or however much Mom tossed out that day.

On the subject of whisky bottles, I remember well one day Mom sending me over to the liquor store to buy her a bottle of her favorite. The trouble was I was only seventeen, and the store clerk asked me for ID, and of course I did not have any. I proceeded home without her whisky only to be given a lesson on why I could not talk the "stupid" clerk into selling it to me. My mother always had a tremendous amount of spunk, so she asked me to drive her back to the store to get the whisky, as she was in no condition to drive. When we arrived at the liquor store, she demanded I go in with her while she told the same clerk she was an idiot to not let her son buy it. Pretty funny, maybe a bit sad too.

Children, you are all very self-aware and intelligent, so please form your own thoughts on what anyone could learn from growing up amid the havoc of whisky bottles.

WHAT LIES BEYOND OUR CONTROL

Please remember that when we are edging toward a more controlling manner of living, this usually ends up in a poor situation for us and the things or people we are trying to control.

Attempting to control too many things around us that are out of our control can waste a lot of energy and time, as well as damage relationships and ourselves.

How many years did I spend thinking I could fix or control people and things outside of my control? Once I started to understand the reasons for my controlling behavior and how it began in childhood, it was easier to start shifting away from it. When we grow up in a family that is totally dysfunctional, unpredictable, and out of control, most of us will learn to take care of ourselves by taking back a bit of control. Unfortunately, it took me years to connect the dots here, but when I did, letting go of things I shouldn't try to control (and couldn't even if I tried) was much easier.

Once I came to understand I did not need to try to control everything, I found it much easier to happily accept my partner's way of doing things. This has also made me so much happier and, with that, given me a more amicable life. Highly recommend you try it.

EMINENT STOIC PHILOSOPHERS WRITING ON CONTROL

Epictetus surely said it much better than most could when he said, "Freedom is the only worthy goal in life. It is won by disregarding things that lie beyond our control."

At the time he was considered the most powerful man on earth, Marcus Aurelius said, "You have power over your own mind, not outside events. Realize this, and you will find strength."

COMPETITION

REFLECTIONS ON COMPETING IN FAMILY AND BUSINESS

As I was about halfway through these notes to you, children, I noticed a theme that popped up a few too many times was how competition and jealousy really destroyed my family's happy times together. I wrote about some of this in the opening chapter, when reviewing my early years, but I will explore my reflections on competition more here.

Because both my parents had so little and had come from such difficult backgrounds, they believed hard competition between kids would push us to success in this world. There is no doubt in my mind they meant well. However, the result of this approach was devastating for us five kids as teenagers and later on in life. This amount of competition made it next to impossible to have healthy relationships among the five of us.

How much resentment is needed before people can see the light? How much depression and how many suicide attempts does it take to realize this competitive approach is not the way to go? What happens to the family dynamics when those who were first in the pecking order are now in third or fourth? Things change, situations change, we grow up at different times, our luck changes. I do not blame my parents or any of the five of us for the resulting pain this competition caused; I just know it is not the way forward for any of us.

Having said that, competition in the real world is real, and we have to learn how to deal with it. I just do not think it belongs in any family. Thinking through this issue of competition and jealousy had me write some notes on it; hopefully, they resonate in some small way.

Whether we choose to like it or believe it, it is my experience that competition is often what drives people to work exceedingly hard to reach their goals. Almost every executive I've ever met in my career who has been extremely successful is also extremely competitive. Any athletes I have met who have also reached the top of their sport are also highly competitive. We may not like a world where competition drives so much of our behavior and actions, but it's clear to me this is simply the truth, and a hard truth at that.

Unfortunately, if you're not somewhat driven by competition, regardless of what arena you are competing in, you will likely fall by the wayside pretty quickly. Of course, there are a small number of occupations that would not require one to be so competitive, but they are in the minority. Competition and comparing myself to others fueled me as well; however, there is a limit to how much it fuels you and how much you become consumed by it.

As someone who was raised by parents to be really competitive and a person who has spent much of my life in an extremely competitive business, where we are ranked in order of our successes every single day, I can unequivocally tell you if not personally managed, too much competition in our life situation will make us miserable. And at some point, that misery will be debilitating to us and contagious to those we love who are watching us live like that.

It is also much easier to preach about not being so competitive when you have already risen near the top of whatever field you are working in. For instance, it is easy for me today to say that competition no longer motivates me in the least. However, that is somewhat disingenuous, considering I spent years building my life and company, and without the drive, inspiration, and the competitive fuel, success would not have come my way. Children, it is imperative that you are driven to succeed if you hope to reach the really high goals you have set for yourself. If your goals are to be somewhat successful, then obviously your drive and competitive nature can be somewhat less. And that is also a wonderful way to live; just make the decision on whatever's best for you.

For my business today, we simply need to have all our senior executives across the country really driven, like I was years ago, to have success. I have the luxury of not living in that world as much in the day to day, but the team does not. The team needs not only initial effort but also second and third rounds of effort, while we hope our competitors will not push quite as hard through the roadblocks and obstacles along the way.

We must do whatever it takes to stay ahead of our competition with hard, smart work and diligent study on new processes and technologies coming at rapid speed. Complacency will kill us very fast. Without being extremely competitive, it does not matter whether it was my time or the younger team's time today, we will not win in the marketplace.

The best lesson I can teach you if you are living and working in this competitive world is to do the best you can at work each day and let it go when you are at home. That is all we should expect of ourselves. Family is so important, and we need time to be with them. This is advice I did not follow enough at a younger age.

Also, I think it's important to note that we pay all our senior people in the company on performance against the market they're competing in. Some could say it is unfair that we set our targets and goals to be in the top 5 or 10 percent of each market we are in. Thus, even our compensation packages are based on competition. Try running a public company in a retail industry when the board and the financial markets rate you on each statistic each quarter against your competitors. I have never heard a board member echo anything along the lines of, *Let's not go too hard on our competitors because we are nice people.* While discussing the topic of competition, I cannot say this strongly enough: I do not believe competition should ever include our siblings; we should always wish and hope the best for them.

This is the sad reality of living and working in retail and was the biggest motivator for me to improve my self-awareness and perception of how I look at things. Without the hard work I talk about in my notes to you, kids, it is next to impossible to survive intact or have a kind, loving, happy, and prosperous life.

HOW DESPERATION AND BUDDHISM HELPED ME IN A COMPETITIVE BUSINESS

I do not know what other leaders in the industry have done to survive and even thrive in the competitive world of automotive dealerships or other businesses they are in. My approach, which might be considered a little different, resulted from a combination of two areas of desperation:

- I was desperate to not be in the financial situation my parents always found themselves in and the dignity they lost dealing with this.
- Years later when I found financial success and freedom, I was desperate to find out why my happiness did not necessarily follow it.

Looking back over so many years, it is clear to me now that I had to do the mental and emotional work early on to improve the skills and drive that I needed in order to win at auto retail. Later on, in order to find happiness to go with it, I had to do even more work and study, which often took the form of Buddhist thought and action. I'd tried other ways to improve myself, but none of these ever stuck for me, as most of the other reading I had done or courses I had taken seemed to work for only a few days or weeks. Whether it was trying to be happier, trying to be more patient, trying to be less angry, trying to be less edgy, trying to drink less, or trying for anything else most humans want, I simply could not make the changes I needed to make stick before I started reading and studying the Buddhist way.

One of the primary issues we have focused on as a company from day one is training—training on selling and training on keeping a good and aware mindset.

Starting in my late teens, I worked on the mental and emotional part of the game of selling. Sales trainers' slogans and canned pitches came and went for me, but real study and training works in the long term. Much of this earlier mental and emotional work is still effective today, even though the business today is completely different compared to when I started out.

Before COVID-19 devastated so many in this world, I did much of the training myself and in person. One of my favorite jobs is meeting with our teams across the country. Most people are kind, courteous, and want what's best for everyone at their company, including themselves, which is why they are usually highly receptive to learning new ways of keeping a positive and healthy mindset so that real happiness can follow their successes.

In this brutally competitive business, we try to teach our teams and ourselves that happiness comes from being the best

we can be in our career and our family life. A core belief we
emphasize in our training is that all you can do is your honest
best at home and at work and then let it go. Even though we
live and work in competitive environments, we are not trying
to be better than anyone else; we just try to be better than our
old selves. I have learned so much from so many on our team,
and we all believe we attain better results this way, including a
more pleasurable journey along the way.

The approach I use is somewhat unique in that it combines
a Buddhist-type mindset with the reality of working and living
in a North American form of extremely cutthroat capitalism.
Even so, our successful team results tell me this approach can
help anyone who puts a bit of effort into doing their absolute
best and then letting it go when it's time to let it go.

A VISION FOR OUR FAMILY GOING FORWARD

Sometimes I envision how I would like to change some of the
harmful aspects of the family legacy I saw as a child for our
family now and going forward. As well as stopping alcoholism,
I pray we all see these things as important values we need to
try to uphold:

- We want to be humble, community-minded people who care about and support the communities
  we live and work in.
- We want to treat everyone with respect and
  kindness.
- We want to celebrate our family members' successes and support each other through challenging times.
- We want excessive competition between family
  members to end with this generation.

We will never be perfect, but let's always try to be moving in the most positive direction, keeping these values in mind. This is very important to Diana and me.

DIANA'S WISDOM

PLEASE, GO AHEAD

I have learned innumerable life lessons from Diana. She grew up in a complex family situation. When her parents divorced, she put herself through university, where she had outstanding grades while working two jobs. While also being a mother of two young girls, she unfortunately battled cancer at thirty-six years old. Despite these challenges, she has always remained upbeat and positive with everyone around her.

Patrick and Diana in San Diego, 2021.

She does two things when in a conversation so often that have impacted me in a meaningful way and really forced me to learn how to be a bit quieter and say thank you more often.

After Diana and the girls moved to Edmonton in 2009, assuming I was home, we would always gather for dinner as soon as Lauren returned from swimming each night at about seven. When any of the three of us would be about to speak at the same time as Diana, she would perpetually say to us, "Please, go ahead."

Unfortunately, it took me almost a year to catch on to this, as our family did not grow up this way, but it made me more aware of how polite and respectful it was to the girls and me. It also made me understand how the kids really felt listened to. It's sure funny today when I hear both of them say it so often now, just like their mom. Since then, I've even added the value of saying "Please, go ahead" to our sales training.

The second expression Diana always used was "Thank you," and that is a powerful message. It seems pretty basic, but we often do not say it enough. I added saying "Thank you" to my sales training notes as well, and most people say that's a good reminder in our meetings. In our lives, if you often let the other person speak first and say thank you a bit more, people will feel respected and in turn respect you so much more.

SETTING THE MOOD

A number of years ago Diana found a pillow for the family room in our Vancouver condo that says "Today is a great day." This twenty-five-dollar pillow tries to set the mood in our house each day. Find your own mood-setter, children.

CRAVING

"Buddhism maintains that the common reaction of the human mind to pleasure and to achievement is not satisfaction; it's craving for more. Hence, no matter what we achieve, it only increases our craving, not our satisfaction."

Yuval Noah Harari

"There is no end to craving. Hence contentment alone is the best way to happiness. Therefore, acquire contentment."

Swami Sivananda

THE HUNGRY GHOST

Kids, I believe it's perfectly fine and normal for us to want to achieve more. We just need to know that endless craving never benefits us. I wish I could tell you how many times craving what other folks had played with my emotions and certainly not in a good way.

It is still vivid to me when as a thirteen-year-old kid I would visit friends at their houses, and it was easy to figure out things were just a tad nicer over there. Their houses looked like mini mansions compared to ours, and at face value, things appeared to me so much more normal than our place. Craving often hit me hard as a young teenager, and jealousy would spring into action. Many years later I would realize what you see from a distance is not necessarily the way things actually are and that these families were not so perfect after all.

When I was a young man of twenty-five, another form of craving came my way as I was trying to start and operate a first-generation business with no availability of any surplus cash for the rainy days ahead. It ate me alive to watch our wealthy competitors having a much easier time riding out a difficult financial period because the banks always cull their loan portfolios of any businesses with no outside assets first. Unfortunately, in 1981 and 1982 we had no other assets. It may be true that craving to be as fortunate as they were was quite normal; however, it never helped me solve the issues we were dealing with.

After spending too much time over the next fifteen years or so still craving what other people had, it took my beginning to study Buddhism to eliminate most of these cravings.

From my readings I learned that an interesting and easy way to contemplate craving in ourselves was to look at the Buddhist concept of a realm of existence called the hungry ghost. These ghosts who love to eat are depicted as having extra-large stomachs and extra-small, constricted throats. Essentially, this is a life sentence of insatiable and unsatisfied craving for the hungry ghost.

We must contain our cravings, or we as well are sentenced to a rather unsatisfying and unfulfilling life. The hungry ghosts in us are continuously fed by advertisements, fed by TV and movies we watch, fed by what our friends and family seem to have, fed by work colleagues we see in better positions than us, fed by what we perceive our neighbors have, and on and on we go. Everywhere we look we see false and misleading remedies for our emotional pain and cravings. Living will teach us the only cure for the hungry ghosts resides inside ourselves.

I spent far too many years of my life craving things other people had or appeared to have, and this was most destructive to me and those closest to me. Thinking that when we get this, obtain that, and so on, we will then be happy is simply a delusion. I realize most of us do not want to admit craving what others have, but, kids, I tell you from a feeling of embarrassment how much I once did in the hopes it will help you to not do it. I sincerely hope these notes can help you eliminate most of the cravings in your life sooner than I did.

UNHAPPINESS GUARANTEED

I believe craving things we do not have or think we do not have is the number-one reason for unhappiness in the world. This has probably been the case for hundreds of years and through virtually all cultures. This yearning or craving is actually only a feeling, albeit a scary and miserable feeling. Craving what we do not have makes us feel we have too many unmet needs and longings, and, until we get them, happiness and peace will be elusive for us.

Unfortunately, the outside world is very unlikely to fill this craving in us, as whenever we receive what we've been wanting, we inevitably want something else. How many times have each of us finally got the girl we wanted, the promotion we wanted, the house we wanted, the cool friends we wanted, the financial security we wanted, only to want something more in a few months?

Obviously, it is perfectly normal to strive for a better life, and we should work hard to achieve these things, but at the end of the day, we must learn to be satisfied with what we have.

Sometimes not getting what we want is a bonus for us. Believe me, kids, craving is the ultimate treadmill of delusion.

A SIMPLE FACT

A most important fact to remember about craving: It's not usually the object or person we crave that is the problem. It's the craving itself that makes us suffer so much.

In most cases if we start thinking deeply about our craving for more possessions, we will discover we already have enough to make us truly happy. Most often, today, right now, at this moment, we already have enough.

Epictetus said so many years centuries ago something that still stands true today and will stand true when all our grandchildren are senior citizens: "If a little is not enough for you, then nothing is."

Plenty to reflect on here, children.

CHANGE

"He not busy being born is busy dying."

Bob Dylan

GETTING BUSY BEING BORN

That powerful line in a song has rung through my head for forty-plus years. You have to think about it very carefully and let it sink in.

Remember, no one's life gets better by chance; it gets better by making small changes and sticking to the changes. These choices and changes make us who we are. We need not stress if the results are not perfect, as nothing ever is. As we all get older, we often want the same kind of happiness and excitement we experienced at a younger age. To achieve this, we really need to keep improving and making small positive changes throughout our entire lives.

Here are some simple examples that have helped me and may help you get busy being born instead of busy dying:

- Continually learning to be a better listener
- Learning to find more empathy for others

- Learning to stop feeling as bitter about a few things
- Learning to find a little more discipline in life
- Learning to count blessings a little more often
- Continually learning to be happier because of the above

THE "FIVE TO TWENTY YEARS FROM NOW" EXERCISE

In the late summer of 1993, we were living in Winnipeg, and I was feeling angry, very beat up, lacking in confidence, in a poor place financially, somewhat depressed, and everything that went with that. Sorry again to Susan and the kids for how you all were affected by my negative mindset then. We had moved there eighteen months earlier, and things were not at all going as planned.

On advice I read or heard somewhere, I spontaneously decided to lock myself in a room for forty minutes with the lights out to make the room as dark as possible. I closed my eyes, pictured all the things that I didn't love in my life, and tried to imagine a scene in life five years from then, assuming I did nothing to change or fix the situation. I thought about how it would affect the kids, our marriage, my pride, and many other things. I put myself firmly in that situation, became part of that scene, and deeply felt how I would experience the same problems and pain. Then I felt deeply about what ten years would look like, then twenty if I did nothing to change the situation. Ouch, that process hurt more than I could ever have expected.

When I seriously felt this pain, I let it sink in for a few minutes more before I emotionally woke up and brought myself back to the present time. This was truly a life-changing moment for me because I stopped feeling sorry for myself, started making some changes and executing some well-thought-out plans, and shortly after had a very fortunate break come our way. Soon we were off to Edmonton to start a new life with new opportunities for us all. I'm not sure the big break I received would have happened if I had not done the exercise and committed to changing my attitude significantly.

About five years later I did the same exercise again when I was struggling emotionally. Once again it woke me up and helped me make the changes necessary to have the life that I dreamed of having rather than the inevitably miserable life I would have if I stayed stuck where I was.

I can't say for sure how this exercise would impact you, but doing this has shaken me to the core. I believe this exercise can be applied to any aspect of our lives that we know isn't healthy for us and have ignored for too long.

Perhaps use drinking as an example. If you drink a bottle and a half of wine each day at thirty-five, sit in darkness and silence and ponder what drinking that much wine every day for another five, ten, or twenty years would do to you. We know the truth is we would be serious alcoholics with many financial, emotional, and health issues, along with marriage and family issues. Perhaps we would be known as the drunk grandpa or grandma by our grandchildren.

Try the same with anger over five, ten, twenty years; try it with being dissatisfied with your job; try it with being in an awful relationship; try it with being in a terrible financial situation that likely will be much more difficult to remedy at sixty. Please consider trying this approach with anything you might want to improve on. Doing this exercise, we discover that the present moment is truly wonderful as we realize we still have time to change our future and appreciate the miracle that we can begin improving our lives right now.

FORGET YOUR PERFECT OFFERING

I think it is crucial to understand that any time we are attempting to change our lives for the better, looking for perfection can be our enemy. I believe we want to always be moving forward in the proper direction, knowing it's OK if we fall back some days. We simply let it go and get back to our positive thoughts and actions. An example of this could be controlling our jealousy. If this was on our mind most days, and we are improving to the point of it occurring only once a week, let's not beat the heck out of ourselves for a momentary slippage.

> Ring the bells that still can ring
> Forget your perfect offering
> There is a crack, a crack in everything
> That's how the light gets in

I think Leonard Cohen is correct in this celestial song when he infers that none of us or any situation in life is perfect, only that we should "ring the bells that still can ring" or take some accountability for our actions to improve things. The problem is if we look for perfection, we will end up disappointed and perhaps give up on trying to make the necessary changes. My life experiences working with people teaches me that looking for perfection in anything is a near-certain recipe for failing to improve what we are working on as we become very discouraged. Better to "forget your perfect offering" and instead remember the light that the cracks let in.

GRANDCHILDREN AND IMPERMANENCE

Many of us can benefit from looking at change and impermanence from a different view. For instance, while we tend to view impermanence with suspicion and fear, a perfect example of impermanence being a benefit rather than a stressful thing is to consider our own children or grandchildren. While of course we love them so much as a two-, four-, or six-year-old child, without life constantly changing, we would miss out on so, so much. We could miss watching Evie, Mack, Emily, and Miles grow up to be beautiful and thoughtful teenagers and adults as well as parents themselves.

From left to right: Miles, Emily, Mack, and Evie, 2022.

Children, if we accept the fact that change is inevitable and everything in life is impermanent, we will appreciate what we have in the moment while looking forward to a wonderful future.

THE SACRED BONUS

If change is so easy, why is it so hard for most of us to do what we need to do to make life changes? I have pondered this question for years upon years, wondering what the heck is holding me back. Many times in my career I have watched excellent people who could not or would not attempt to make a few small changes that would materially change their life for the better.

These are a few of the reasons that seemed to come up an awful lot in our conversations:

- We are comfortable with what is familiar even if it is not working for us in many ways.
- We feel the need for instant gratification, as most of us want to see things change immediately. This is simply not true with making changes in ourselves. I believe the only way to successfully change ourselves is one step and one day at a time.
- Sometimes we overthink our goals. Let's set our goals and spend more time actually working toward them. Obviously, after a long-enough time with no results, it is prudent to rethink our approach.
- Pride often gets in our way as we think we do not need to change, and it's the world around us that needs to change. I have been fortunate enough to fail on many things along the way, so I've learned to not let pride interfere with the changes I need to make now. Too often I let pride stop me from making serious changes because making them would force me to admit I was on the wrong side of significant issues.

- Another major roadblock in trying to make lasting change is we often simply give up too soon along the way. Our old self will often fight back against change, becoming a discouraging voice in our head. This has happened to me far too many times. If we are committed, we will succeed in whatever we set out to accomplish. Please do not give up too quickly, as anything worth having takes time.

These are some of the reasons that change is difficult for all of us. When we are starting to make a few small changes, let's remember to have a little fun and enjoy the journey; otherwise it's a bit painful to be waiting around hoping change will happen quickly. Some can happen immediately, but many take much practice and diligence to reach fruition. Let's remember change may seem difficult at first, but anything worthwhile is a bit difficult to achieve. I can't say resolutely enough that learning and improving ourselves and our loved ones' lives is a lifelong journey, so let's try to enjoy the ride.

If we continue to stay positive, have belief that God is on our side, and stay committed, our lives will change for the better. And what a beautiful sacred bonus that your children and grandchildren will learn this life lesson from you.

LEADERS CHANGE OR FADE AWAY

Inflexible leaders who are not willing to learn and embrace new concepts do not possess opinions as strong as they think. Perhaps their opinions actually possess them and hold them back.

Leaders that are not open to change inevitably get left behind, often led by their own tunnel vision. Often, they cannot see the obvious trends, which competitors open to positive change see, and thus get overtaken in their markets. Believe me, what worked in our business five years ago may not be very useful today, including our management style.

George Bernard Shaw said, "Progress is impossible without change, and those who cannot change their minds cannot change anything."

Children, please think carefully about this as you progress through your careers.

SAW MYSELF ON TV

Recently we were watching a TV series where the lead character's role really touched me because he was someone with immense talent, intelligence, and a good work ethic. Unfortunately, alcohol trouble was always brewing close by. It made me think of many days gone by when I used to watch someone in a movie and recognize myself in the role of the drunk person or the angry person. Always think that it's a good opportunity for self-reflection when I can see on the screen how being drunk or angry hurts my loved ones as well as me. After a number of years, I had seen enough of me in the shows or movies to catapult change.

When we are dealing with any very negative issue and then see it play out on a TV series and pretend it's us doing the same thing, it forces us to at least contemplate some change.

On the other hand, let's take ourselves when we are happy, content, and enjoying life. Let's watch a show where the main character is playing that role and we think we would sure like to have that life. Well, perhaps we can have that life right here, right now, with a bit of work and a new viewpoint. Watching a thought-provoking series can really help us adjust our view.

I have often suggested to people I was coaching to try to

use this way of seeing our behavior on a big screen with someone else doing what we are doing. It's often very effective.

REFLECTIONS ON CHANGE

Barack Obama said, "Change will not come if we wait for some other person, or if we wait for some other time. We are the ones we've been waiting for. We are the change we seek."

Andy Warhol said, "They always say time changes things, but you actually have to change them yourself."

Napoleon Hill said, "Don't wait. The time will never be just right."

Erica Jong said, "I have accepted fear as part of life—specifically the fear of change . . . I have gone ahead despite the pounding in the heart that says: turn back."

Taylor Swift said, "This is a new year. A new beginning. And things will change."

Charles Darwin said, "It is not the strongest species that survives, nor the most intelligent, but the one most responsive to change."

Helen Keller said, "Life is either a daring adventure or nothing. To keep our faces toward change and behave like free spirits in the presence of fate is strength undefeatable."

Rumi said, "Yesterday I was clever, so I wanted to change the world. Today I am wise, so I am changing myself."

Lao Tzu might have said it best when he said, "If you do not change direction, you might end up where you are heading."

Children, I gathered these quotes for us because they reflect much of what I believe about change. Please consider the wise words above.

CHARTING THE COURSE OF CHANGE

"Would you tell me, please, which way I ought
to go from here?"

"That depends a good deal on where you
want to get to," said the Cat.

"I don't much care where—" said Alice.

"Then it doesn't matter which way you go,"
said the Cat.

"—so long as I get *somewhere*," Alice added
as an explanation.

"Oh, you're sure to do that," said the Cat,
"if you only walk long enough."

When contemplating even making some small changes in our lives, we really need to have a pretty good idea of where we want to be. It is difficult to have enough motivation to make changes when we know where we want to go, let alone if we are not sure. As the cat inferred, how can we pick a road to somewhere when we don't know where we are going?

To make lasting change, we have to have some idea where we are going. We also can never be one hundred percent certain, but we must have some vision. George Harrison wrote a song with the Alice in Wonderland theme, singing, "If you don't know where you're going, any road will take you there."

I can tell you with a tinge of regret that anytime in my life when I did not have some idea of where I was going, it generally led me to negative emotions like jealousy, anger, or regret.

Time has also taught me we can't change the course of our lives if we don't first change our minds.

"LATER ON WON'T WORK NO MORE"

It was usually easy for me to see what changes needed to occur and understand why I needed to make those changes. Getting the motivation, discipline, and consistency to make those changes was always more difficult.

Over the years I've thought of what ultimately pushed me to make hard changes, and I've come to realize that often certain songs would continue to play in my head, and listening to them repeatedly would be the catalyst to drive me to move forward with some of these necessary significant changes.

It was the late summer of 2006, we had just gone public, and I was riding high from the success of the IPO, but I could already sense dark clouds on the horizon with a number of manufacturers. Stress and pressure were part of the game, and many people in our industry were watching us, with most of them hoping we would fail.

Alcohol seemed like a good way to cut the edge a bit, and living on my own did not help either. Tom Petty's *Highway Companion* was released, and I was sure looking forward to listening to it. After hearing the song "Square One" a few times blasting in my family room, the line, "Later on won't work no more" stopped me in my tracks. I knew big changes in me were necessary to survive and prosper in this new world of running a public company, fighting with my brother on a regular basis, and now being alone after so many years of marriage. Making changes later on simply was not good enough.

Recently divorced and running a new high-profile company was plenty enough to worry about when anxiety already ran through my veins. While running a private company with way less scrutiny, I learned how to fake my way through a lot of situations, and if I was feeling off my game, I could change schedules easier, etc.

This new reality was just enough to keep me half-sober

and sober of mind. However, adding in massive family fights with my twin brother and later my three sisters was more than enough to kill the nice plan of staying half-sober of both mind and body. All I really wanted was to have a deep and kind relationship with my kids, be halfway content, have some peace in my life, run a good business, and not need alcohol to try to sleep at night. Unfortunately, the toxic family situation made those plans impossible, or so I believed.

Within a year, pressure was mounting everywhere at Auto Canada, as the auto manufacturers and competitive dealers were doing everything they could to not accept us as buyers of their stores, and investors were frustrated. I don't think all the resilience I learned growing up would have been enough to get me through this period of monumental business problems on top of weekly family hassles about that business. Fortunately, that is when I made the decision to stop drinking completely before I totally fell apart.

I thank God I received the strength to get myself together in time to avoid a potential collapse on many fronts. Just as importantly, I intensified my daily Buddhist studying and working on my inner sense to find some peace and happiness.

"Later on won't work no more" helped me see the change that needed to happen now. Not later. We all need some inspiration to change the course of our lives a bit or a lot. Thanks, Tom, for helping me find mine.

OPTIMISM VS. PESSIMISM

SAND AND STONE

I can't remember where I found this quote, but it was in some older notes and still resonates today:

"Write in sand the bad things that have happened to you.

Carve in stone the good things that have happened to you."

For too many years I would carve in stone the bad things happening to me and write in sand the good things happening. Surely a foolish way to think and live. I am so fortunate that I was able to adjust my thinking and change course. Children, let's please think about this as we ask ourselves truthfully what we practice here.

THE SCIENCE BEHIND OPTIMISM

Children, I can tell you as I moved through the difficult task of starting a business with very few financial resources, I often let myself drift into being a little too pessimistic and feeling sorry for myself. Please understand, never once did this help solve any of the obstacles and problems I faced on this journey. It was only when I said, "Enough is enough with the negative feeling-sorry-for-myself talks," that I made significant progress and started to experience more success in the industry.

Having experienced the power of optimism firsthand, as a young manager and leader, I often would try to train our teams on being more optimistic than pessimistic. However, the results were good, but not exceptional and certainly did not have the lasting effect I wanted on most of the people. This all changed about twenty-five years ago when I fully realized the scientific positive effect this had on people who lived the majority of their lives in an optimistic manner. I spent time in these meetings putting real-life, measurable differences up on a large board. We discussed the truth that optimists truly have a better life than pessimists. For instance, pessimists are eight times more likely to be depressed over life circumstances that are difficult and unfortunate.

Here's the simple way I explained it: Harvard Health Publishing states optimists do better in almost every health area, including a lower rate of death from disease and surgery, less chance of a heart attack, better blood pressure, a longer life, a much better chance of overcoming depression, and experiencing less stress. If we want to do much better in every phase of our lives, we simply must follow the evidence.

Once I started explaining all this in meetings, there was an instant change in how the teams looked at this for their lives. When faced with the undeniable facts about how we view this world as an optimist vs. a pessimist, almost everyone would make a serious commitment to trying harder to be more optimistic. Not a perfect optimist, just more of an optimist. Being a beautiful example for their children often made a big difference in their desire to improve, as so many of us grew up with pessimistic parents whose lives had beaten them down through war, depression, scarce resources, and many other factors.

Children, please accept the convincing scientific evidence here. This optimistic view is simply one of the few absolute no-brainers we will see in our lifetimes. Much of what I write about in this book is somewhat hard work, but being more optimistic is not only easy, it's fun.

TIPS ON OPTIMISM

Here are some tips about being more optimistic that I have shared in hundreds of meetings:

- Optimism feels good. Quite simply, it makes life feel more pleasurable and the future more promising, no matter what comes our way. Even Albert Einstein said, "I'd rather be an optimist and a fool than a pessimist and right."
- Optimism can be relearned. How many of us were not optimistic as three-year-olds?
- Self-defeating thoughts make us more pessimistic.
- It is always easier to stay optimistic when things are going well. Let's try to keep it up when we are going through a rocky path.
- Talking positively to ourselves will gradually become a dominant habit that leads to optimism.
- It takes a bit of time and practice to become more optimistic; keep at it.
- Keep in mind the life-changing effect our positivity can have on our children and grandchildren.

- Remember, we all slip back into being negative sometimes, and that is normal; just take a few breaths and get back on the optimism train.
- Let's just work every day to be on the positive side of the ledger.

JEALOUSY AND ENVY

THE SEVEN "GREAT" THINGS
JEALOUSY AND ENVY DID FOR ME:

- Jealousy and envy bred serious suspicion in me.
- Jealousy and envy hurt my relationships.
- Jealousy and envy made me miserable.
- Jealousy and envy lowered my self-esteem.
- Jealousy and envy often made me controlling.
- Jealousy and envy caused me even more anxiety.
- Jealousy and envy added to my temper.

Children and grandchildren, please take heed of what these two highly negative emotions did for your father (or grandfather). Please work hard to make sure it does not happen as much to you. Nothing good ever comes from these two intruders of the heart and soul.

SHOPKEEPERS' TALE

About forty years ago, I read a tale about two shopkeepers, which hit me hard and made me contemplate why I was thinking and indeed feeling like I was. Perhaps it will have a similar effect on you. It went something like this:

Two shopkeepers were bitter rivals, and their stores were right across the street from each other. Each shopkeeper would spend considerable time watching customers come and go from the other's shop; if one sold something, they would flaunt it to their rival. The competition and jealousy between them were inconceivable.

One late night an angel appeared to one of the shopkeepers in a dream and said, "I will give you anything you ask, but whatever you receive, your competitor will receive twice as much. You can be very, very rich, but he will be twice as wealthy as you. You can wish for a long and healthy life, but his will be longer and healthier. Whatever it is you want, I shall grant it to you." The shopkeeper frowned and thought about it for a minute before saying, "Here is my request. Please strike me blind in one eye." This story has stuck with me for over forty years.

With the amount of jealousy that flowed through me for years, it's amazing I did not have myself blinded in one eye. When meeting someone from a wealthy background, I would often feel they were so much luckier than I was, and I could truly feel the envy in my soul. What a terrible way to live and act, and years later all I can acknowledge is how truly lucky I have been compared to almost anyone on earth. Of course, I am not proud of my former jealousy, but I tell you this humbling fact about myself to hopefully help you keep your jealousy in check along your journey.

WHEN JEALOUSY CREEPS IN

Jealousy is a complicated and paralyzing emotion that tends to haunt many of us in this world. Clearly, this bothered me for years, but as much as I wanted to be first so badly, I never rooted against the other person as long as they were in second place. When I started working in a highly competitive environment at seventeen, it was much the same. I always wanted my competitors at the dealership to make as much as possible, as long as it was less than me.

Jealousy really came knocking on my door as we got into our first business, and it hit me surprisingly hard. My consistent teenage thinking that the rich really had a life advantage over the rest of us was proving to be very on point. When the economy started reeling from blow-by-blow interest-rate increases in 1981, things went from a hopeful future with the move from Edmonton to London, to the possible loss of our only business and everything I had. This would mean starting over and working for someone else again, and that was not something I could stomach.

Just as interest rates reached 22 percent and massive unemployment was everywhere, the bank came banging on our door in December demanding a loan payout. Trouble was definitely here. Thank God we had Chrysler's support, or we would not have made it to the other side.

During this time, it felt impossible not to be jealous of the long-term-wealthy family-dealer competitors who did not mind quietly rubbing it in our faces that the banks were going to foreclose on people like us, not them. There was nothing more that I wanted to do than to kick their pompous asses. We were doing that in sales but not in financial stability, as they could continue to fund losses, while we simply had no money or assets to give the banks as collateral. I've come to believe that in certain situations jealousy is a bit unavoidable.

Even today, with all the work spent trying and mostly succeeding in eliminating jealousy from my life, it still creeps back in from time to time in some form. There are still times when we are trying to purchase a business that's extremely expensive and the other company that's bidding on it just needs to have their multibillionaire family wire them the funds from overseas to outbid us that a tinge of jealousy creeps in for a few minutes.

As it pops into my thoughts, I simply say something like *Hello jealousy, not today, thanks.* I also quickly remind myself to be thankful that we can even look at the business in the first place when there are thousands of good people with top-end drive and inspiration who can't afford to buy a company 1 percent the size because of their family situation. Sometimes we all need to get a grip on how good our own reality actually is.

As I started studying Buddhism again when I was around forty-five years old, Thich Nhat Hanh's teachings guided me to understand how devastating the emotion jealousy actually is. He helped me understand that craving what other people have is life's easiest journey straight to unhappiness. I learned to not give my jealousy the attention it so dearly craves in my thoughts, and to learn to care for my jealousy in a kind manner.

So many people say greed runs the world, and in many sad ways, it does. However, Warren Buffet says, "It is not greed that drives the world, but envy." It is also my belief that even the wealthiest business leaders are often more preoccupied with jealousy and envy than their own situation.

FOCUS

WIN THE SHIFT

When I was given my first sales manager's job, I had a strict routine to get our team motivated and ready to go to war before each shift. "War" to our team meant outselling the other three sales teams, each and every day. We would hold a thirty-minute sales meeting that was like preparing a team to go to battle for our eight-plus-hour shift. Going through my notes while assembling this book, I found a typical page of notes I used in a meeting from way back in 1985. In some ways this was similar to the meetings I would do today.

Inevitably, one of the things I would say is *I know we all have a lot of things in life to deal with, but we are here for eight or nine hours today, and we really ought to try and sell some cars and make some money while we are here as we are going to be here anyway.*

This was an important theme for staying focused and being successful, as we were going to be at the dealership anyway. One could always make the argument that I would rather be at the beach or ball game, but we did not have that choice to make. Our choice to make was simple: Either focus on working hard and smart for the next eight hours, make some sales, make some money, and go home happy. Or put a half-assed effort into our eight hours, take a bunch of shortcuts, and hope it turns out OK. This would most likely turn out to be a shift with little success, and we would go home disappointed.

Most of the team would fully comprehend that and understand that we would have a better time at home that night if we had a fruitful day at work. The choice wasn't whether we were going to be here. We had to be at work, so the choice was *Are we going to put in an all-out effort and focus on winning the shift or put in a half effort and lose the shift?*

Our mission was to be on our A game all day with every customer we met and win the sales derby. The fact was and still is if we win twenty of our twenty-two shifts for the month, we will win the month. If we win eleven of twelve months, we win the year. Breaking it down shift by shift is a simple but highly effective way to win the sales game each day, each week, each month, and each year. To this day, I have no idea why no one who trained us looked at things this way when I started.

This is a summary of thousands of sales meetings we had:

- Let's focus on having a great day today.
- Let's focus on whether it's our choice to see the good or bad in every situation we face today.
- Let's focus on each customer we are dealing with today and not worry about yesterday's or tomorrow's customer.
- Let's focus on doing every step in our process today without skipping steps on the road to a sale.
- Let's focus on leaving our problems at home (this was easier without cell phones because if we were with customers, phone calls were not allowed to be put through to us) and just focusing on our shift.
- Let's focus on how you would like to be treated as a customer today.

NOTES FOR THE CHILDREN   217

- Let's focus on the process, not the result, and we will likely achieve the results we want today.
- Let's focus on having a little fun selling cars today.
- Let's focus on the fact we are the best team at the dealership, and we help each other out.
- Let's remember if we do all the above, we can go home satisfied that we did the best we could and hopefully have made good money as well. Game on.

BLINDERS ON

The importance of focus was another lesson I was fortunate to learn at a young age. I remember one of the managers whose crew I was not on explaining it to me while we were standing outside.

I can't remember exactly whom he was pointing out to me while they were trying to sell a car, but he said to me, "He has no focus at work and will never be a hitter."

I asked something like, *What exactly do you mean by that?*

He said something along the lines of "Pat, we all have problems at home and at work, but there is no value in mixing them up. Like a racehorse, put your blinders on at work and stay 100 percent focused on selling cars. When you get home, stop thinking about work and deal with your home issues."

It was terrific advice from someone I did not even work for at the dealership. Years later I say, "Thank you again, Tony."

From then on, I would drive into work with my most motivating music on extremely loud in my car and put my "work blinders" on from the moment I arrived at the store until I departed the dealership that evening. I left my personal problems at home, and when I was home, I would try to leave my work stress behind, which was not always easy. I am certain

I endured the same sort of issues most of the staff had, but the advice to keep them separate really differentiated me from many others who could not seem to do that.

Unfortunately, I am still working on this type of focus today and fully realize I will never be perfect here, but getting 80 percent to "blinders on" is much better than 50 percent. Experience also taught me if deep down we know we gave our best effort at work that day, we will be less likely to bring our problems home that night.

CAN'T HEAR THE OUTSIDE NOISE

When thinking about the topic of focus, I can still remember an afternoon in 1983, around four thirty, standing at the front door of our dealership in London, Ontario. It was a beautiful afternoon, and there were about four sets of customers outside working with our salespeople, and our fleet manager was standing next to me. I was around twenty-seven, and he was very old at about forty-five. (Ha ha! Time sure changes our perspective.) Anyway I was his boss, but we were very friendly to each other, even though Herb was a consummate square who wore a bow tie every day, and I was a long-haired rebel. I have fond memories of us going back and forth at each other's ways.

This night he was standing around, watching what was going on outside the showroom just before he went home. He said something to me, and I did not really hear him, as I was very focused on the action at the store. If anyone looked like they were going to say goodbye to the salesperson, I would likely walk over and see if I could help sell them a car right there.

A minute or two later he said to me, "Did you not hear what I just said?"

I said, "Sorry, no, I was paying attention to the potential sales happening."

He gave me an incredulous look of disbelief and said, "I just told you Dollie died."

Of course, Dollie was his wife, and I was not sure what to think besides the fact he would not be standing in the showroom if that had actually happened.

"Well," he said with a smile, "I was just testing you to see how you would react. You are surely the most focused person I have ever met in my life." He went on to say something along the lines of *You are going to be incredibly successful in life, Pat, but not sure I would want to be you.*

Still not sure if his words were a compliment or not, but I can say being focused drives results. It's also hard for our teams not to be focused and committed when the boss is driven. Children, please trust me as it is a very competitive world, and if we want to win, we need total focus and commitment.

LET'S KEEP OUR FOCUS WHERE WE ARE

Focus is another of my early fundamentals of any training program I have ever run. I found early in my career that many of my coworkers and I really had trouble focusing on the tasks at hand during the workday. Many would talk incessantly about problems at home with their partner, their children, their family members, dwindling finances, etc. By no means do I mean to belittle anyone or believe they did not have these troubles, as I surely had mine. However, the point of focus is that if we are going to be successful in our careers, we must focus 100 percent of our effort at work on our daily tasks and actions, which in turn will drive our results.

When we are off work and at home, I learned that we need

to keep our work problems at work and focus on our families. I fully understand this can be difficult for all of us, but if we stay focused on what's important in each place when we are physically there, we end up having far fewer problems in both places to deal with.

I so sadly remember times when the kids were young and they would be talking to me in such an excited way, but my mind would be on why we did not sell ten cars that day. Often, I did not listen to Susan as well as I should have because I was thinking about having too much used-car inventory or some other work-related issue. During too many periods of my life, I neglected my own advice here and am very sorry for this behavior. Hopefully, children, you can do better at this practice than I did.

DAILY HABITS

"Your words become your actions, your actions become your habits, your habits become your values, your values become your destiny."

Gandhi

THERE IS NOT A LOT OF TRAFFIC ON THE EXTRA MILE

I was extremely fortunate to learn at around twenty-six years old a classic lesson on getting things accomplished in life. An excellent sales trainer who did seminars across North America taught me this when I was in London, Ontario, and our financial situation was tenuous, with record-high interest rates. It has stuck for forty-plus years, and I have shared this with our teams in thousands of meetings and one-on-ones: "It's the little things you do that you do not have to do that make a big difference when it's too late to do something about it."

It is really a pretty simple habit to work on, as it says most people are willing to do a fair amount of work in the process of a sale, but the truly superior salesperson always does those little extra things that make a difference to the customer. When the customer is making a decision after spending a couple of hours with you, they will remember those little extras you did that competitors usually do not do. An hour in, when the sale is looking bleak, it is usually too late to go back and try to do those little things. Experience has taught me that if you do the little extra things no one is asking you to do, it can make a huge difference in the outcome. Surely this applies to most everything in life, not just selling a car.

The Hall of Fame star and Dallas Cowboys quarterback Roger Staubach said, "There is not a lot of traffic on the extra mile." I have always agreed with that quote because, for me, it parallels doing the little things others won't. Children, if you practice this on a habitual basis, your results will change for the positive.

DAILY REMINDERS FOR ALL OF US

Please remember we are never faultless, and we are only looking to improve our daily habits, and sometimes just starting a new habit takes us halfway there. These are specific things I try to focus on each day:

- Count my blessings, at minimum, each morning and before bed.
- Do walking meditation at home and work.
- Actively listen to understand, not to react to others.
- Remember how much my mood affects others at work and home.
- Continue to read and learn from others.
- Be aware how important resilience is to my day.
- Remember to practice "I Like You."

Children, if we do these practices each day, I truly believe our lives will be moving in the right direction. Of course, add your own things and replace some of these with your own daily habits that are positive and make you feel better. The point here is to be self-aware of what you need to think about and actually do each day to find your happiness and career goals.

WHAT WE DO EACH DAY

"We are what we repeatedly do. Excellence, then, is not an act but a habit."

Aristotle

Often in my career, when I have tried to figure out why a certain employee who seemed to have talent and character was underperforming, I would often ask them something important. *Please tell me in a bit of detail what you actually do each day from start to finish?* This taught me very much about how important daily habits are, as inevitably, they would be missing some crucial habits needed to be successful. Often a few small changes make a significant difference in the results.

What we do each day, including our regular habits, has a profound effect on our ability to achieve our dreams and goals. Poor habits are very hard to break, but with insight, personal awareness, and commitment they can change for the better.

I know this seems obvious and basic, but a bad habit that took me years to break was almost being late for every meeting. If a meeting started at eight thirty, I would plan to arrive at eight twenty-five, never really considering external events such as unexpected traffic. Most of the time I arrived by the slimmest of margins, but unfortunately, a few too many late arrivals made me look disrespectful and immature. Just as bad was the extra stress, worry, anxiety, and guilt I would feel racing to be on time. This was a good habit to change.

Of course, if we are not consistent with our new, better habits, the old ones can reappear quickly. This is something I have had to really work on through the years, as my bad habits would reappear if my self-awareness and discipline were lacking.

DAILY HABIT OF LEARNING

Children, I cannot tell you in any stronger words my belief that to be very successful and stay happy in life, we need to make it a daily habit to become lifelong learners. As I have said in other notes, we can never think we have reached the limits of our understanding, our knowledge, our wisdom, or our emotional intelligence. The smartest minds in the world were saying this thousands of years ago. Seneca wrote sometime around AD 49 that if we are to live well, we must be students of life. Here are a couple of his many penetrating insights:

- "As long as you live, keep learning how to live."
- "No man was ever wise by chance."

Epictetus wrote sometime around AD 120 that it is impossible to learn what we think we already know. He preached that we need to learn from everyone and everything. Here are some of his other sage insights on knowledge and learning:

- "Be careful to leave your sons well instructed rather than rich, for the hopes of the instructed are better than the wealth of the ignorant."

- "Don't just say you have read books. Show that through them you have learned to think better, to be a more discriminating and reflective person. Books are the training weights of the mind."

Please make it a habit of learning something daily so that you can become lifelong learners, children. Through this path you will find prosperity and happiness and, even more importantly, pass the lessons you learn on to your children. What a blessing for them to see this example.

A FEW DAILY HABIT TIPS

Children, it is always a good practice to do a regular deep dive of our own habits, being very truthful with ourselves. Self-control creates a lot of our good habits. Here are some tips I've learned during my ongoing efforts to let go of destructive habits and add more positive ones:

- The habit of being organized with structure is beneficial, as it creates an atmosphere of less stress and more relaxation.
- Complaining to others is a poor habit; it makes us feel bad as well as the person we are talking with.
- Good habits really improve our diet and exercise programs.
- The habit of negativity genuinely keeps us from watering the positive seeds in us.
- A restful sleep is one of the most critical good habits we can have.

THE BENEFITS OF DAILY PRACTICE

Our success comes from the daily actions we take on a consistent and disciplined basis. If this were so easy, everyone would do it. I remember someone telling me forty-five years ago: "You can only use what you practice, not what you know."

Boy, was that terrific advice that I have passed on to thousands of folks over the years. I really feel bad saying this, but the truth is most humans will not put in the last bit of hard work, sacrifice, and discipline needed to reach their dreams. The sad part is most of us are already doing about 85 percent or so of what is needed and just need to make that last bit of effort. Remember, it's not what we profess, it's what we practice that makes the difference. People who prefer to take the easier way over what is necessary to get our jobs done well usually do not have much self-discipline when it comes to daily practice and as a result will not experience the success they are seeking. I say this to make sure you are not in this trap now or succumb to it in the future. Attitude, resilience, and the discipline to practice daily will get you there.

SUFFERING

"He who learns must suffer. And even in our sleep pain that cannot forget falls drop by drop upon the heart, and in our own despair, against our will, comes wisdom to us by the awful grace of God."

Aeschylus

WE ALL SUFFER

I am not trying to be negative in any way, but it is very important that we understand and accept that every human being will suffer in some form or another. All of us suffer: our children suffer, our mother and father suffer, our grandparents suffer, our family members suffer, all our friends suffer, all our work colleagues suffer, all our mentors suffer; in fact, everyone we do not know in this world suffers. Suffering is truly part of the human condition and comes to everyone. Children, to help us with our own suffering, we need to acknowledge that all humans suffer, and living in Canada as we do, we likely suffer much less than most.

In fact, without suffering, we would not know what happiness and peace are. We need to embrace our suffering, as it can teach us so much about ourselves and the world we live in. So let's have compassion for our suffering and trust that from suffering great things will come our way. How would we know true love, true happiness, and pure joy without suffering?

I could not in my heart believe more that some suffering in life is the only way to happiness and success, and this I tell you from sixty-six years of living. I do not regret a moment of my suffering, as it has helped me grow and find true love and happiness. However, let's not keep making the same mistakes that have us continue to suffer as the Buddha says in the next note.

SUFFERING AND LIFE

Everyone feels suffering; even though every person in this list comes from a different place, they all share this feeling.

"Suffering is an ineradicable part of life, even as fate and death. Without suffering and death human life cannot be complete."
Viktor Frankl

"Suffering has been stronger than all teaching, and has taught me to understand what your heart used to be. I have been bent and broken, but—I hope—into a better shape."
Charles Dickens

"There are two kinds of suffering: the kind that leads to more suffering and the kind that brings an end to suffering."
Buddha

"I hated every minute of training, but I said, 'Don't quit. Suffer now and live the rest of your life as a champion.'"

Muhammad Ali

"A disciplined mind leads to happiness, and an undisciplined mind leads to suffering."

Dalai Lama

THE HAZARDS OF RELIVING SUFFERING

In the past many of us have been abused in some way and treated very poorly, sometimes by people close to us. These events are buried within our consciousness, and we often can't seem to get over them, so of course this causes us even more suffering. We often relive these sad occurrences over and over, and each time we do, we are somehow abused again.

For far too many years I relived the same painful memories again and again. Forget who was to blame for a minute. Why did I spend literally years of my life reliving the pain of losing my twin brother and best friend since birth combined with the incomprehensiveness of this situation? This was terrible pain and anguish that the memories continued to incite for years on end. What good did it do me? What good did it do Susan? What good did it do the kids? What good did it do my mother and sisters? What good did it do my friends who could not stand listening to me? What good did it do my business? And many years later, what good did it do Diana? The only difference is Diana implored me to move on with my life and helped me get through the raging darkness inside me from years of this. Together we made it to the light, a very happy place to be.

To get to that light, we all need to be vigilant with our mindfulness as we move forward. This was my path from suffering to happiness and will be yours as well. A life fact is that suffering will occur in all our lives at some time, and we have the choice to relive it all the time or not. Children, this is an important life lesson I took far too many years to learn. Please be aware and mindful if this creeps into your life at any time.

THE SUFFERING THAT IS FAMILIAR

For us to suffer a little is completely normal and fine. In fact, if we learn to take care of our suffering, we can keep it to a minimum and enjoy much more happiness.

As usual, Thich Nhat Hanh says it with such clarity, and I can attest to his words personally: "People have a hard time letting go of their suffering. Out of a fear of the unknown, they prefer suffering that is familiar."

I wish I had a tenth of Thich's wisdom, but I've surely learned so much from him. Honest to goodness, it's hard to believe, but for so many years I chose suffering because I was used to it and thought I was tough and could handle it. Why would I not want to address my sorrow? Perhaps I thought it was selfish somehow. After studying for a long period and having some difficult moments in life, I learned from Thich's teachings the way to take care of my own suffering.

Sometimes we just have to cradle this anguish like we do our own child. Take it and gently say to it, "It is OK, I am here for you." Especially for a man this may sound weak, but it is the exact opposite. The ability to take care of our suffering makes us so much stronger as human beings. This also assists us in helping others we care about and being more present for them when we are not spending too much time living inside our own heads. Earlier when I spoke of anger, I said we have to compassionately care for our anger as we would for our children. The same is true for our suffering—we really need to be the compassionate mother of our own pain.

I believe the biggest reason we often do not take care of our own suffering is reflected in a story I once heard. Let's say we are living in a pigsty, and we have been there for so long it begins to smell normal to us. One delightful day we are freed from our pigsty, and we live for a week in a beautiful place with fresh air and an ocean breeze in our faces. We can't believe how much better life is here, and wow, no smell at all, we have found our paradise. Unfortunately, circumstances often of our own making put us back in our own personal pigsty. Lo and behold, a few days later we are back in our old, smelly situation thinking, "Hey, this is not that bad." Way too often we stay with or return to a situation we know is not good for us, and yet we stay with it because it is familiar and what we are used to.

Something worth pondering, kids.

IMPERMANENCE AND SUFFERING

Another crucial thing I've learned over the years about suffering is that mindfulness will really help us recognize ours, and this is very important. We can then take care of the suffering so it can go to a much lower level and perhaps disappear for most parts of our life.

To learn and recognize that everything is impermanent and that it will change in time helps us keep our suffering down and helps us appreciate what we have today. It's also a wise practice to work a bit with our mindfulness when things are going really well, as things eventually change for all of us, and this mindfulness preparation will help us when we really need it.

LET'S TRY TO UNDERSTAND OUR SUFFERING

Suffering is a misunderstood emotion that we all have to learn to deal with throughout our lives. Whether it is our fear of losing someone we love, or the fear of struggling with sickness, old age, money problems, family problems, or anything else that causes heartache, there is a better way to view suffering. Clearly, I spent too many years not understanding my suffering, the roots of it, or a better way forward to deal with it.

Only after studying the way Buddhists look at suffering was I able to begin moving forward on the right path toward eliminating much of the suffering we all face. Children, I hope these notes here will help you along your path earlier on your journey.

The Buddha taught the following when trying to help people look deeply and shine the light of mindfulness on our suffering. They are referred to as the Five Remembrances:

1. I am of the nature to grow old. There is no way to escape growing old.
2. I am of the nature to have ill health. There is no way to escape having ill health.
3. I am of the nature to die. There is no way to escape death.
4. All that is dear to me and everyone I love are of the nature to change. There is no way to escape being separated from them.
5. My actions are my only true belongings. I cannot escape the consequences of my actions. My actions are the ground on which I stand.

It seems logical to me that if we only looked at the five verses above as terrible warnings of our true future, more misery could come our way. However, it is best for us to accept these facts of life, smile a bit at them, and use mindfulness to make the most of every situation every day of our precious lives. Life is short for us and our loved ones, and enjoying each present moment will keep us in a positive emotional state and cut our suffering immensely.

HAPPINESS

ICE CREAM

Besides having enough for our families to live a reasonable life, we really need only a couple of things to be very happy and content. We need a life partner we adore, and we need some small things we like or like to do. In my case, I just love being around the house at night and seeing and being with Diana. I also love the fact I can wander over to my freezer and pick from ten different pints of ice cream.

Here is some life advice for my children:

- Please find and keep your Diana.
- Please find and love your ice cream.

MAGIC AND LOSS

This brilliant song "Magic and Loss" by Lou Reed is a contemplative take on what real life is composed of. We all win, we all lose, and when we can accept that, learn from our mistakes, and take some accountability to improve ourselves, life is pretty special.

Here are some excerpted lyrics from the song:

When you pass through the fire, you pass
    through humble
you pass through a maze of self-doubt
When you pass through humble, the
    lights can blind you
Some people never figure that out . . .

As you pass through the fire, your right
    hand waving
there are things you have to throw out
That caustic dread inside your head
will never help you out . . .

When the past makes you laugh and you
    can savor the magic
that let you survive your own war
You find that fire is passion
and there's a door up ahead not a wall . . .

Please look up all the lyrics and listen to the song someday
and ponder the fact there is a bit of magic in everything and
then some loss to even things out. We simply have to accept
that, and we will likely find more doorways and less walls in
our lives.

HAPPINESS AND SUFFERING

Buddhists rightly believe an important life lesson: we cannot
have true happiness without some suffering. This is something
I have worked on for years and continue to do. I wrote the following in my notes many years ago and try to remember them
regularly:

- We simply can't have one without the other.
- Let's try to keep the suffering down.
- Let's try to get the happiness up.
- Always remember that our happiness is most important to us and our loved ones.
- Happiness can fade if we are not keenly aware and mindful of it.

Children, when your happiness does fade a bit, as it surely will from time to time, let's make sure we try to not go too far to the suffering side. If we fall too much to that side, let's work to find out why we are experiencing it and, hopefully, get some answers to help us on our journey back to happiness.

HAPPINESS PILLS

We all want happiness. We should all also want to know what often prevents it. Thich says if we are living with jealousy, envy, and delusion, sustained happiness is not possible. As long as these poisons are in our hearts, true happiness is simply not possible. My sixty-six years of living confirms this is correct in my case; I suspect it is the same for all of us. Freeing ourselves from these negative emotions is surely easier than finding a happiness pill.

Children, let's all take this to heart and always remember no one is in charge of our happiness but ourselves.

PEACE AND HAPPINESS NOW

"Peace can exist only in the present moment. It is ridiculous to say, 'Wait until I finish this, then I will be free to live in peace.' What is 'this'? A diploma, a job, a house, the payment of a debt? If you think that way peace will never come. There is always another 'this' that will follow the present one. If you are not living in peace at this moment, you will never be able to. If you truly want to be at peace you must be at peace right now. Otherwise there is only hope of peace someday."

                                        Thich Nhat Hanh

This is another of Thich's quotes that touched me deeply. These are wise words to study well for all of us. Waiting for everything in our lives to be as we want them in order to find happiness will never work. During moments throughout our lives when we find these thoughts coming at us, let's please read the words of a master.

RANDOM THOUGHTS ON HAPPINESS
TAKEN FROM OLD NOTES

We generally do not become happy overnight, but with patient good practices day after day we can find lasting happiness. Here are some examples:

- Most of us have to change ourselves a bit to be-come happy on a consistent basis.
- A healthy mind will generally make us a lot happier.
- Happiness is also a product of how we interpret the world, since most of the time it's not possible

to change the world, but it's possible to change the way we look at it.

- If we enjoy inner peace and happiness, we are not broken by failure or inflated by success.
- If we crave recognition and adulation from others, happiness will be elusive for us.
- Happiness is an exceptionally wise and solid foundation to live with.

LEADERSHIP

EVERYONE NEEDS A LITTLE SOMETHING

An excellent leadership tip I learned many years ago was that each and every person who works with us needs a little something from us most days. If we want to be superior leaders, we must give it to them. Perhaps some of these suggestions could get us started here. Let's try to give them the following:

- Our undivided attention
- Respect
- Dignity
- A little of our time
- A little wisdom if we can
- A heartfelt thank you
- A heartfelt "Nice job"

This respectful behavior by leaders saves us from a lot of staff turnover and makes us proud we could help someone else succeed a bit. I often cover this subject in our manager training meetings. Please find your own leadership list, kids.

IT'S GOOD TO BE KING

Some basic leadership traits I learned very early on have stuck with me for years on end. As a young man, I had the good fortune to observe many styles of leadership, but in our business, the most prominent style was that the leader is king of everything. It amazed me how some of the senior leadership where I worked in 1975 had the impression that if you were the boss, you were the king, and many of the folks in the dealership were simply treated like peasants.

As I started working my way up in automotive retail, it quickly became clear to me that this style would not be effective for me at all. Two reasons why this wouldn't work were obvious.

First off, I was a nineteen-year-old kid tasked with running a team of people between the ages of twenty-five and sixty-five. Human nature told me there is no way they would have responded well to a young leader with that type of attitude.

Second, it was not in my nature then or forty-seven years later to lead this way. I firmly believe exceptional leaders actually care about how the individual members of the team are doing, as well as how the entire team is doing. If we had ten people on our team, I wanted each one to have as good a month as possible, which of course means the team will do well and hit all our targets. Too many leaders only care about the total team number to be attained and just keep replacing the lower performers. This is simply wrong, as each team member deserves the leader's attention if they are putting the effort in.

In the early days of my automotive career, the owner would tell the four sales managers to fire their bottom 20 percent each month, which was a very stupid and immoral thing to do. He also found it very entertaining, as if it were a symbolic gallows in the old west. The only difference was he didn't hang them, he just embarrassed them in front of the team and had us fire them. Perhaps the cowboy hat he wore inspired him to lead this way. Fortunately, I learned many lessons from this ridiculous way of managing. An ironic thing here was his business did reasonably well for a number of years before it crashed and burned. Here are some early lessons learned before I was twenty-one years old that have stuck with me for nearly fifty years:

- Never embarrass anyone in front of another person.
- Be wary of peaks and valleys in a sales cycle, many salespeople who are performing in the bottom 20 percent one month can improve significantly with a little help.
- Do not celebrate our victories too much, as our team does not need a cocky person leading them.
- Do not mope around too long after some losses; our sales team deserves a positive leader at all times.
- Instilling fear in any team does not lead to long-term success.
- Regardless of whether we win or lose today, always move forward, steadily practicing what we know works.

KITCHEN-TABLE LEADERSHIP LESSON

My father was a very troubled man in almost every way, but he was kind to me most of the time and very smart. Forty-seven years later I can remember his words to me about my first sales meeting. I was nineteen and was so proud to tell him that the owner had just promoted me to sales manager. I had already written out a draft for my first sales meeting the next day and proudly read it out to him. I remember most of its content to this day. I was going to tell each sales-team member that they can sell thirty vehicles a month, and that kind of thing.

Sitting at his kitchen table, he listened for a while and then said in a very straightforward manner, "How long do you think these people are going to work for you?"

I was like, "This is a clever speech; it's very motivating."

He said that it might be motivating, but it will not work. His point was I received the job because my drive to succeed was intense, but he explained to me that you have to manage ten people who all have different dreams and goals and skills from you. He explained that each individual has different needs and desires and therefore will put in different amounts of effort and focus to achieve their goals, not yours. As leaders, we must learn what makes them tick, what motivates them, not us.

I thought about it for a few minutes and figured I better change course quickly here. Turns out that was a good lesson, and I rewrote my entire first sales meeting. As I had been selling about twenty-eight cars a month, and most of my new team was selling around ten to twelve each month, we instead changed the sales meeting to try to get everyone to work on improving their own numbers by about 30 percent instead of trying to press them hard to sell twenty-eight a month each, which would have failed spectacularly. Our new goal was to try to improve the whole team by about 30 percent each month, but the most important thing was to help each salesperson try to improve by that number.

Many salespeople, in fact, started selling twelve to sixteen cars a month rather than nine to twelve, which was a major success for them and the whole team. It's a lesson about bottom-up success that Dad taught me: if your individual team members win, we win. It's a lesson that still works today when we forecast each person and each store. Thanks, Dad.

MAGICAL MYSTERY TOUR

When I started as a sixteen-year-old lot kid at Chinook Chrysler in Calgary, I was mostly around for the paycheck I received. I had very little interest in washing cars, changing rusted-out license plate brackets, getting hamburgers for the salespeople, or doing the myriad other jobs. But I sure was clueless to what was really going on at the dealership. I certainly knew the sales crew were a collection of hard-as-nails people who played by a different set of rules compared to the university crowd I was hanging around with during the day.

One of the outrageous things I was told to do as a lot man was to find the dealership vehicles that were advertised in the daily newspaper and fill them with a bunch of garbage, usually leftover food. Obviously, the customers who came to see these vehicles did not feel too good about buying a new car looking and smelling like that. Now the salesperson's job was simple: try to sell them a different vehicle with more profit in it that did not look like it was being lived in. Even with all that trickery and more going on, I had no real idea what I was about to get into as the dealership management asked me to start selling cars a couple of months before my eighteenth birthday. In hindsight you would think my father might have warned me a bit more, but he must have thought it was kind of normal, as he had been around it for too many years.

As they had an enormous amount of turnover of the salespeople, I think management withheld the good stuff from them until they had been there at least a month. Nothing totally abnormal happened in my first month or so, except I truly surprised myself by selling thirty-one vehicles and leading the team for the month. Believe me, no one was more shocked than me, and I suppose at this point I was now allowed to enter the club of real salespeople and managers. It was a Friday afternoon just before the two-until-ten shift, and our sales manager finished his fifteen-minute tirade of a sales meeting. He told about two-thirds of us to stay back a minute, which was the first time I was allowed to stay back, and I was really shocked at what came next. He reached into his desk drawer and proceeded to give each of us a speed pill, which the guys quickly took. I was a very nervous kid and said I am OK without it, but the boss said you will need it to win in this business, so take it.

Can't remember exactly what happened, though I did not take it that Friday, but I will never forget what happened the next day as he convinced me Saturday morning that it was really necessary for the team to have a big day and I took Saturday's pill. This was at about nine a.m., and I spoke to my first customer about thirty minutes later. Lo and behold, if the customer did not turn out to be an RCMP officer from British Columbia who was in Calgary to shop for and buy a car.

My paranoia was racing through me as I found him a big four-door Chrysler Newport for his family, and we took it out for a test drive. Thank God, he was really nice, and when we returned twenty minutes later, I asked him if he would buy it today if we came up with a great price for him. He said yes, and I pulled out my purchase order to get the serial number off the front dashboard by the driver's window, but in the stoned state I was in, I started looking for it on the driver's side of the hood. The customer, who was about fifty years old, said "Son, the serial number is by the glass; don't you know that." I said, "Sorry sir, I just started a couple of weeks ago," and off we went to the showroom to write up a deal. Scared the hell out of me, and I sure did not like amphetamines and did not do it again. Wish I could say the same about a few other bad habits, but we are only human.

Another eye-opening experience for me to witness at work each day occurred around three p.m. when the dealership's unofficial bar and drug emporium opened for business.

Operating out of a trunk of one of the new vehicles near the back of the property, a salesperson would operate as bartender for an hour or so of their shift. Whether you wanted whisky, rum, or vodka with your particular mix, it was all available, including ice. Found out a few weeks after starting my sales career that it cost about five or ten dollars a week to join the action. A "bud tender" was also available, but that was à la carte pricing for weed, hash, or some kind of speed. I often wondered if my dad thought it was quite normal to drink a bottle and a half of Canadian Club whisky a day, considering what most of the staff was consuming in alcohol, speed, and cocaine virtually every day.

One thing I certainly learned about leadership during this period was if these people could lead by acting and doing what they were doing, better leadership should not be impossible for me or any of us to learn.

Looking back today, I've come to find that many of these folks who were drinking heavily and doing numerous drugs each day died young and mostly broke. I suspect many died lonely as well. I am so fortunate to have gotten out of that environment mostly intact. The start to my automotive career certainly felt like we were living in the Beatles' epic 1967 album, *Magical Mystery Tour*, a druggy psychedelic journey.

PREPARATION AND LEADERSHIP

Inspiring leadership is just as much about preparation as it is about action. Inspirational leaders do the work on changing themselves before they try to change and improve the lives of others. Most everyone wants to play the leadership game, but not as many of us want to practice and prepare. I would never go into a meeting in front of many people without a little practice, as it's simply disrespectful of their time.

A simple example of preparation was in May 2006 when we were preparing to hit the road for our two-week roadshow to try to sell over $100 million in stock. We not only wanted to play the game but also practiced for a number of extra days to make sure we were prepared to answer a staggering number of potential investor questions. The bankers would pepper us with tough questions and respond harshly to many of our poor answers during practice sessions, which was much better than stumbling in actual meetings. They even brought in a speech coach for half a day. The preparation and practice certainly paid off for us, as we sold every last dollar of stock we wanted to. Extra preparation will pay off for you in your careers as well.

LESSONS FROM DETROIT

Leaders need to execute their business plan, not just talk about it. A fortunate life lesson I learned early in my career was from a gentleman from Chrysler in Detroit who used to visit our store every month. Every time I saw him, I gave him five exciting new ideas we were working on. At twenty-four I thought this idea or that idea was great and could not wait to get going.

He stopped me in my tracks about five months after knowing me and said, "Man, you have some great ideas, and I really don't think I have ever met someone as motivated as you. However, have you actually implemented the last twenty ideas you gave me?"

I realized quickly that he was right, and I was getting things to the finish line about only 50 percent of the time. Ideas are extremely important, as is motivation to win, but let's finish each one first. If it is such a good idea, let's implement it before we rush to the next five.

LET'S PROTEST ANYTHING

I was very fortunate to learn some early leadership lessons as a young teenager that benefited me years later. Though Mike and I were the youngest kids in grade twelve, we did not especially like the rules and attitude the teachers would lay on us, so we were determined to do something about it.

The world was full of protests in the late sixties and into the seventies, and we decided to hold our own protest. We proposed a student walkout to protest something that was going on (I have no idea what it was), likely something stupid like lunch hours. It was an interesting day as we organized and then led about three hundred students to walk around the school perimeter from noon on, with protest signs saying we were not going back to school until the teachers started treating us better.

When the bell rang at 12:45 p.m. to go back into class, we told the other students we cannot give in, or we would look like idiots with no jam. We implored them to keep the protest going until the school gave in to us. After the bell rang, the teachers went outside and told everyone to get back into class, and we lost about fifty at a time, who ran for cover and back into class. Ten minutes later the loudspeakers warned students they would be in big trouble if not in class immediately, and by one thirty there were only about five other students walking with us. We lost the battle and the war that day, but we never lost our pride, and I was happy with what we had done. That said, I received a couple of gifts from the protest:

- I, along with five others, was suspended for a couple of days.
- I learned a lifelong leadership lesson: we need to get people totally bought into our plans. Hoping

they will follow you without a full commitment on their part is wishful thinking.

LET'S WORK BESIDE OUR TEAMS

An influential leader not only tells someone how something should be done but also shows them. Being on the field or floor working with our teams for a significant part of each day will have an influential impact on the team and results. Let's never forget what it's like to be a crew member when we are the captain. As Einstein said, "Example isn't another way to teach, it is the only way to teach."

LEARN TODAY

To lead tomorrow, we must learn today. Leadership is developed daily. The good news is our leadership ability will continue to improve as we work at it month after month and year after year. Today is the best time for us to start improving our leadership skills and continue throughout our lifetime.

I have seen many good leaders who ended up having something called destination disease. Basically, they felt when they got to a certain position, they could stop learning because they already knew everything. This simply does not work if you want to be a phenomenal leader. Even though I'm sixty-six, I believe that the day I stop being committed to learning is the day I should sell our business.

PEOPLE FOLLOW CHARACTER

I've come to believe that people will follow leaders because of

who they are and what they represent. Therefore, our character and actions are extremely important in retaining really
good people. I also see trust as a huge part of the foundation
of leadership. People will forgive occasional mistakes, but they
won't follow someone whose character they do not trust. By
violating their trust, we will likely never win them over again.
Good character communicates to your team that you can be
trusted on a day-to-day basis to do the best you possibly can
and help them in every way.

For instance, I don't think we can succeed in life if we work
hard only on the days when we feel really good and everything
is going our way. We must have the discipline to push through
the tough days, as that is a big difference between real leaders
and those who hope to lead but do not want to pay the price.
Our people will see through our character and actions here
very quickly.

CRITICAL LEADERSHIP TRUTHS

These are qualities that most leaders share that took me years
to learn and accept as truth. I have presented these at training
sessions for years on end:

- Leaders generally don't feel sorry for themselves
  because they know that is a waste of time.
- Leaders don't shy away from change in a world
  that is changing faster than at any time in history.
- Leaders don't focus on things they can't control;
  they focus on what they and the company can
  control.
- Leaders lift up other people around them.
- Leaders don't fear taking calculated risks that are
  well thought out and mapped out.

- Leaders learn from the past and don't dwell on it. They don't keep making the same mistakes over and over again.
- Leaders simply do not give up after the first, second, or third problem or obstacle arises.
  My life experiences taught me that the average salesperson gives up after about 50 percent of the objections that customers give us, really good salespeople at about 75 percent, and true leaders at about 90 percent.
- Leaders generally don't feel the world owes them anything.
- Leaders don't expect immediate results, especially on big issues involving change. They realize you have to keep working on it.
- Leaders never want to be the smartest person in the room; we need to surround ourselves with smart people.
- Leaders work on their mental and emotional strength, the key words here being they work at it. I can tell you from personal experience that the minute I stop working on my mental and emotional strength and mindfulness is the minute it all gets worse, even after these many years.

LEARNING FROM THE BEST AND WORST LEADERS

They say money runs the world, and I know in a sick way it does, but I also believe this is not something any of us are going to soon change. What we can change is how we feel about it and try to keep a bit of our greed in check. Money is a perfect example of our craving. Often the more we make and consume, the more we crave.

As an eighteen-year-old salesman, I worked for a fellow by the name of Frank, who was my first boss in sales. He certainly was not a top-end leader to learn from, but I didn't know better at the time. Sometimes we would sit in his office, and he would philosophize with me about many things in life. About four months after I had started, he realized being his top salesman was my destiny, and he tried to help me a fair bit, which I appreciated. One of the things he felt was important to teach me was how to deal with banks and personal loans.

Frank would say that I was heading to make $25,000 this year, so they would loan me such and such. He would then say to me, "Hey, I am making around $35,000, so they will loan me more." The real trick, he would say, is to start with a small loan you don't need, say $2,000, and pay it back well before the due date, then wait nine months or so, and they will lend you $6,000, and then you pay it back early as well. Wait a bit longer, and next time they will loan you $15,000, as you will be making more money at work, and you have already paid back two loans.

"With your attitude and skill," said Frank, as he continued to get excited, educating me, "about four years into your career, you will likely be a senior manager making a ton of money."

He declared it was my chance for a career- and life-changing moment. I sat in anticipation of a brilliant answer and thought, *Boy, he is a lot smarter than I thought he was. What could he know that most of us don't?*

Well, the answer to that question came soon enough. "By then," he told me, "you will have paid back five or six loans you never needed and will qualify for much more money in loans." He then said, "Go in, talk to your banker, and borrow fifty thousand from them, then leave town, never pay it back, and live the good life."

Brilliant leadership. This was the moment it occurred to me that someday I could do a better job than Frank on career advice.

He was my first leader, and at the beginning I looked up to him but soon realized he was all talk with no substance, or as the cowboys say, "Big hat, no cattle."

On our career journey we will all have some outstanding leaders and some poor ones. The good news is we can learn much from both types. Our career path should not be determined by the odd poor leader we worked for. The best leaders take accountability for their own situation.

EMPATHY IN LEADERSHIP IS A STRENGTH

Empathy is an immensely important character trait to have in life. Experience tells me if two people are very close in so many ways in their career paths, but one has empathy while the other lacks it, I will promote the employee who shows more empathy to others one hundred percent of the time.

To be able to emotionally understand what your coworker feels and be able to "put their hat on" when deciding which way to go on any project is a desirable skill, as is the ability to communicate that understanding back to them. Empathy in a leader adds to the company culture and embodies the famous saying "Culture eats strategy for breakfast." Of course, empathy also benefits all our relationships outside of work as well. Most importantly it is an admirable human trait to have.

LEADERSHIP AND ADVERSITY

The following are some of my thoughts on how we have led teams to deal with adversity, but of course, it pertains to how we lead ourselves through personal adversity too:

- Everyone on the team needs to fully understand the problems we are dealing with and look outside the box for solutions.
- We spend about five minutes a day complaining about the adversity and twelve hours looking for solutions.
- We do not keep people on the leadership team if they are good at pointing out problems but not so good at finding the solutions.
- Though every team needs a leader, everyone on the team is also a leader, and we play as a team; everyone has a role in our success.
- We insist on a consistency of effort throughout the project.
- We do things one step at a time each and every day.
- Our team realizes that treating people well every day is not only the right thing to do but pays off in times of severe adversity, as we may need outside help from people we have dealt with before.
- We hope our hard work and skill in solving problems brings a little luck with it, which we all need sometimes.

PERSONAL COST OF LEADERSHIP

Leaders who succeed in their field and rise to the top fully understand this equation: the higher your position and the higher your responsibilities are, the higher the level of commitment is needed. Part of this higher level of commitment requires higher levels of personal sacrifice, which inevitably includes our personal time.

When it comes to commitment, leaders understand that employees are watching us and watching our own commitment level. They understand if the boss comes in late all the time and is always cutting corners, employees will do the same thing.

Our children watch what we do and copy it, just as employees watch what we do and emulate it. Kids, I do not want to be tough here, but if we want to be a leader, wherever we are, we have to show ourselves to be as committed as we want our employees to be. Simple leadership fact of life.

HAND IN HAND

AN EARLY INSPIRATION

I remember living in River Heights when I was around fourteen years old and seeing this couple about thirty-five years old always walking on the street we lived on. Their house was about ten doors down from ours on the other side, and so often I would be walking at night and see them out walking together. Many things about them hit me hard:

- They always walked hand in hand, looking like they were without a care in the world. This was a significant departure from the chaos I usually left at home.
- They always seemed so loving to each other while talking and laughing. Our house definitely didn't have that loving vibe between our parents.
- They never seemed to be sniping at each other.

This was really my first real experience seeing a couple who seemed to be so in love. Back then I realized for the first time that this was what I would want for my life.

Thanks to Diana, I have it.

SOULMATE

I was nineteen when Jackson Browne released the brilliant album *Late for the Sky,* and for so many years his songs of epic love combined with life's disappointments often seemed real to me. It really made me aware that having your true soulmate with you along the ride was the only way to happiness.

He wrote, "I thought of all the empty miles, and the years that I'd spent looking for your eyes." Wish I could say it that well. Children and grandchildren, through the beautiful days and through the dark nights, please remember:

> We don't want to be walking through the
>   beautiful days alone
> We don't want to be walking through the
>   darkest days on our own
> We don't want to be walking through this
>   life alone
> So try to find your desired partner and
>   soulmate

And when you do, work hard every day on the blessings of this relationship and thank God each day for them being with you on this road through life.

TWO DAYS WORKING IN VEGAS

October 2021
It's 11:30 p.m. in Las Vegas, the last place I want to be tonight, but the company is good with my son Daniel and a number of our partners and friends at Toyota. I came here from La Jolla to attend the Toyota New Vehicle Show and try to put together

the largest deal we have ever done, with Daniel by my side. In fact, it would be the largest deal in Canadian history for automotive retail with a value well over $1 billion. Having said that, the hotel room I am staying in is the worst I have been in, even having made at least twenty trips here over the years.

I phoned the front desk and asked for a kettle so I can make some tea in the morning; however, their customer service philosophy is to put you on hold or transfer you to someone else so many times you just plain give up. Even though I write a lot in this book about not giving up too quickly, sometimes you just need to know when to tap out. I guess my morning tea will be made using hot tap water, which is a pretty disgusting way to treat enjoyable green tea. I do not have it in me to pay the fifteen dollars the hotel will charge for hot water in the morning, besides which my tea will taste better when I'm home on Saturday.

Many people here in Vegas might be putting up drunk selfie after selfie of what a fun time it is here, but that reality is far different for me. After attending the Toyota social tonight, Daniel and I met with our potential acquisition partner until about eleven p.m. It was nice that he was a fun person to be around. The truth is it has been all business all day and a late one at that.

Very serious family and lifestyle decisions will have to be made soon. What was I actually thinking about at eleven thirty in my dark room with half the lights not working while listening to an *Edmonton Journal* hockey podcast on YouTube? My thoughts were filled with the fact that at this moment, at this time, I'm more in love with Diana than I've ever been with her or any other person in my life. That's a pretty special feeling at sixty-six, and the hopes and worries over a monumental deal kind of disappear, and the room does not seem as dark and gloomy.

Love is all there is, it makes the world go
    'round
Love and only love, it can't be denied
No matter what you think about it
You just won't be able to do without it
Take a tip from one who has tried

Bob Dylan and Johnny Cash, 1971

COVER ME

A terrific and supportive life partner can make a world of difference both at home and of course at work. Trying to succeed
and reach your goals and aspirations in an extremely competitive world is almost impossible without having a partner who
is with you all the way. From the beginning of our relationship,
Diana and I would use the Bruce Springsteen song "Cover Me"
as a way of saying we cover each other all the way through life.
What a beautiful way to live.

Some partners actually criticize and mock their significant
other enough that their partner loses confidence and second-
guesses themselves. Of course, we all need some gentle criti-
cism from home once in a while, but a steady stream is very
hard to take. Be careful, as this is a hard habit to break once
started, and the other party often becomes extremely resent-
ful over time. Covering each other is a much better practice,
which took me too long to understand. A loving relationship is
also a tremendous example for your children to see.

An exalted love in our life makes us capable of inspirational courage. Any journey through this world is much easier
with our loves by our sides.

A SWEDISH PROVERB

"A shared joy is a double joy; a shared sorrow is half a sorrow."

Wise words to remember when we are in love.

CHOICE

CHOOSING OUR INNER STORY

It is perfectly normal to be upset when we make mistakes, or even fail completely, while trying to do something important for ourselves, whether at home or work. I have seen many people fail miserably and yet come back much stronger than ever. Unfortunately, I have also seen far too many who have let a few failures or mistakes really demoralize them, often endlessly beating themselves up.

A choice we have in life is to accept that everyone makes mistakes and often big ones, and everyone fails sometimes. The only genuine thing we control is how we respond to these setbacks. The truth is our mistakes and failures can become the inner stories we continually tell ourselves, or our resilient comebacks from life's inevitable setbacks can become our inner stories.

That choice is ours alone to make, kids, and I hope that some of the notes in this book will help guide you to stop beating yourself up and choose to tell yourself a more empowering story.

WE ALL USE SO LITTLE OF OUR ABILITY

"Thousands of geniuses live and die undiscovered—either by themselves or by others."

Mark Twain

Many experts on human behavior believe the average human being uses about 20–25 percent of their actual potential. I am not sure what the exact numbers may be, but from the beginning of my career, I've thought if the average is at about 25 percent, I would be way ahead of the pack if I could use 35–40 percent of my potential.

Given the fact we are likely using a relatively small percent of our potential every day, we would routinely challenge our teams to move it up by ten points, as this is something we can actually accomplish, and most would agree. When we look at human potential and the science behind it, it's much easier to convince our teams to reach a little higher. It can be a life-changing choice for us to move up a bit from average, and believe me, we can do this.

It's wonderful to know that if we can move our progress to using even 30–35 percent of our actual potential, we can be leaders in our chosen fields. When we all choose to stretch and meet more of our potential, we usually win.

IT'S REALLY OUR CHOICE

For the last fifty or so years, I have been fortunate to know that it really is each person's choice every day whether to have a good day or a poor day. I can't remember exactly whom or where I learned this from, but I know that it was when I was in university. Obviously, a very unusual or hurtful event can make having a good day impossible, but we can control only what we can, and 95 percent of the time, we have the choice to decide what kind of day we are having.

I vividly remember a discussion I had with Laura when she was around thirteen years old—a time when she was always grumpy in the morning. Finally, one day I told her, "It's your choice on what kind of mood you are in each morning. Let's get out of bed with a good attitude and make the choice to have a great day." She actually got so sick of me walking in to tell her this most mornings that she would yell from bed before I could say anything, "It's going to be a good day, Dad, please get out of here." I'm not sure if this helped at all, but she finished her master's degree with honors and is the best mother possible.

When we get out of bed in the morning, we really need to make it our choice what kind of day it's going to be. Often there are two choices we can make: one might offer immediate satisfaction that never lasts, and the other choice is harder at first but helps us accomplish our goals, which leads us toward more lasting happiness. If we make the right choice each day, each week, and each month, we will follow the same fruitful pattern to more happiness. It's not the events of the day or week that will determine our success; it's the actions we take that will enable us to take advantage of the opportunities presented or to overcome the serious obstacles put in front of us.

The truth is, kids, if we don't make our own daily plans for success, someone else will have plans for us that likely will have very little in it for us. Laura is a classic example of making the right choice.

SAGE ADVICE FROM GROUCHO MARX

Groucho Marx once said, "Each morning when I open my eyes, I say to myself, 'I, not events, have the power to make me happy or unhappy today. I can choose which it shall be. Yesterday is dead, tomorrow hasn't arrived yet. I have just one day, today, and I'm going to be happy in it.'"

It's a fascinating world when a famous comedian sounds like a Buddhist with these insightful words. Let each of us have these words ringing in our ears as we pass through life.

GUILT

ALCOHOLIC FAMILY SHAME

Children, I think it's best that I tell you how damaging my guilt was and how agonizing it was for me in the hopes of helping you avoid this painful trap. When I looked deeply inside and did the hard work on what had caused so much guilt from as early as twelve years old, it became pretty clear. Why would I continually feel guilty and have so much shame as a teenager for my father's drinking and embarrassing actions? Why, after my father died and someone would bring up his name, would I immediately panic and feel so guilty? Why, at thirty years old with children of my own, would I be walking into the service department of our dealership in London, see someone who looked like a person my father and I knew from years ago, and then quickly start walking the other way to avoid the pain of a potential conversation? These were obviously deep, agonizing memories for me, and the guilt was nonstop for years on end. Imagine living like that for forty years as I did, and so many others do.

Wow, what a state to live in and what powerful emotions to have. How does this come to be? How could we feel so much guilt and a bit of shame? Sometimes we can only guess, but unless we do the work on ourselves, we will likely never understand it. Although I no longer spend any time at all watering the seeds of guilt in myself, it is still a bit of a challenge many years later.

Let's remember to not carry the burdens of others, which are not ours to carry, as guilt can manifest itself here very quickly. I carried the guilt and the effects of my father's drinking until I was about forty-five years old. I suspect part of the reason children often feel guilty about their parents being alcoholics is due to us feeling pretty anxious most of the time, while trying to present a false face to the world, a face that pretends we are quite content and serene. So when we are not truthful to ourselves or anyone else, guilt usually visits us nonstop. We must also consider how guilty our parents felt knowing what they were doing was hurting their children. Of course, they did not mean to do this but simply could not stop. This is not a peaceful or happy way to live.

I believe my parents miscalculated badly on causing their children to have so much guilt, but that is what they were taught, in part by the Catholic Church and by their parents, so that is what they taught us. They certainly loved us and never meant to hurt us, so I do not blame them for any of it at all. As adults, it's up to us to see who we really are and make the changes necessary for a happy life.

With all respect to the Catholic Church, being an altar boy also did me no favors as far as guilt goes. Perhaps the message that the devil is out to get us is the wrong one and can really screw us up. The exceptionally good news is that years later I came to realize God is with us, wants to be on our side, and does not want us to live with enormous guilt.

Children, if you are honest, kind, considerate, and hardworking, you have no need to ever live in a state of guilt. No one expects you or anyone to be the perfect person, perfect parent, perfect partner, perfect grandparent, or anything else. Just continue to do your best, learn, and let it go.

SOME LIFE TRUTHS ABOUT GUILT

Guilt actually has a couple of good characteristics to it, though I am talking about living with a small bit of normal guilt. It demonstrates to us we have a conscience and helps us recognize we have said or done something wrong. Guilt also allows us the opportunity to say we are sorry and to make amends for things. The point here is that a little bit of healthy guilt is not a bad thing at all, but a lot of guilt makes living very, very difficult for us.

Here are some characteristics of people whom I've worked with for years who live with too much guilt (Unfortunately for too many years, I was one of them.):

- Very sensitive
- A bit introverted
- Often like to keep the peace
- Do not stand up for themselves quite enough
- Often learned this feeling of guilt from certain types of parenting or religion

Here are some other poor results we are likely to feel from having too much guilt, many of which affected me as well:

- Guilt can make us anxious.
- Guilt can make us sad.
- Guilt over a long period can make us depressed.
- Guilt can make us more stressed.
- Guilt makes us more prone to beating ourselves up.
- Guilt can damage our self-esteem.
- Guilt makes it harder for us to have fun.

- Guilt can make us second-guess a lot of what we want to do or say, fearing that may be the wrong thing to do or say.
- Guilt can also cause stomach and sleep problems.

When we look deeply into our guilt, we need to understand that feelings don't always reflect the truth. In fact, the negative feelings that we all have are often not true whatsoever. Negative emotions are usually caused by harsh self-evaluation, or, of course, the judgment of others.

Please remember that the judgment of others, just like our harsh judgments toward ourselves, may not be correct. There is a big difference between feeling guilty and being guilty, and it took me years to understand the difference. If we are too much of a perfectionist, generally our guilt is even worse. It is also a difficult beast to tame. Children, please always be mindful and very self-aware if your guilt is going in the wrong direction.

LISTENING

LISTENING AT WORK

Many employees' biggest frustration is that they believe senior management does not listen to or care about their ideas. Over the years I learned to emphasize this with our management teams and have tried to remember this daily.

Listening does all the following, and more:

- Improves work relationships
- Improves productivity
- Improves teamwork
- Improves problem solving
- Improves morale

If we need more reasons to improve our listening skills, please remember effective listeners often become exceptional leaders. Kids, be that kind of leader.

LISTENING WELL

If I can share another important note with you on the power of listening, this would be it. I have shared this for years with our teams: listen to understand, not to react.

In many situations we think we might have the correct answers, but it's best to take the words in, pause for a second, and then speak softly so the other person will feel listened to and respected. Many of us are too ready to respond to what the other person is saying before we let them finish. This can make a big difference in our lives and is the right and respectful thing to do in any conversation. I can't tell you how many times I have been excited to say something and forgot to listen properly. This is also astute advice for parenting, and I regret not listening enough as a father.

I distinctly remember many times when the children were younger, being completely preoccupied with work and family issues and not being really invested in what one of the kids was trying to tell me. So many times I was reeling from another family fight and not able to listen with enough understanding and compassion. This is completely my fault, and I certainly wish I could have a redo there, but life does not work that way. I am so sorry for this, and hopefully, you all can learn from my mistakes. The one good thing about our mistakes as parents is if we learn from them, we can do better as grandparents.

A LISTENING SALES MEETING

I am not an expert on the subject, but having sold thousands and thousands of cars, I have learned what works and what doesn't. Here are a few basic tips to practice enhancing our listening skills that we talked about at too many meetings to remember:

- Keep an open mind when another person is speaking because if we are quickly judging them, it's difficult to actually understand what they are getting at.

- Try not to interrupt the person speaking; this is challenging to do for all of us—even more so for us salespeople (ha ha).
- Try to look directly at the person talking and maintain a bit of eye contact without staring at them.
- Be present and mindful of your presence in the conversation. Just because we are there does not mean we are actively listening. Do not think about other things while listening, as the other person will likely pick up on this. It does take some effort to quiet our thoughts when someone is speaking, but they deserve our full attention.
- Nodding, smiling, and being mindful of our body language, such as leaning in a bit, goes a long way to having the person understand we are really listening.

This sounds so obvious, but you would be amazed how many people sneak a look at their phone when listening to someone else. This is fine in a normal fun conversation with a friend or coworker, but it is rude in a business situation or an important relationship discussion.

In business situations, I've trained myself to always listen to what the other person has to say and then repeat back to them the important points they brought up. I know this is not always possible, but if you're sitting across from each other, on a Zoom call, or even on a telephone call, we certainly can try to do this. There has never been a person upset with me after I repeated back to them some of what I thought they had said. More often than not most would say, "Someone is finally listening to me."

A perfect example of this was when a customer would come in with a major issue with the servicing of their vehicle and be very upset, to the point of yelling at someone on our team. I would introduce myself and say, "I am going to try to help you," and then get them to speak for a bit on the problems they were experiencing. Having written down the important points and then slowly repeating these back to them, I would attempt to solve the issue.

I can honestly tell you if people think you actually listened to them and cared a little (putting their shoes on), many will become our best customers, and they always phone me a few years later to help them buy a new vehicle from us.

WHAT DIANA TEACHES ME ABOUT LISTENING EVERY DAY

The good news is I have really learned to be a better listener over the last fourteen years; the bad news is Diana had to teach me to really listen, and that's kind of embarrassing.

She taught me the most about how good listeners actually listen. Listening at the kitchen table, listening as we walked, listening during a car ride, listening while I talked too much, listening everywhere. I saw how influential this form of listening could be for those of us she was listening to, as it was often empowering, knowing someone we loved was truly listening to us.

Good listening as she does is all about being present in the listening, not just about being there and quiet. The funny thing about it is she never said much to me about my lack of listening enough; it was her powerful example that taught me. Good listeners are hard to find, and the effort put in to improve our skills here, as I have had to do, can make a gracious and material difference to our lives. Although I was always a good listener at work, it proves it does not mean we are doing the same at home.

YA, BUT

When I was eighteen, we had approximately thirty-five sales-people working in the showroom, and sometimes you would learn something even from the worst of them, though this fellow was not that. We had a salesperson working with us who had impressive talent and a superior résumé, and when he started, I thought he would be tough competition, and a couple of the bosses ribbed me really good and said, "He is going to outsell you every month." I really liked him, as he was personable and an authentically nice person about ten years older than I was. Out of respect, I will not name him because, hopefully, he is alive and doing well somewhere.

Unfortunately, any time he was engaged with a customer, he simply could not wait for the person to finish what they were saying before he would say, "Ya, but . . ." This would happen so often it got to be a running parody on the showroom floor. Other salespeople in the showroom watching him were taking two-dollar bets on how many times in ten minutes he would use the phrase. He meant well but could not contain himself, and pretty soon his nickname at the store was Ya But, and everyone called him that, which was pretty tacky, and the poor guy resigned within a month or so of starting.

The takeaway here is all the other skills you have amount to very little in sales if you can't listen properly. Many years and many regrets later, I have realized "Ya, but" does not help our personal relationships much either. I have made listening one of my original fundamentals of training ever since those days, and in every meeting I have ever held, using the words "Ya, but" makes people laugh, but they really get the message of how important listening is. Who would ever think the words "Ya, but" could have such a profound effect on one's life?

LISTEN, LISTEN, LISTEN

When I first started selling cars way back in 1973, one skill that was completely overlooked by our trainers was listening to the customers. Perhaps I was blessed being so shy that I was often really quiet with customers and mostly listened to their needs.

Because I was shy and nervous with the customers, especially at the start, I would ask them to take a seat at a small desk in the showroom, and I would open a clean sheet of paper and ask them several questions to find out what they really wanted and needed. This turned out to be very effective, as many of our competitors listened very little. When I received my first sales manager position, leading a crew of eight to ten, one of my first priorities was to coach our team on the benefits of actively listening to our customers before we led them around the lot looking for a vehicle.

It appeared to me even back then that having them fall in love with the fanciest, most expensive vehicle on the lot was a poor strategy because if you had spent ten minutes actively listening to them, you would have realized sooner what their budget really was. Once we knew that, it was best to then show something even lower priced and then move them up to the vehicle they could afford. It was always easier to move them up to a nicer vehicle than to tell them the one they loved was too much and here's a model that's not quite as nice.

Today I would think everyone in the industry would be doing this as customers would demand they be listened to, and it is the right way to do things. The funny thing about this technique I used early on is I didn't do it because I was smarter than anyone else but honestly because I was so nervous and shy that it was easier to ask them questions than talk nonstop. Of course, once I had done most of the listening, customers would warm up, and I would usually make the sale.

This has been an early fundamental that I have focused on till this day. I remember having so many meetings with investors where we had a plan and full presentation to give during the fifty-minute meetings, but a smart investment firm's people would often interrupt us and try to get us off our script.

After a number of these meetings, someone on our team who wasn't the best listener would inevitably say to me, "I was just trying to push our agenda, so that's why I kept going on and on." I would reply something like, *Well that is nice, unless they ask you about something else, as they were the buyer and we were the seller.*

Sometimes I would remind our team and myself that we have to actively listen to them to make the sale. If we wanted to win, we had to listen carefully to their questions before we started talking too much. At the end of the day, there's no clear difference between selling a $6,000 car or $20 million in stock.

EXCELLENT LISTENING ADVICE

"Never miss an opportunity to shut up."

                                        Mark Twain

I laughed many years ago when I read this quote, but it does give us a lot to ponder here. Even if we are not talking about being a better listener, Mark Twain's words should be wise advice for most of us. How many times have we seen a friend, a work colleague, or a family member go on and on and dominate the conversation in the room to the point of embarrassment? Sadly, when I was drinking, I could be one of them, and

I am sorry and a bit embarrassed for those times. Even at sixty-seven I still have to watch myself here.

A perfect example of my occasional lapses in listening skills as a young manager happened back in about 1984. A very good person and employee of ours needed to be demoted and had just returned from a two-week Florida vacation. I was waiting to tell him the bad news when he came up to my office and asked to chat. After a few minutes of small talk, he looked like something important was on his mind, but I figured I might as well give him the news. After about ten minutes of discussing his flaws and the reason for his demotion, I stopped talking. He looked at me and said he had come up to tell me his young family had decided to move to Florida full time, and he was to become a teacher again, as the car business was not right for him.

Had I just simply listened to him for two minutes, the firing would not have been needed and we both would have felt better. This was terrible leadership on my part, and forty-some years later, I vividly remember it—what a wonderful life lesson. And to boot, he was a really good man. I can't even use drinking as an excuse here, I just a missed perfect opportunity to shut up.

On the bright side, had I not been embarrassed and ashamed by my behavior, perhaps I would not have done the work I am talking about in these notes to you.

EXECUTION

WE CAN ONLY USE WHAT WE PRACTICE

Our work and career success are often driven by how we execute our or the company's plan. In this light, we all must realize something I was fortunate to be taught at a young age. We always have to be aware that "We can only use what we practice, not what we know."

Arguably the greatest NFL receiver of all time, Jerry Rice, said he practiced daily more than anyone: "I do today what others won't so that tomorrow I can accomplish what others don't." He understood knowing is nice, but practice makes the difference.

Yamamoto Tsunetomo would say, "Having only wisdom and talent is the lowest tier of usefulness."

Children, this life lesson is urgent for all of us. If we simply rely on what we know and do not practice our craft, to improve each day, success will be more elusive for us.

NO BATTLE PLAN SURVIVES CONTACT WITH THE ENEMY

We all know many people who have what they think are

concrete plans for a successful business. In fact, some of them probably are quite good. However, a life lesson learned through some abject failure on my part has taught me that the actual execution of the plan is often more important than the plan. Of course, the plan has to be in line with the markets we are dealing with, but more good plans are defeated by a lack of execution than the plan itself.

Business and strategic plans, no matter how impressive, are only as good as the actions taken to execute them.

Military strategists often say, "No battle plan survives contact with the enemy."

Former boxing legend Mike Tyson said, "Everyone has a plan until they get punched in the face."

To take a plan to a successful completion, we need to have our teams buy in at the highest level, believing in the plan. We also have to be open to a few changes to the original plan when reality in the real world sets in.

I also believe a successful idea that is executed well is far more likely to happen if you bring a number of people in the field into the discussions early, as they are the ones who need to execute it, and if brought in, they always take ownership of that plan.

I learned this as a twenty-year-old kid ordering new vehicles for the dealership. I would have the salespeople who sold the vehicles to our customers help me order them so when they arrived two months later, they could not say, "Who ordered these options and colors? We can't sell these."

It was hard to believe most of the dealerships at the time never did this. If anyone over the last forty-five-plus years complained to me about our inventory, I would say, "Come on, you ordered it with us, let's go sell it."

Clearly, many businesses do not survive because they have the wrong business plan, including the wrong product or services. However, most fail because they don't execute the plan. Always remember, the plan is very important, but the execution of the plan even more so.

COMMITMENT AND SUCCESS

SURVIVOR

I have never watched the reality TV show called *Survivor*, but from what I have heard, Mike and I investing in a Chrysler Canada dealership with $8,500 each in 1981 certainly had the same concept and theme. This was my first small ownership position in a business and came with a move of 2,200 miles and the risk of losing what little money I had.

At the time, General Motors, Ford, and Chrysler had programs for outstanding general sales managers of large dealerships to help them invest, as otherwise they would not have the money to buy a store. Most of these young people were in the thirty to forty age range, with a fair amount of experience combined with a good track record of leading the sales teams to sell cars at their previous dealership.

The only people buying dealerships back then were old-money families that had owned a business for years; often they would purchase additional stores for a couple of their children to operate. The manufacturers wanted to sell cars and thought that good competition from somewhat desperate young people wanting to be dealers would be good for them. All three manufacturers were completely right about this, and many of the best auto dealers and groups in Canada today came up through one of these programs. Similar to shows like *Survivor*, the winners did really well in the OEM programs, and without them, I would not be here in this situation today.

I learned about real-life business survival in 1981 as a twenty-six-year-old kid with that $8,500 investment, which was everything I had except the down payment on a $60,000 house. Chrysler had about thirty-five dealerships nationwide in this program and told us that fifteen to eighteen failed each year. We received our chance because someone else lost their life savings trying to turn around a losing dealership. I convinced Susan, my soon-to-be-wife, to take a massive chance with everything we had and move across the country from Edmonton to London, Ontario, which neither one of us had ever seen.

The dealership had lost approximately $350,000 in 1980 (in today's dollars, over $1 million) and we were praying to turn this around to a small profit in 1981. We started with high hopes, but again, reality set in as interest rates were going up weekly in a frenzy not seen before until the prime interest rate reached 21.5 percent. Try running a business where your customers have to pay 22 percent interest rates to buy a car, and our inventory costs to stock our vehicles on our lots were completely unaffordable at that rate. We begged, borrowed, and prayed that we'd end the year at a $100,000 loss, which is a third of what they lost in 1981 before interest rates skyrocketed. Even losing money, this turnaround might have been the best job I have ever done in my career.

We thought things were reasonably good until Chrysler informed us late in 1982 that we had to reinvest our part of the loss, which amounted to the same $8,500 each. Failing to do this would mean we would join the list of many who went home broke and despondent. When I informed Susan of this, I think she thought I was unhinged and wondered if we would have to do this every year, even worse with our first child,

Daniel, having been born in June. I believe she would have favored moving back home and me getting a job working for someone again—a job in which we wouldn't have to give back more money every year. This was not an option I considered at all; I knew I could not start working for someone again at twenty-seven, lest my fate end up a lot like my father's. This was something I simply could not stomach.

As Susan was always reasonable, she agreed to sign with me on the new loan of approximately $8,000, and I thought we were ready to roll. Unfortunately, our bank turned down the loan and said no bank would loan us money to invest in a Chrysler dealership in 1982.

I pondered another heavy setback for a day or two, not knowing if I was depressed or just plain desperate, likely a combination of the two. I phoned the loan officer back and asked for another meeting. Her name was Jean Campbell, and she had known me for about fifteen months, since we moved to London, and was always nice to me. She was nice again but firm and said there was no chance of this loan happening. I am sure she could sense my desperation as I told her I was finished without the loan approval.

She sat back, thought for a minute, and asked if I would like a basement loan, which of course I wasn't looking for, as finishing a basement was the last thing we could afford to do. Jean said, "I am going to change your file to a home loan and just tell me you are using the money to upgrade the house, and I wish you luck at the dealership." That was life-changing, and we were fortunate she was in that chair during this period, as few others would have done it. I'm not sure what fate has to do with good luck, but it was on our side that day.

When I think about it, the only way I ended that season of my life as a "survivor" was through tenacity, commitment, and accountability to my business and my dream. If I did not accept full commitment for my work, regardless of the adverse market conditions and the adversity we were facing, we would have been completely broke, and I would have had to start over doing who knows what.

I'm not telling you this story to boast about my skills because as you can tell, it wasn't all my doing here—there was certainly much luck and blessings involved that helped this all work out. But I want you to know that this was one of my first opportunities to face seemingly insurmountable adversity, dig deep, and make even more personal commitments to make sure we were one of the survivors. An unwavering commitment, some seriously inspiring music, and a lot of luck sure helps.

A ONE-STORY TOWN

As I was saying, soon after Mike and I took on the ownership of our first dealership, interest rates and bankruptcies were skyrocketing everywhere. The truth was hope and motivation were hard for me to find, especially in '82. Back then, bankers were willing to work with old-money families in our industry, as they had other assets, but they were not so keen to work with folks like us, as one banker reminded us one day in my brother's office. "You two are broke without the dealership, as that is your only asset, and we are no longer interested in working with you."

I had lots of desperate talks throughout the days and many of the evenings, often with Mike. Fortunately, around this time, Tom Petty released a classic album called *Long after Dark*. I listened to the album opener "A One Story Town" hundreds of times that year, and it was a pure shot of inspiration and adrenaline that certainly helped in maintaining my commitment level during those truly trying times. That song helped me to tap a commitment level in my career and my ambitions that I did not know I had before this experience. Added bonus, I had a new band that I pretty much knew I would be listening to forever. Here are some lyrics from the song:

> I'm for standing up, I'm for breaking free
> I don't want fate handed down to me
> Yea, I'm for moving on, try another town
> Time ain't changing nothin', take a look
>   around
>
> Oh, I'm lost in a one-story town
> Where everything is close to the ground
> Yea, the same sh*t goes down
> Nothing turns around
> It's a one-story town

Remember, children, just because we were not always committed, does not mean we cannot find a whole new level of commitment and desire. I am sure the meaning of the song was much different to him, but to me, it meant going back to work for someone else who could fire you on a whim was like being "lost in a one-story town where the same sh*t goes down and nothing turns around." "The same sh*t goes down" was a metaphor to me that the wealthy who really did not need much help were the only ones the bankers would protect in a crisis. My total commitment meant we were going to make it in London and not even ponder anything else.

NO RULES FOR HIGH SCHOOL

A funny example of trying hard vs. commitment happened when I was around fourteen years old and heading into high school in Winnipeg for grade ten. It was the first experimental school in Manitoba, where you did not have to go to class, as they were trying to prepare us for university. Naturally, this experiment did not work well for all the students, and I was the poster boy for failure. I believe my grades for the first semester were in the 33 percent range, and I am pretty sure you had to put in quite an effort to get that low a grade.

My parents were disgusted with me, borrowed money from a relative, and rewarded me by sending me to an all-boys Christian Jesuit school for the second term. I am certain you have heard of these schools, which during that period of time were awful to any students misbehaving. They threatened me when we signed up that if I ever talked back to any of the teachers, punishment would come my way. Even then, I had to question why priests and other religious people at the school liked to show you who was in charge by using force. However, the more interesting fact about this religious school was it was adjacent to my high school and friends. The difference being we were fenced in at my new school and not allowed out until school was over at four.

What a contrast at recess and lunch, nice girls and boys having fun beyond the huge fences and idiot teenage boys looking for a fight at our school. I could not wait to get out of this so-called prison. My marks in the second term were close to ninety. What was the main difference even at age fourteen? I was trying the first semester when my results were pathetic and committed the second term when ninety was the result. It is amazing what real commitment can do for us when we are desperate, the tricky part is to maintain that type of commitment when we are not desperate.

Many times in my life I have tricked myself into believing my commitment level was soaring when in fact I was only trying hard. Life experience tells me so many of us fool ourselves into thinking trying hard is the way to achieve something important to us when only a serious commitment will likely get us where we want to be.

PRESIDENTIAL ADVICE

Three American presidents' words to consider carefully:

"I find the harder I work, the more luck I seem to have."
Thomas Jefferson

"Things may come to those who wait, but only the things left by those who hustle."
Abraham Lincoln

"Nothing in the world can take the place of persistence. Talent will not; nothing is more common than unsuccessful men with talent. Genius will not; unrewarded genius is almost a proverb. Persistence and determination alone are omnipotent."
Calvin Coolidge

Children, with the exception of the forty-fifth one, we can learn from America's presidents.

HUSTLE

Like President Lincoln believed, the choice to hustle a little more than our competitors can make all the difference in the world for our ultimate success. I truly never felt that I was the hardest worker in the country and obviously wasn't, but I truly believed I hustled a little more than most of the competition from the beginning of my career. That being the other sales-people, the other managers, and ultimately, the other busi-nesses we were competing against when owning dealerships. I have used the "eighty-five/fifteen" discussion in thousands of meetings throughout my career. I truly believe most of us give an 85–90 percent effort, which is really good; we just need to do a little more to be exceptional. We do not have to reinvent our work ethic; usually we do not have to work more hours; we simply have to keep learning, growing, and be committed enough to find that extra 10 percent or so.

While most things certainly change in life, some things actually remain the same two centuries later. Children, we all need to be very aware of our own actions. We all can make the choice to give 10 percent more. We can choose either to be among those who commit and really hustle or among those who think they hustle.

MY FAMILY EATS

I was about to watch a world championship match a couple of months ago but wondered if an underdog fighter moving up in weight named Oscar Valdez would be competitive with Miguel Berchelt, who was bigger and punched much harder. Having followed boxing for over fifty years, I knew this was a big mountain for Oscar to climb, and the oddsmakers shared this opinion, as betting odds the day before the fight had climbed to 4.55 to 1 for Miguel.

ESPN was carrying the fight, and they did a terrific job on the backgrounds of the fighters and with their interviews. When I listened and watched Oscar's interview, I knew this fight would be worth watching. "This is my opportunity; I'm not going to go in there and not give it my all. I'm going to do whatever it takes. If I have to box, I'll box. If I have to bang it and brawl it out, then I'm willing to do that too."

Later in the interview he also said, "I have fought with broken ribs and a broken jaw, and I am undefeated in thirty-four fights. Either his family or my family eats. I am going to win tonight, and I will be closer to my goal of being one of the three greatest Mexican fighters of all time." You simply cannot get more committed than Oscar is, and he won a fight-of-the-year candidate with a tenth-round knockout in a big upset.

Hall of Fame boxing champion Marvelous Marvin Hagler, who had made a lot of money by then, said that it's simply your choice how committed you are. "It's hard to get up at five in the morning when you are sleeping in silk pajamas."

For fifty years I have always admired the courage, skill, and commitment of the world's most gifted boxers. I have often asked myself, *If they can do this in the face of all their challenges, how can I not be committed to my much easier goals?*

"I AM THE BOSS" SYNDROME

Commitment to our position and career is an area that often makes a significant difference to our success. If this is so obvious, why do many of us miss it? One type of behavior I have seen often throughout my career is that many people get a few promotions and think they are the boss who now does not have to do much.

One such encounter happened to me in Edmonton when we brought a partner in to essentially be the managing partner of a new dealership we had just purchased. After a couple of months and a few discussions, it appeared clear to me that the business was not going in the proper direction, and the employees did not seem happy at all. One management style I would often practice to help people was to have them map out what they actually do each and every day and discuss it with them.

Many were a little inexperienced in the new role they had undertaken and just needed a few tips on little things that turned into big things they were not doing. In this particular case I was perplexed at his answer to my question, "Can you please tell me exactly what you do each day, and hopefully, we can find some answers."

He looked straight at me without a worry in the world and said, "I am the boss and part owner here. The employees do the work, and I just tell them to hit the numbers every day."

Not only did I realize that this was not going to be a successful venture, but I was also immediately mad at myself for promoting him, even though he was very competent at his lesser position. It's not only a senior position type that has this attitude sometimes. I remember distinctly thirty years or so ago when we had six lot men who moved and cleaned cars, etc., and I decided to put one in charge. Not a smart move by me in this case, since we basically lost one of the six, as all he did was yell at the other five to do all the work, which, as you would know, caused nothing but resentment from the team, and production declined significantly.

Many exceptional leaders know that employees may listen to what the leader says, but they usually believe more based on what the leader actually does. We can make all the motivational speeches and send out all the memos in the world, but if people in the organization don't see us putting forth our best effort every single day, they won't either. Kids, this type of effort is what commitment is about if you want to reach the top of your profession.

HOPE

HOPE AND A GOOD PLAN

Many times I would be in my good friend Steve Rose's office at work, and he would say to me, "You are so much like my dad, always so full of optimism and hope. Hardly ever met anyone like you two in that manner." Hearing him say that during the credit crisis of 2007/8 when we were on the brink of survival really made me ponder if and why I was so full of hope.

Well, first off, when growing up, I was always hopeful that things would change—and I think it helped me survive some of the troubles we endured, but ultimately, it led to some problems, which I speak to in the next note. But I was always hopeful at the office because I thought that during times of severe crises, the team would already be frightened enough; they really wouldn't need the CEO to be walking around preaching Armageddon. Obviously, they would be scared for the company, but more importantly, they would be scared for their family if the company were to go out of business. I was always realistic when we were in trouble, but still confident we would survive if we had both hope and a well-thought-out plan. Our team also believed if we had both, we would survive and then prosper.

Any company needs a serious, well-thought-out plan that has a good chance of success and, of course, some hope that it will succeed. However, if our plan is mostly built on hope, and the people we are dealing with on the other side of the table have a serious plan of their own that does not include us, then clearly hope is not enough to make our plan work.

In any business plan, we have to put the other person's hat on and understand clearly whether the plan we present to them would really change what they're thinking about our situation. For instance, when we were dealing with Cerberus Capital during the financial crisis, we knew that whatever plan we were presenting to get our credit reinstated needed everything possible, plus some hope. Knowing the absolute arrogance of people who, because of their positions at work, are encouraged to have no human heart whatsoever when making decisions, you quickly come to understand your plan must be bulletproof, as one small mistake or omission will give them license to put you out of business with a smile on their face.

Children, we must always have hope in business and life, but let's have a well-thought-out plan to go with it.

HOPE AT HOME

In our personal lives we certainly need hope, but on its own, I am sad to say to you kids that I believe it's really not worth that much. Growing up, I was continually hopeful things would get better and turn out nicely, like it was supposed to with our family. Hoping people will change and the situation will get better on its own is a foolish and even risky way to think and live. Perhaps the situation will improve, but more likely, history tends to repeat itself, especially when it comes to human behavior. Unfortunately, this also includes our own behavior.

Hoping we will change for the better is not enough on its own either, we have to do the work.

The life experiences I have had with certain people would clearly point this out in an illuminating fashion. My continuing hope that our family dynamic would change and everyone would be happy and peaceful in the family was simply foolish. It was only when Diana and I came up with a well-thought-out plan to deal with the situation that things changed for the better. Of course, we were hoping it would work, but we needed the substance of a good plan to be successful.

I suspect it's no different when we as parents are trying to assist our children with a bit of advice and knowledge in helping them out through problematic situations. We clearly want hope, but we better have a concrete plan or help them develop their plan.

Children, I have always tried to live with hope running through my veins in all life's journeys, but it took me a long time to realize hope needs a well-engineered plan alongside it.

SINCERITY

FAKING SINCERITY

Sincerity is described as being free from pretense, deceit, or hypocrisy. It also means having honesty of mind or intentions. Sincerity might best be summed up as the quality of being honest, true, and real. No wonder people like to follow leaders who practice being sincere each day.

It is important to build trust with others, as people who work with us will follow our lead and vision if we are perceived as being sincere. In the long run, people will follow only leaders who are perceived as sincere with them and with others.

I remember a nice fellow who worked with me about twenty-four years ago, and I can still recall his words to me one day because they were so impactful. He was struggling with success and would often come into my office hoping to find some answers. One morning I suggested to him that he might try being a bit more sincere with customers, as my perception working with him was that he seemed to be overacting with them.

His exact words to me were: "No one acts more sincere with customers than I do, nobody can fake sincerity better than me."

A little shocked at his words, I took a minute to think and

wrote his words on a piece of paper and asked him to read them out loud and think deeply about them. He then knew full well his fake sincerity was not really working as he thought it had been. With some reflection and change, his results improved measurably. Though he moved on long ago to another industry, he still sends me a text every year at Christmas.

Children, always be sincere, and if you can't be, please do not try to fake sincerity, as it never works and is also a bit deceitful.

SINCERITY AND LEADERSHIP

Working with different leaders over the years has taught me many things about leadership and what is most effective. Seeing excellent leaders up close has made it clear to me that the majority of these top leaders shared an important quality, and that is they were sincere people. Most of these men and women were honest, transparent, and authentic, and this made their teams loyal to them because they trusted them more, which of course made them have less turnover and superior results.

Unfortunately, I have also worked with a few who thought they could fake their way through being sincere and caring about their team. In almost every case, long-term stability with staff and long-term success never happened.

I firmly believe people will always rally around you if sincerity is a big part of your leadership style. A good example of sincerity in our retail business is when a leader compliments a coworker by saying things that reflect her true feelings, not some BS she thinks will inspire them. We simply cannot fake our way here for very long, otherwise our credibility soon erodes, as will results. These types of leaders and coaches might be able to fool people for a while, but it never ends well.

TRUTH MAKES FOR GOOD BUSINESS

It's fascinating that I can still remember a night in Calgary in 1975 when my father was talking to a customer complaining in his office. Unfortunately, it was around seven in the evening, and he was a little more drunk than usual, so I was sure hoping it would end up OK. I walked by his showroom office a few times to kind of keep an eye on things, and he looked completely oblivious to the customer's concerns and raised voice. By the third or fourth pass, I realized we had a problem that was not going to solve itself. My father had leaned back in his chair in a drunken slumber, snoring while the customer was yelling at him.

For a solitary moment I thought perhaps I should keep walking and avoid a serious confrontation with this angry man. No one on the sales floor stepped up to help, so I took a deep breath, walked into his office, and said hello to the customer. As I was a very young salesman with long hair, he thought the joke was getting worse on him, and saying he was angry would be an understatement as he told me to go to hell and that this dealership was the worst and on and on. Unfortunately, I had to stay standing, as my dad was asleep in his chair, and I wasn't sure I should sit right next to the customer on the other side of the desk while he was screaming at me. Life had already taught me that listening was helpful to de-escalate any situation, so I tried it here. After about three straight minutes of hearing his raised voice, I simply told the truth, "I am really sorry about the situation you are facing here with all the problems with your car and this type of service you are receiving tonight. The boss sleeping here is my father, and he is not feeling well." Considering his alcoholism was a serious illness, I didn't feel like I was stretching the truth.

There's a good lesson here on being sincere and honest about a situation, as he calmed down and a minute later said,

"He's your dad?" I said yes again, and now we could solve his problems as he must have felt sorry for me and began acting amiably.

RESILIENCE

TWENTY-FOUR HUNDRED AND NINETY-SIX WEEKS OF BEING JUDGED BY WHAT WE SOLD

During my one year of university, my favorite subjects were philosophy and psychology. That was likely a good thing, as throughout my entire career, I continued to read and study and take a keen interest in what motivates people and how we motivate ourselves in a business as brutal on our emotions as auto retail.

Every single day of our careers we get judged on precisely how many new vehicles we sell, how many used vehicles we sell, how many service hours we sell, and how many parts we sell. If we have a body shop at the dealership location, it gets measured just the same. It's all sales results—all day, all week, and all year, and believe me, this wears on you. The auto manufacturers rate you every day on these sales numbers compared to your competitors, who are trying to take your business and your good people. To make it even more stressful, you do not get paid if you do not sell. If you own the business and you don't sell enough, you go bankrupt; it's that simple.

In merging what I learned about human psychology in university with what I've learned about handling sales pressure, I have come to believe that resilience plays a huge role in surviving this kind of pressure and staying motivated. There is no possible way any of us can be successful in our chosen field without dedicating ourselves to cultivating resilience. This is something I continue to work on every day.

NINE THOUSAND MISSED SHOTS

You simply cannot be a GOAT basketball player like Michael Jordan without having an unimaginable amount of resilience. His words should resonate with us all. "I've missed more than nine thousand shots in my career. I've almost lost three hundred games. Twenty-six times I've been trusted to take the game-winning shot and missed. I've failed over and over and over again in my life. And that is why I succeed."

A resilient person believes setbacks are temporary and we can change things; it's just a setback along the journey.

A nonresilient person often thinks the setbacks are going to undermine everything we do and will last a long time.

Children, let's always choose to be resilient. Again, the choice is ours to make.

THE BOUNCES EVEN OUT

Remember, it's not just us who lose sometimes. It's not just us feeling we just got punched in the face sometimes. It's not just us getting embarrassed sometimes. It's everyone who has ever lived on this earth who faces these challenges.

If we remember this fact, we will not take it so personally, and we will find better ways to overcome these obstacles both at home and at work. Many times in my life I felt that my luck was worse than others, but life experiences tell me that was simply not true. Saying to myself that my luck was worse than others does not make it true. Remember, despair is easy, resilience is powerful.

Life is very much like a hockey season, the bounces usually even out over the season. The only thing that really matters is how we respond to these bad bounces, challenges, and setbacks. We are not defined by our hard days, we are defined by how we come back from them.

RESILIENCE SALES TRAINING NOTES

For years on end, I would spend considerable time training and sharing tips on overcoming obstacles and having a strong, resilient nature. Over the years, thousands of people would participate in these meetings and tell their stories of resilience, and many of these stories shaped my training on the subject. Most of the points below were learned from resilient team members—thanks to all of you. Remember before online shopping became so prevalent if we failed 70 percent of the time with customers, we were a star. The average closing rate for walk-in customers averaged around 15 percent. Think about that. Here are five themes about resilience that continued to come up:

- We need to fully appreciate the importance of resilience in determining our success.
- We need to continue to learn how to deal with our negative thoughts that hold us back and make us less resilient.
- We need to believe in our own abilities to overcome significant setbacks.
- We need to always be on the side of being somewhat optimistic, rather than a bit pessimistic, to overcome resilience.

NOTES FOR THE CHILDREN   299

- We need to embrace adversity, as it will surely come. If we have prepared for it, we will deal with it much better.

Kids, resilience plays a major part in anyone's success. Sometimes we just need to get our courage up, leave our victim role behind, take responsibility, believe a bit more in ourselves, and move forward.

PARENTS

OUR PARENTS' SHOES

There is no more important role we can play throughout our lifetimes than that of being a parent. Unfortunately, this is a role we receive no formal training for and because of that we (subconsciously) tend to remember how our parents raised us as a guide. As much as we might love them, how can we know they had the correct approach to raising us? Or were they more likely to follow their parents, who may have been severely mistaken in their approach?

We also have to be aware of the times they lived and grew up in. If the Great Depression or either of the World Wars were part of that upbringing, it is obvious this would have affected them significantly and not necessarily for the best. We also need to understand how much dealing with addiction, depression, and anger could have hurt them. Perhaps a scarcity of money and goods, including food, affected them as well. If this was the case, then their guilt in not being able to help us more could well have hurt their parenting abilities. We must try to walk in our parents' shoes before we get too mad at them and blame them for our misfortune.

A Native American proverb I learned so many years ago

applies well here: "Never criticize a man until you have walked a mile in his moccasins."

HELPING OURSELVES REALLY
HELPS OUR CHILDREN

As for our own parenting, I wish I had more advice for you, but there is no one perfect way to handle it. I surely made far too many mistakes, especially early on, as I was mired by too many of my own issues to truly understand what it took to be an excellent parent. I can honestly say I loved my children as much as anyone ever could and really tried my hardest for you, although my actions were frequently wrong. Far too often I was overly angry and short tempered in our home. Far too often I was too preoccupied with work and family issues to be present enough for you. And for this I am very sorry. I was fortunate that Susan was such a good mother, and that really helped the situation for all of us.

When Lauren and Kaedra came into my life, it was a bit smoother because I had done more work on myself years before that. I was also twice lucky with Diana, as she is just a phenomenal mother who kept our new group together with her kindness and wisdom.

Children, the one unequivocal thing I can say about being a better parent is that the more work we have done on ourselves and the kinder we are to ourselves, the better parent we will be. When we make changes to better ourselves, we help ourselves and our children. Please remember our children only have one childhood, let's try extra hard to make it a special one.

WINTER

(For Daniel, Laura, Jenna, Lauren, Kaedra, Evie, Mack, Emily, and Miles)

The following lyrics about a daughter and father came from a brilliant song that was released in 1992 on an absolute gem of an album by Tori Amos.

> Snow can wait, I forgot my mittens
> Wipe my nose, get my new boots on
> I get a little warm in my heart when I
>   think of winter
> I put my hand in my father's glove
>
> I run off where the drifts get deeper
> Sleeping beauty trips me with a frown
> I hear a voice. "You must learn to stand up
> For yourself 'cause I can't always be
>   around"
>
> He says, "When you gonna make up your
>   mind?
> When you gonna love you as much as I
>   do?
> When you gonna make up your mind?"
> 'Cause things are gonna change so fast
> All the white horses are still in bed
> I tell you that I'll always want you near
> You say that things change, my dear . . .
>
> Mirror, mirror, where's the crystal palace?
> But I only can see myself
> Skating around the truth who I am
> But I know, Dad, the ice is getting thin

When you gonna make up your mind?
When you gonna love you as much as I
    do?
When you gonna make up your mind?

The power and emotion of the song hit me hard the first time I heard it, and all I could feel listening to it was the love I felt for all three kids. Daniel was ten, Laura eight, and Jenna seven at the time.

From left to right: Jenna, Daniel, Laura, around 1990.

I also realized that they would all have their own challenges pretty quickly as they moved into the teenage years, and I wished I could help them more, but I knew, as Tori's dad had said, they had to love and believe in themselves as much as I loved and believed in them. Many of these feelings came back to me when I watched a thirteen-year-old Kaedra and a fifteen-year-old Lauren move to Edmonton from Richmond, Virginia, knowing the challenges they would surely face.

As my kids always did, Lauren and Kaedra faced their

problems with courage and grace, and I could not be more proud of them all. I am so fortunate and grateful to Diana and Susan for being thoughtful and caring moms. I know all our grandchildren will benefit immensely from the love and care of their parents, and Laura and Daniel have started as excellent examples of that.

GRANDPARENTS CAN BE VERY INFLUENTIAL

When my brother and I were between the ages of eleven and thirteen, my parents would have us leave Winnipeg and go stay with our grandparents in Burlington, Ontario, for the summer. They had moved from the old house on Fairleigh Avenue to Burlington, and Mike and I very much enjoyed leaving home and spending our summers there until about age fourteen when, lo and behold, girlfriends came into the picture back home in Winnipeg.

Both Nana and Baba, as they were called, were Hungarians who had come to Canada to enjoy a better life. Nana worked for years as a seamstress and also worked extra hours in tobacco fields and picking fruit. Unfortunately, she thought we might learn something from doing that, and she had us do our fair share of picking fruit, which was not a fun way to spend the days of summer, but she was correct that it was good for us. Baba was a construction worker, then a foreman, and we enjoyed him taking us down to some of his work sites. They were both very kind to us, and living there was a big change from the chaos at home.

Nana was very strict, but Baba was a kind soul who would act really strict around Nana, but if she was out of the picture, things got a whole lot easier. He loved to get out a couple of nights a week to have a bit of a break from the tight routine at home that Nana set, and off we would go. He would take us out for a pop and a drive, which Nana thought was OK. The three of us would laugh as we headed out of the driveway with our escape plan. (Inside joke, Jenna.)

He loved to stop at the tavern called the Pig and Whistle for a couple of "pops." He would buy us each a real pop and let us keep the music on in the parking lot where we waited. We were twelve the first year visiting and just starting to listen to a bit of music, so the radio would play all the new songs in 1967, which we loved on summer nights. Forty-five minutes later he would be back in the car with a big smile on his face, and we would rush home feeling pretty good. Our instructions were clear, we really enjoyed the pops and the drive Baba took us on. He was the best grandfather you could have, who was very proud of Mike and me and knew something wasn't quite right in our home without ever saying it. He regularly told us we were going to amount to something in this world. This type of honest faith in you makes you believe you can actually accomplish something in life. A beautiful lesson learned on how to talk to my grandchildren today. Thanks so much, Baba.

My grandmother was really tough but so kind as well, and many years later she would laugh and tell me, "You think I did not know all those years ago in Burlington that Baba went for beers when driving you two around."

Baba would also buy us the three cheapest seats we could find at live wrestling shows every two weeks when the tour stopped in nearby Hamilton. We would get there by seven for an eight o'clock start and get the best seats in the upper section, and he would regale us with all the things the good and bad guys were going to do that evening. Still not one hundred percent sure if he thought the wrestling was real, and although he was quiet man, he would yell at and boo the bad guys. Years later when he was very sick and in a wheelchair, I would drive from London to see him on the odd Saturday, and the day always revolved around watching wrestling on TV in the afternoon. Nana would look at us with a smirk on her face as we enjoyed ourselves, and she later told me that in those moments he was the happiest he had been in a while. I could not be more grateful for the help and love my grandparents provided me along the way.

THE BEAUTY WAY

The Navajo have a beautiful closing prayer from their Blessing Way ceremony they often recite. We could surely learn so much from it. So will our children. Here are the opening lines:

> In beauty I walk
> With beauty before me I walk
> With beauty behind me I walk
> With beauty above me I walk
> With beauty around me I walk
> It has become beauty again

Walking through life in the beauty way means walking in harmony with all living things. If we practice the beauty way a little more in our lives, our children's lives will be blessed when they follow our example.

ACTIVELY LISTEN FOR FIVE MINUTES A DAY

Children, my best advice for you on this crucial role of parenting comes from years of unequivocal love and pride in you, learning from unfortunate poor behavior from myself, and studying and watching the way we all parent. Having watched Laura and Daniel as parents, it amazes me how good you both are and how proud I am of you. I am also extremely confident that Jenna, Lauren, and Kaedra will be wonderful parents if and when they choose to have children. I will leave you with some of my thoughts:

- Please accept the fact that we all need to work on ourselves to improve our mindset, attitude, and state of mind. We must learn to water the positive seeds in ourselves if we are to be the most caring and thoughtful parents and role models for our kids.
- It is beneficial for children to grow up in a home with two parents who are loving to each other, not sniping at each other.
- Please try not to argue in front of your children; this is a mistake I made and regret as much as anything in my life.
- Please do not belittle your spouse or egg them on in front of your children—another mistake I made and am not proud of.

I believe so strongly in the following two actions that I have tried to share both of them while training our employees for years on end. I share these with you, not to sound like an expert, but because someone was kind enough to share them with me almost forty years ago, and I pass that favor and advice on to others:

- Please try to actively listen to your children for even five minutes a day from the time they are two years old; this means really listening intently. This means listening to understand, not correct them. We have plenty of other ways to correct or scold them. This is time well spent, and the child will learn that we want to listen to and care about them.

- Please remember to tell each child as often as you can how proud you are of them. This is extremely important for their confidence and emotional well-being. Kids get emotionally beat up on a regular basis, and this reassurance is crucial. It is amazing to me how many people I have tried to help and motivate during my career that have openly and honestly said to me, "My parents were never proud of me." Perhaps those parents were, but they never thought to tell the kids who often craved this. Children, I cannot tell you enough how proud of you I am.

GRATITUDE

"When we live in the spirit of gratitude, there will be much happiness in our life. The one who is grateful is the one who has much happiness, while the one who is ungrateful will not be able to have happiness."

Thich Nhat Hanh

WISE WORDS

Children, I cannot stress to you enough how true I've found the words of this Buddhist master to be and how they can change our lives.

FINDING PEACE THROUGH GRATITUDE

Researchers believe gratitude enhances self-esteem and increases psychological well-being, as well as improving our chances of not being depressed. This powerful emotion helps us feel less inclined to be envious and jealous, and it keeps us more resilient. Gratitude will also make us all better human beings who are more likable and have healthier relationships with our families and friends, and it makes us healthier. I am not aware of any pharmaceutical drugs that can do for us what gratitude will.

The researchers' conclusions have surely proven to be accurate for me. Living in a state of gratitude has made my life much easier, less stressful and worrisome, more satisfying, and just plain happier. Please remember we are not going to be living in this state of gratitude every minute of every day, but if we can move significantly closer to more time residing in gratitude, we and those closest to us will be much happier.

I would suggest that of all the positive emotions we are trying to water in us to improve our lives, gratitude would be near the top. Another encouraging fact is that this powerful emotion can be practiced until it becomes a habit for us.

Children, this is something to never forget and why this book has these two distinct chapters, one on counting our blessings and one on gratitude.

BY THE WAY, I FORGIVE YOU

A PRECIOUS GIFT

Forgiveness is a rare and invaluable gift that we can give ourselves. It costs absolutely nothing: we do not need to write a check for it, we do not need to use our debit card, we do not need to hand over cash for it. We simply need to forgive people who have hurt us at some time in our lives. If we choose to forgive and make peace with our past, we can live happily in our present.

STUCK IN OUR OWN PRISON

"Before you embark on a journey of revenge, dig two graves."
Confucius

"We must develop and maintain the capacity to forgive. He who is devoid of the power to forgive is devoid of the power to love."

Martin Luther King Jr.

"True forgiveness is when you can say, 'Thank you for that experience.'"

Oprah Winfrey

Forgiveness is something that took me years to understand and appreciate, especially its power to heal us. When this enlightenment happened, my life changed for the better in so many ways. I had people who were residing in my head because I had not forgiven them. Once I forgave them, they were rarely thought of again. Finding forgiveness is a gift to ourselves and the ones we love. I have also experienced Oprah's words on numerous occasions.

Here are some notes that I had written and shared in training sessions about forgiveness over the years:

- Our ability to forgive others cannot be achieved unless we can learn to forgive ourselves.
- If we forgive what someone has done to us, it does not mean they did not do something wrong. It just proves we are able to rise above that action.
- I believe we have to be strong people to forgive others; forgiveness is never a sign of weakness.

There is no possible way my words on forgiveness can compare to what Nelson Mandela said, but from experience, I know this to be true. After spending twenty-seven years in prison for being a terrific human being, Nelson wisely said, "As I walked out the door toward the gate that would lead to my freedom, I knew if I didn't leave my bitterness and hatred behind, I'd still be in prison."

Children, often our freedom is waiting for us, but we are not ready to take it. Please be aware how we perceive forgiveness, and never forget the power forgiveness leaves us with.

REAL HURT

My parents grew up in the Depression and of course were profoundly affected by that; the only way they taught us to get ahead was to fight for everything you can. My father was a very intelligent man who often made good money but was bankrupt a few times through the years and died completely broke. His life was extremely difficult, and I suspect he beat himself up considerably. This devastating cycle continued when he often beat up a couple of my sisters with brutal, unkind words that scarred them.

Forgiveness was not something we talked about at all. Going through my notes, I found so many of them were written in small doses over the last fifteen years. It appears to me that I was about fifty years old when I really started thinking about how forgiving others was the only possible way forward for any of us; in fact, I learned it was the only way for me to move forward from my own suffering.

I am very thankful for everything my parents did for me, as I know they did the best they possibly could in their circumstances. My mother and I spent many hours together after Dad died, often in grocery stores, where she would do a rigorous price check on anything she would purchase. Pretty funny days, as she would be so proud to tell the cashier her son had made it and was paying for her groceries. Believe me, she did not need me to pay, she just liked being a proud mom.

Truthfully, I have never blamed my parents for their actions because the life they grew up in hurt them so much. Combining those demons with the ultimate curse of alcoholism surely gives me reason to forgive them for anything and everything. Mom and Dad, thank you for all you did for us, love you forever.

FORGIVENESS IS HAPPINESS

A number of years ago, when I had finally understood what true forgiveness really was, I wrote the words below precisely this way in my notes. I am not sure where this came from and kind of wish I had looked at them a little more frequently over the years, as they were found when I was searching through old notes for this book. I can also truly understand why each was written twice.

> There is great happiness in forgiveness
> There is great happiness in forgiveness
> There is wonderful peace in forgiveness
> There is wonderful peace in forgiveness
> There is wonderful healing in forgiveness
> There is wonderful healing in forgiveness

> What are we waiting for?

ONE STEP AT A TIME

CROSSING THE HIMALAYAN MOUNTAINS

Many years ago, I read a Buddhist tale that made me reconsider whether I was indeed accomplishing my goals doing things one step at a time. The story goes along the lines of a Buddhist monk who had successfully navigated the incredible journey of passing from one side of the Himalayan mountains to the other. When the local villagers saw him and asked him how he had crossed over from the other side, they were perplexed as to how he could have done this. His simple reply was, "One step at a time." I do not know the veracity of this tale, but its meaning is pretty clear and direct and certainly helped me focus better on doing things one step at a time.

For the life of me, children, I cannot understand why so many times we continue to walk along the path to our goals, not realizing that the only way to the other side is one step at a time. We simply have to put one foot in front of the other each day until our goal is reached. Then we move on to the next challenge. Whether we are crossing the mountains or trying to excel in school or at work, let's do it one step at a time.

FIVE-MINUTE INTERVALS

Playing goalie in the NHL is one of the most difficult jobs in sports, similar to being a pitcher in MLB or a quarterback in the NFL. Successful goalies often play a sixty-minute game in five-minute intervals. This is done in the same manner as doing things one step at a time because they realize if they are going to win, they must simply focus their entire being on winning each five minutes until you reach the end. Twelve five-minute intervals done one step at a time.

Most everything we hope to accomplish can be broken down into intervals and one step at a time.

LET'S PUT ONE FOOT IN FRONT OF THE OTHER

As I so believe in doing things one step at a time, I reviewed hundreds of notes written over the years about doing exactly that and the people who inspired me from their words. Perhaps you will learn as much from them as I have.

The first one I remember reading as an eighteen-year-old salesman came from a car-sales legend from Detroit named Joe Girard: "The elevator to success is out of order. You'll have to use the stairs . . . one step at a time."

Other famous people and spiritual leaders have spoken to this concept as well:

- Helen Keller: "I long to accomplish a great and noble task; but it is my chief duty and joy to ac-complish humble tasks as though they were great and noble."
- Muhammad Ali: "I have learned to live my life one step, one breath, and one moment at a time, but it was a long road. I set out on a journey of

love, seeking truth, peace and understanding. I
am still learning."

- Mark Twain: "The secret of getting ahead is
getting started. The secret of getting started is
breaking your complex, overwhelming tasks into
small manageable tasks, and then starting on the
first one."
- Lao Tzu: "A journey of a thousand miles starts
with a single step."
- Chinese Proverb: "It is better to take many small
steps in the right direction than to make a great
leap forward only to stumble backward."
- Buddhist saying: "There is no large and difficult
task that can't be divided into little easy tasks."

Many times along my personal journey when I was in
doubt, worried, and a little depressed, I just took the next small
step and then the next one until things started improving.

COUNTING OUR BLESSINGS

SAVE THE CHILDREN

We like to think that childhood is a beautiful time for playing, learning, and just plain growing up while being loved and
nurtured by our family. We like to think our children, if they
work hard, have a positive attitude, and generally do the right
things, they will find happiness and contentment in their lives.

Man, oh man, I am reading this now, and it's hard to believe that the dream above we have for our kids is not the
real situation for many children. There is a vastly disparate
growing-up experience for hundreds of millions of kids worldwide. The humanitarian aid organization Save the Children
has reported that 25 percent of all children grow up in a terrible situation, born in "particularly impoverished, discrimi-
natory, conflict-ridden places, may die early, or see their own
chances of success drastically reduced because of preventable
health issues, malnutrition, poor schools, violent home lives or
early pregnancy."

The *Lancet* medical journal reported on CNN that in 2015
"263 million children were out of school, 168 million were involved in child labour, and nearly 28 million were forced to
leave their homes globally."

Children, these startling and tragic numbers must teach

us that our family must continue to always give a percentage of our company's earnings to those less fortunate than us. I know all five of you will insist on continuing this long after Diana and I are gone. I also believe we must continue to understand how fortunate we are not to have been born into these circumstances and to count our blessings every day. Anyone growing up in a situation where there is some hope is surely better off than hundreds of millions worldwide who are born into a completely hopeless environment.

Who of us could believe in 2021 we could watch desperate people hanging off airplanes and falling to their death to escape the ruthless rule of the Taliban in Afghanistan? How could this happen, live on TV, in front of our eyes? These scenes and many more like them will happen in my time on earth and continue through my grandchildren's years on earth.

Despicable behavior has caused significant pain from the beginning of humankind and is highly likely to continue unabated. Let us always remember the unfortunate worldwide, especially the children, and try to do some good in this world while counting our blessings each and every day.

EVERY DAY

Every day I thank God for my wife Diana, who I always say to myself was heaven sent.

Every day I thank God for my three children, who are the greatest kids a man could ever have.

Every day I thank God for my two stepdaughters, who make me think I won the Stepdad Lottery.

Every day I thank God for our four grandchildren, Evie, Mack, Emily, and Miles, who bring us so much joy and love.

Every day I count my blessings, which make all of life's daily struggles worthwhile and easier.

BLESSINGS FOR WHEN THE DAY IS DONE

Children, I know this is quite personal, but my goal is to try to help you, and if one little thing resonates here, I will be happy. I have this on my iPhone and read it for about two minutes each night when I go to bed. Perhaps you could come up with a personal message of your own.

> Thank you, Lord, the day is done
> I have done my best
> I have had a calm and aware mind today
> Sleep
> Gratitude
> Amazing and Beautiful Diana
> Amazing Children, amazing Grandchildren
> Wonderful company and friends there
> Keep your positive thoughts going
> If a negative thought comes up, just say
> Not now, thank you
> We simply can't control everything
> Ten percent of our thoughts are useful
> Biting tongue with teeth helps stop un-
>   wanted thoughts in bed and
> brings us back to the now
> Water the seeds of gratitude, not fear
> Enjoy the luxury of the bedsheets
> What else could we possibly want?

Patrick, around 1960.

Patrick and Diana on their wedding day, April, 2009.

Patrick's grandsons, Mack and Miles, 2023.

Patrick and Diana with their granddaughters, Evie and Emily, 2023.

From left to right: Lauren, Justin, Jenna, Laura (pregnant with Emily), Evie, Patrick, Diana, Daniel, Kristen (pregnant with Mack), and Kaedra, 2017.

AFTERWORD

SONGS TO LISTEN TO AT LEAST ONCE

Children, I would like to leave you with a list of songs that have inspired, motivated, and comforted me. They have been some of my most beloved companions as I've traveled the tumultuous road of life. As I said in these notes, I encourage you to create your own playlists that bring you similar joy, inspiration, and companionship. I also hope that at least once you listen to each of these songs and see if they touch something deep inside you as they have deeply touched me. Perhaps some of these will even become lifelong companions. Here they are, in no particular order:

"Fisherman's Blues," The Waterboys (1988)
"The New Life," The Waterboys (1993)
"We Will Not Be Lovers," The Waterboys (1998)
"My Love Is My Rock in the Weary Land," The Waterboys
    (2000) *(Thanks, Diana)*
"Peace of Iona," The Waterboys (2003)
"Once Were Brothers," The Waterboys (2022)
"The Return of Pan," The Waterboys (1993)
"In My Time on Earth," The Waterboys (2019)
"Long Way to the Light," Mike Scott (1995)

"She Is So Beautiful," Mike Scott (1998)

"Where the Streets Have No Name," U2 (1987)

"One," U2 (1992)

"I Still Haven't Found What I'm Looking For," U2 (1987)

"Fortunate Son," Creedence Clearwater Revival (1969)

"Who'll Stop the Rain," Creedence Clearwater Revival (1970)

"Lodi," Creedence Clearwater Revival (1969)

"Have You Ever Seen the Rain," Creedence Clearwater Revival (1970)

"You're So Vain," Carly Simon (1972)

"Fire and Rain," James Taylor (1970)

"Black Day in July," Gordon Lightfoot (1968)

"Year of the Cat," Al Stewart (1976)

"Yesterday," The Beatles (1965)

"Strawberry Fields Forever," The Beatles (1967)

"A Day in the Life," The Beatles (1967)

"While My Guitar Gently Weeps," The Beatles (1968)

"Across the Universe," The Beatles (1969)

"I Me Mine," The Beatles (1970)

"Help!," The Beatles (1965)

"Ticket to Ride," The Beatles (1965)

"Here Comes the Sun," The Beatles (1969)

"Let It Be," The Beatles (1970)

"I'm So Tired," The Beatles (1968)

"How I Roll," Bob Geldof (2010)

"Tweeter and the Monkey Man," Traveling Wilburys (1988)

"I Don't Live Here Anymore," War on Drugs (2021)

"Gimme Shelter," The Rolling Stones (1969)

"You Can't Always Get What You Want," The Rolling Stones (1969)

"Sister Morphine," The Rolling Stones (1971)

"Sympathy for the Devil," The Rolling Stones (1968)

"Paint It Black," The Rolling Stones (1966)

"Miss You," The Rolling Stones (1978)

"Doo Doo Doo Doo Doo (Heartbreaker)," The Rolling Stones
(1973)

"Memory Motel," The Rolling Stones (1976)

"Street Fighting Man," The Rolling Stones (1968)

"(I Can't Get No) Satisfaction," Rolling Stones (1965)

"Angie," The Rolling Stones (1973)

"Winter," The Rolling Stones (1973)

"Curse of the Mummy's Tomb," World Party (1997)

"Always on My Mind," World Party (2000)

"Father and Son," Cat Stevens (1970)

"Oh Very Young," Cat Stevens (1974)

"Sitting," Cat Stevens (1972)

"I Was Drunk," Alejandro Escovedo (1999)

"Keep Me in Your Heart," Warren Zevon (2003)

"Visions of Johanna," Bob Dylan (1966)

"Like a Rolling Stone," Bob Dylan (1965)

"The Times They Are A-Changin'," Bob Dylan (1964)

"Positively 4th Street," Bob Dylan (1965)

"It's Alright, Ma (I'm Only Bleeding)," Bob Dylan (1965)

"Dirge," Bob Dylan (1974)

"Sara," Bob Dylan (1976)

"Tangled Up in Blue," Bob Dylan (1975)

"Every Grain of Sand," Bob Dylan (1981)

"Idiot Wind," Bob Dylan (1975)

"A Hard Rain's A-Gonna Fall," Bob Dylan (1963)

"Hurricane," Bob Dylan (1976)

"We Better Talk This Over," Bob Dylan (1978)

"Slow Train," Bob Dylan (1979)

"Where Are You Tonight," Bob Dylan (1978)

"Tryin' to Get to Heaven," Bob Dylan (1997)

"Don't Fall Apart on Me Tonight," Bob Dylan (1983)

"Masters of War," Bob Dylan (1963)

"Not Dark Yet," Bob Dylan (1997)

"Key West," Bob Dylan (2020)

"Shelter from the Storm," Bob Dylan (1975)

"Black Diamond Bay," Bob Dylan (1976)

"When the Night Comes Falling from the Sky," Bob Dylan (1985)

"Girl from the North Country," Bob Dylan (1963)

"Man in the Long Black Coat," Bob Dylan (1989)

"Most of the Time," Bob Dylan (1989)

"Ring Them Bells," Bob Dylan (1989)

"Wedding Song," Bob Dylan (1974)

"Knockin' on Heaven's Door," Bob Dylan (1973)

"What Was It You Wanted?," Bob Dylan (1989)

"Things Have Changed," Bob Dylan (2000)

"Red River Shore," Bob Dylan (1997)

"Ain't Talkin'," Bob Dylan (2006)

"Gimme Some Truth," John Lennon (1971)

"Working Class Hero," (Acoustic) John Lennon (2004)

"Steel and Glass," John Lennon (1974)

"Watching the Wheels," John Lennon (1980)

"I'm Losing You," John Lennon (1980)

"Instant Karma," John Lennon (1970)

"How Do You Sleep?," John Lennon (1971)

"Mind Games," John Lennon (1973)

"Out the Blue," John Lennon (1973)

"(Just Like) Starting Over," John Lennon (1980)

"Cold Turkey," (acoustic) John Lennon (2004)

"Nobody Told Me," John Lennon (1984)

"Imagine," John Lennon (1971)

"Jealous Guy," John Lennon (1971)

"Hotel California," Eagles (1976)

"Night Moves," Bob Seger (1976)

"Mainstreet," Bob Seger (1976)

"Against the Wind," Bob Seger (1980)

"Roll Me Away," Bob Seger (1982)
"Let's Not S— Ourselves (to Love and to Be Loved)," Bright
     Eyes (2002)
"Land Locked Blues," Bright Eyes (2005)
"Waste of Paint," Bright Eyes (2002)
"When the President Talks to God," Bright Eyes (2005)
"Born to Run," Bruce Springsteen (1975)
"Downbound Train," Bruce Springsteen (1984)
"No Surrender," Bruce Springsteen (1984)
"The Promised Land," Bruce Springsteen (1978)
"Darkness on the Edge of Town," Bruce Springsteen (1978)
"Streets of Fire," Bruce Springsteen (1978)
"Independence Day," Bruce Springsteen (1980)
"The Ghost of Tom Joad," Bruce Springsteen (1995)
"The River," Bruce Springsteen (1980)
"Better Days," Bruce Springsteen (1992)
"Cover Me," Bruce Springsteen (1984)
"Lucky Town," Bruce Springsteen (1992)
"If I Should Fall Behind," Bruce Springsteen (1992)
"Atlantic City," Bruce Springsteen (1982)
"Empty Sky," Bruce Springsteen (2002)
"You're Missing," Bruce Springsteen (2002)
"Death to My Hometown," Bruce Springsteen (2012)
"Wrecking Ball," Bruce Springsteen (2012)
"This Depression," Bruce Springsteen (2012)
"Beauty Way (Live)," Eliza Gilkyson (2007)
"Jokerman (Live)," Eliza Gilkyson (2007)
"Landslide," Fleetwood Mac (1975)
"Dreams," Fleetwood Mac (1977)
"Wasteland," Dan Bern (1997)
"Black Tornado," Dan Bern (2001)
"Everything Falls Away," Gretchen Peters (2015)
"Hello Cruel World," Gretchen Peters (2012)
"Blackbirds," Gretchen Peters (2015)

"Arguing with Ghosts," Gretchen Peters (2018)
"Disappearing Act," Gretchen Peters (2018)
"Blanket," Gurf Morlix (2007)
"Hard Road," Gurf Morlix (2009)
"Late for the Sky," Jackson Browne (1974)
"Sleep's Dark and Silent Gate," Jackson Browne (1976)
"The Late Show," Jackson Browne (1974)
"Running on Empty," Jackson Browne (1977)
"The Pretender," Jackson Browne (1976)
"Lives in the Balance," Jackson Browne (1986)
"Sky Blue and Black," Jackson Browne (1989)
"Rain on the Scarecrow," John Mellencamp (1985)
"Pop Singer," John Mellencamp (1989)
"Void in My Heart," John Mellencamp (1989)
"Wasted Days," John Mellencamp (2022)
"Save Some Time to Dream," John Mellencamp (2010)
"Country Gentleman," John Mellencamp (1989)
"Minutes to Memories," John Mellencamp (1985)
"Help Me," Johnny Cash (2006)
"On the Evening Train," Johnny Cash (2006)
"Redemption Day," Sheryl Crow and Johnny Cash (2019)
"All Some Kind of Dream," Josh Ritter (2019)
"Thin Blue Flame," Josh Ritter (2006)
"Girl in the War," Josh Ritter (2006)
"Lawrence, KS," Josh Ritter (2001)
"Old Black Magic," Josh Ritter (2019)
"The Torch Committee," Josh Ritter (2019)
"Train Go By," Josh Ritter (2017)
"Me & Jiggs," Josh Ritter (2002)
"Anthem," Leonard Cohen (1992)
"You Want It Darker," Leonard Cohen (2016)
"Happens to the Heart," Leonard Cohen (2019)
"Hallelujah (Live in Dublin)," Leonard Cohen (2014)
"Waiting for the Miracle," Leonard Cohen (1992)

"The Future," Leonard Cohen (1992)

"Everybody Knows," Leonard Cohen (1988)

"The Future (Live in London)," Leonard Cohen (2009)

"Going Home," Leonard Cohen (2012)

"Show Me the Place," Leonard Cohen (2012)

"My Oh My," Leonard Cohen (2014)

"Come Healing," Leonard Cohen (2012)

"Ain't No Cure for Love (Live in London)," Leonard Cohen (2009)

"Closing Time," Leonard Cohen (1992)

"Stairway to Heaven," Led Zeppelin (1971)

"Going to California," Led Zeppelin (1971)

"The Battle of Evermore," Led Zeppelin (1971)

"Losing My Religion," R.E.M. (1991)

"Oh My Heart," R.E.M. (2011)

"I Don't Sleep, I Dream," R.E.M. (1994)

"Everybody Hurts," R.E.M. (1992)

"Überlin," R.E.M. (2011)

"Bang and Blame," R.E.M. (1994)

"Tiny Dancer," Elton John (1971)

"Your Song," Elton John (1970)

"Crucify," Tori Amos (1992)

"Winter (Live at Montreux)," Tori Amos (1991)

"Me and a Gun," Tori Amos (1992)

"The Sound of Silence," Simon and Garfunkel (1966)

"America," Simon and Garfunkel (1968)

"The Boxer," Simon and Garfunkel (1970)

"Won't Get Fooled Again," The Who (1971)

"Baba O'Riley," The Who (1971)

"Behind Blue Eyes," The Who (1971)

"Hand in My Pocket," Alanis Morissette (1995)

"Reasons I Drink," Alanis Morissette (2020)

"Wish You Were Here," Pink Floyd (1975)

"Mother," Pink Floyd (1979)

"Hey You," Pink Floyd (1979)

"Comfortably Numb," Pink Floyd (1979)

"4:47AM (the Remains of Our Love)," Roger Waters (1984)

"The Tide Is Turning," Roger Waters (1987)

"Amused to Death," Roger Waters (1992)

"It's a Miracle," Roger Waters (1992)

"Racing the Angels," Matraca Berg (2015)

"Dust of the Chase," Ray Wylie Hubbard (2005)

"In Times of Cold," Ray Wylie Hubbard (2018)

"Rock Gods," Ray Wylie Hubbard (2020)

"My Song," Brandi Carlile (2007)

"The Joke," Brandi Carlile (2018)

"Right on Time," Brandi Carlile (2021)

"Turpentine," Brandi Carlile (2007)

"After the Gold Rush," Neil Young (1970)

"The Needle and the Damage Done," Neil Young (1972)

"Shock and Awe," Neil Young (2006)

"Heart of Gold," Neil Young (1972)

"Revolution Blues," Neil Young (1974)

"Hitchhiker," Neil Young (2010)

"Lookin' for a Leader," Neil Young (2006)

"Love and War," Neil Young (2010)

"Crime in the City," Neil Young (1989)

"Old Man," Neil Young (1972)

"Rockin' in the Free World," Neil Young (1989)

"The Loner (Live)," Neil Young (2021)

"Ambulance Blues," Neil Young (1974)

"Don't Be Denied," Neil Young (1973)

"Comes a Time," Neil Young (1978)

"From Hank to Hendrix," Neil Young (1992)

"My My, Hey Hey (Out of the Blue)," Neil Young (1979)

"Stop Draggin' My Heart Around," Tom Petty and Stevie Nicks (1981)

"Forgotten Man," Tom Petty (2014)

"Square One," Tom Petty (2006)

"Mary Jane's Last Dance," Tom Petty (1993)

"Thirteen Days," Tom Petty (1993)

"Counting on You," Tom Petty (1999)

"Fault Lines," Tom Petty (2014)

"Learning to Fly," Tom Petty (1991)

"Room at the Top," Tom Petty (1999)

"Into the Great Wide Open," Tom Petty (1991)

"You and Me," Tom Petty (2002)

"Runaway Trains," Tom Petty (1987)

"You and I Will Meet Again," Tom Petty (1991)

"A One Story Town," Tom Petty (1982)

"The Last DJ," Tom Petty (2002)

"Finding Out," Tom Petty (1982)

"The Trip to Pirate's Cove," Tom Petty (2010)

Long after Dark, Tom Petty (1982)

"Waiting for Tonight," Tom Petty (1995)

"Angel Dream (No. 2)," Tom Petty (1996)

"Rebels," Tom Petty (1985)

"I Need to Know," Tom Petty (1978)

"Southern Accents," Tom Petty (1985)

"Listen to Her Heart," Tom Petty (1978)

"Don't Fade on Me," Tom Petty (1994)

"Free Fallin'," Tom Petty (1989)

"Crawling Back to You," Tom Petty (1994)

"Love Is a Long Road," Tom Petty (1989)

"A Face in the Crowd," Tom Petty (1990)

"Runnin' Down a Dream," Tom Petty (1989)

"A Matter of Trust," Billy Joel (1986)

"Piano Man," Billy Joel (1973)

"We Can't Make It Here," James McMurtry (2005)

"Fire Line Road," James McMurtry (2008)

"The Horses and the Hounds," James McMurtry (2021)

"Copper Canteen," James McMurtry (2015)

"Trailer," Mudcrutch (2016)

"Scare Easy," Mudcrutch (2008)

"The Same Situation," Joni Mitchell (1974)

"Court and Spark," Joni Mitchell (1974)

"Come Talk to Me," Peter Gabriel (1992)

"Escape Plan," Mobina Galore (2019) *(Thanks, Jenna)*

"Skeletons," Mobina Galore (2015)

"You're Not 23 Anymore," Mobina Galore (2015)

"Dig Myself Out," Mobina Galore (2019)

"Vancouver," Mobina Galore (2017)

"Magic and Loss," Lou Reed (1992)

"Me & My Lover," Matthew Ryan (2000)

"3rd of October," Matthew Ryan (2000)

"Guilty," Matthew Ryan (1997)

"Spark," Matthew Ryan (ft. DJ Preach) (2009)

"Heartache Weather," Matthew Ryan (2000)

"Aspen/These Days," Dan Fogelberg (1975)

"The Last Nail," Dan Fogelberg (1975)

"Part of the Plan," Dan Fogelberg (1974)

"Times like These," Dan Fogelberg (1981)

"Loose Ends," Dan Fogelberg (1977)

"Same Old Lang Syne," Dan Fogelberg (1981)

"Nether Lands," Dan Fogelberg (1977)

"False Faces," Dan Fogelberg (1977)

"Walk through the Fire," Mary Gauthier (2002)

"Falling out of Love," Mary Gauthier (2005)

"Drunken Angel," Lucinda Williams (1998)

"Steal Your Love," Lucinda Williams (2001)

"Out of Touch," Lucinda Williams (2001)

"Essence," Lucinda Williams (2001)

"People Talkin'," Lucinda Williams (2003)

"I Don't Know How You're Living," Lucinda Williams (2011)

"Seeing Black," Lucinda Williams (2011)

"Car Wheels on a Gravel Road," Lucinda Williams (1998)

"Real Live Bleeding Fingers and Broken Guitar Strings,"
    Lucinda Williams (2003)
"Maybe I'm Amazed," Paul McCartney (2004)
"With a Little Luck," Paul McCartney (1978)
"Band on the Run," Paul McCartney (1973)
"Pennyroyal Tea," Nirvana (*MTV Unplugged*, 1993)
"Stolen Car," Patty Griffin (2002)
"Making Pies," Patty Griffin (2002)

ACKNOWLEDGMENTS

I am incredibly grateful to the following individuals who have played significant roles in shaping my life and supporting me through my journey:

Firstly to my wife, Diana, the kids, and grandchildren, whom I love and care for so deeply.

I want to express my deepest appreciation and love to my parents, who have taught me so much despite the hardships they faced.

I would also like to extend heartfelt love and gratitude to my grandparents, John and Teresa, who showed me so much support and faith throughout the early years of my life.

To my sisters and brother, whose intelligence and resiliency have taught me so much. And to their children, my nieces and nephews, who I've had the pleasure of watching grow into such mature and remarkable adults. To my half brothers, Tom and Tim, who came into my life late but for whom I have such deep gratitude.

To Susan, the mother of my three children, thank you for your constant loving presence in their lives.

Furthermore, I want to express my gratitude to the numerous partners and colleagues I have been fortunate enough to work with over the years. A heartfelt thank you goes out to Paul, Art, Eric, Ryan, Joe, Wes, Camille, Steve, Tom, Matt, Chris, Jeff, Rob, Derek, Bob, Alistair, Matt, John, Bob, Clayton, David, Warren, Dave, Natasha, Rick, Lowell, Phil, Scott, Aaron,

Scott, Justin, Chris, Amit, Chris, Cole, Justin, Chris, Lukasz, Jamie, Jason, Troy, Iftikhar, Krysta, Alan, Kimberly, Stacy, Craig, Marc, and others that are too numerous to name.

I would like to extend a special appreciation to Gail Hudson for her coaching and guidance throughout this endeavor. Her expertise has been invaluable, and I am deeply grateful for her support.

Last but not least, my thanks go to my editors, whose dedication and hard work have transformed my words into a polished manuscript.

Once again, thank you to all who have touched my life and helped me become the person I am today. Your support and encouragement have meant the world to me.

ABOUT THE AUTHOR

Patrick Priestner, a Canadian entrepreneur, started his journey to success as a teenager by becoming the top Chrysler car salesman in all of Canada. Over the next fifty years, he founded and developed one of the most successful automotive businesses in Canada, which currently operates thirty dealerships across the country, generating sales of approximately three billion a year. In 2008, he was awarded the Canadian Innovator Laureate, and in 2015, he received the EY Entrepreneur of the Year Prairies award. Priestner's passion for mentoring young employees has helped many achieve personal success. He is also deeply committed to philanthropic work. Priestner currently resides in Edmonton, Alberta, with his wife, Diana, and cherishes his relationships with his five children and four grandchildren. In his free time, he enjoys reading, practicing mindfulness, and indulging in a good bowl of gelato. *Notes of the Children* is his debut book. For more information on Patrick and his charity, please visit www.wellbeing-canada.ca.

Made in the USA
Las Vegas, NV
23 January 2024